DELIVERY OF COMMUNITY LEISURE SERVICES: AN HOLISTIC APPROACH

DELIVERY OF COMMUNITY LEISURE SERVICES: AN HOLISTIC APPROACH

James F. Murphy, Ph.D.
*Associate Professor, Department of Recreation and
Leisure Studies, San Jose State University,
San Jose, California.*

Dennis R. Howard, Ph.D.
*Assistant Professor, Department of Recreation and
Parks, Texas A & M University, College Station, Texas.*

LEA & FEBIGER
Philadelphia 1977

Health, Human Movement, and Leisure Studies
Ruth Abernathy, Ph.D.
Editorial Adviser
Professor Emeritus, School of Physical and Health Education
University of Washington, Seattle 98105

Library of Congress Cataloging in Publication Data

Murphy, James Fredrick, 1943–
  Delivery of community leisure services.

  Includes index.
  1. Recreation leadership. 2. Recreation—Administration.
I. Howard, Dennis Ramsay, 1945–   joint author.
II. Title.
GV181.4.M87   1977   301.5'7   76-41372
ISBN 0-8121-0575-3

Published in Great Britain by Henry Kimpton Publishers, London

PRINTED IN THE UNITED STATES OF AMERICA

Print Number: 4 3 2 1

Preface

The complexity and dynamics of community life in contemporary American society require continual evaluation and assessment on the part of administrators in order that they can comprehend the changing needs and requirements of a highly heterogeneous population to sustain a life support system and enhance the quality of life. The challenge confronting the Recreation and Park Movement involves the ability of its leaders to identify and then implement a diversified, flexible and comprehensive leisure service opportunity system which will embrace the needs of all people living on the frontier of a post-industrial society. The integration of human experience is viewed as an important conceptual approach that is necessary to enable the individual to realize one's potentialities within an environment which allows the person to flourish according to unique interests and capabilities, meet individual needs and find his or her own life solution.

The focus of the Recreation and Park Movement in the future appears to be centered on an understanding of the dynamics of community life and *all* aspects of the environment and whether they can be meshed to create a milieu serving a central goal of human development. This book serves to provide an overview of societal events and factors contributing to social change and how these relate to leisure behavior patterns; humanistic philosophical perspective; operational application of useful traditional and innovative approaches to management; political implications of service delivery; and evaluation of community leisure service agencies.

The major challenge in any leisure service agency is "making it happen." We hope that the text will provide a realistic overview of contemporary events and social issues which have an implication for the operation of public, private and voluntary leisure service programs and through an analysis of community life can furnish a sound philosophical perspective and beneficial "workable" guideline for the operation of leisure service agencies. The text focuses on the recognition of the heterogeneity of community life which requires a varied response through differentiated strategies in providing leisure services; a concomitant need for personnel to look at alternative leadership and management roles and approaches; and an awareness of the interrelationships of the components which make up a community system.

The book is geared primarily to upper division students in leisure studies and park management curricula in community recreation, programming and administration courses. Practitioners seeking new approaches to management may also find the volume of value. We had a mutual interchange of ideas throughout the development and writing of the text and attempted to critically evaluate each other's material throughout the project.

The book is divided into three parts: Section I, Recreation and Leisure: Building a Community Life Support System (including chapters on Leisure as a Segment of Contemporary Society, The Nature of the Recreation Experience, The Meaning of Community, and Human Development as the Primary Goal of Recreation and Leisure Service); Section II, The Dynamics of Managing a Community Recreation and Leisure Service Agency (including chapters on The Setting: The Community as a System, The Delivery of Community Recreation Services and The Program Function); Section III, Summary (includes the chapter, Ecology of Recreation and Leisure Service: New Management Considerations).

We wish to thank Ed Wickland of Lea & Febiger for his faith in the value of the text and his encouragement to complete the project.

San Jose, California   James F. Murphy
College Station, Texas   Dennis R. Howard

Contents

SECTION I

Recreation and Leisure: Building a Community Life Support System

CHAPTER 1

Leisure as a Segment in Contemporary Society

"The provision of community recreation has become a primary source in contemporary American society for fostering individual opportunities for self-expression, mastery and social interaction beyond the social groupings of occupational associations and kinship."

An Overview of Contemporary American Society

We are on the threshold of a new era, similar to the Protestant Reformation, as we are experiencing a rapid shift in basic, previously unquestioned cultural premises, beliefs and values, and its pervasiveness is impinging upon every aspect of social institutions, custom and ways of life. We have reached a stage in which it has become paramount that everyone be concerned about preserving the earth's habitability and about creating societies conducive to each person achieving the highest degree of self-fulfillment. This includes pre-eminently, an image of man and woman as part of a whole, potentially capable of an awareness in which each person's identity with the whole and their awareness as chooser of the experiences that happen to them, become apparent.

We have experienced at an ever increasing rate the breakdown of conditions requisite to human dignity through fragmentation, perceptual change, ideological and aesthetic bankruptcy, and increasing depersonalization of experience. A massive change of

3

consciousness has resulted in a revolution of awareness, of values, of life styles, as a counter to alienation and dehumanization of life; indeed it is broader than cultural change, it seems to be part of the evolutionary development toward self-enlightenment. There is a growing recognition that a "Transformation" of human perceiving, feeling and being in personal, social, political and environmental issues must occur if we are to become spontaneous, empathetic, loving, sensitive human beings. Leonard states:

> *"Institutions and human consciousness obviously reflect each other; one cannot long maintain a new shape without some kind of shift in the other."*[1]

Western society has looked increasingly at Eastern cultures which have kept alive the conceptions of spirituality and social and psychic awareness which are largely in disuse in our own. The transformation to a "New Age" defines wealth, not in terms of acquisition and conspicuous display, but in terms of nature, of process and experience. Jerome warns that there is a need to consider the humanistic value system of the New Age or we may face destruction.

> *"The new scarcities are of unobstructed sunlight, clean air and water, uncontaminated foods, honesty and love in human relations, and the body, with all its riches. These commodities are abundant in the world at large and will be so in our culture when the hang-ups, perversions, and unnecessary exploitations of the old culture are eliminated."*[2]

Culture and Change

The acceleration of change in American society has been unprecedented in the twentieth century. Tremendous social and technological changes, precipitated by advancements in medical science, engineering, computer technology and educational literacy, have had a marked impact on the values, beliefs and knowledge of our American culture. The perceptions of the world at the turn of the century were manifestly concerned about economic security, gaining a measure of material comfort, and achieving a sense of individual identity and prosperity. Contemporary Americans are provided with a reasonable measure of economic security and material affluence. Most people no longer need cope with problems that beset them half a century ago. "Instead the individual faces the hard inner reality of alienation, insecurity, and anxiety, all related to the diminution or even the loss of identity ... Old values have been eroded, new values develop too slowly to replace the loss effectively."[3]

A culture oriented five or six decades ago around horse power, assembly line hardware, rural living, and kinship has been radically transformed into a new society in America dominated by computer software, bureaucracies, television, outer space travel and an instantaneous communication network. Our comprehension of the relationship of people, materials, knowledge and time has created a new consciousness. Kostelanetz states: "the new technologies create a radically different sense of space and a new experience of time . . . change in one dimension capitalizes upon transformations in another until wholly unprecedented potentialities become eminently possible."[4]

A rapidly changing society has created the need for new kinds of understanding and the development of an appropriate value system which will embrace a changed obsession with work to one of at least equal concern with leisure. Sessoms comments on the consequences of this stage of the industrial revolution (one dominated by cybernation) with its emphasis on communication and as a self-correcting mechanism:

> *"We are literally creating new time blocks, new residential patterns, new consumptive behavior, and new approaches to life. We are in the midst of a social revolution where the issue is not scarcity but of having so much around us that we know not where to start."*[5]

Sessoms indicates that the first stage of the industrial revolution was identified with mechanization as the central force and in which work was an integrative activity. The second stage of the industrial revolution saw the rise of the corporate society with its organization for mass production; workers became like machines, elements of the assembly line, in which management synchronized the interdependent parts so that the product appeared whole. Workers no longer used machines as an extension of themselves as they became specialists, with accompanying loss of identity as the rhythm of work became the dictate of the production worker, not the laborer.

At present, there appears to be a search for identity — whether it be in work or leisure—a desire for activity and meaningful existence. Prior to the Industrial Revolution Sessoms[6] indicates that leisure was essentially a philosophical notion. However, in the electric age of the "global village," characterized by more options and more opportunity for diversity, leisure is normally equated with free time. With an abundance of free time, the masses have unprecedented and unequaled access to "the good life" as never known before.

Recreation — A Humanistic Expression

Recreation and leisure service, an integral part of the allied human service profession, reflects the growing humanism, a philosophical justification for providing people opportunities for leisure expression. Humanism reflects a central concern for the dignity and worth of a person and the development of human potentialities. In recreation and leisure service it sees this as the fundamental consideration for human beings — that the individual should have a measure of choice, autonomy and self-determination. Humanistic psychology has become recognized as a "third force" transcending the two main schools of psychology, behaviorism and psychoanalysis. It seeks to study the "healthy personality" and recognize the essence and capacity of all human beings to be unique individuals.

Recreation and leisure service agencies which incorporate a humanistic approach to service would seek to promote the capacity and ability of individuals and groups to grow, to explore new possibilities, and to realize their full potential. For example, the Long Beach, California Recreation Commission, in its 1973–74 Annual Report, captured the essence of the humanistic perspective, by indicating that recreation provided children a sense of wonder, adults a sense of achievement, and senior adults a sense of fulfillment through its various and diverse recreation activities. In other words, recreation serves as a means of human fulfillment.

A humanistic perspective involves facilitation of growth potentials as well as a concern for eliminating barriers which hinder self-development. Typically, social science depicts an image of man and woman in society in relation to a set of institutions which are disposed to serve, control and facilitate human needs. Any conflicts, changes or alternative expressions are usually seen as deviations, not as relevant social processes. A humanistic approach to life seeks to embrace a person's positive capacities, his or her expressions of joy, freedom and self-fulfillment. Humanism is concerned with facilitating a person to become what one is capable of being. It asks, "What are the possibilities of human beings? And, from these possibilities what is an optimum person and what conditions will most probably lead to one's attainment and maintenance of such a state?"

The provision of community recreation has become a primary source in contemporary American society for fostering individual opportunities for self-expression, mastery and social interaction beyond the social groupings of occupational associations and kinship (with its myriad forms). The individual in a technological society lacks the necessary support from traditional institutions to achieve and maintain self-identity. Rather than confront oneself, the individual submits to the lack of privacy, which is a striking characteristic of American life. The individual seeks identity through identification through a constant shifting of peers, work groups, neighbors and family. However, these temporary and shifting groups can provide only a pseudo-identification and uncertain refuge. Social mobility is a demanding and dynamic opportunity which leaves many people uncertain about themselves. "The person in search of identity must continue to live in a culture that provides no 'pause for transition.' "[7] Because society will continue to be so unstable and afford the individual with little external support, institutions and agencies will need to provide opportunities for self-appraisal, more intensive social interactions, and experiences which allow the individual to realize personal aspirations.

In a constantly changing and dynamic society, the social fabric of community life has become depersonalized and fragmented for many and various forms of rituals and ceremony have broken down and collapsed altogether. Community life, representative of work, family and leisure, are inseparable components of living and essential ingredients to human life. Leisure involves social interaction, celebration and self-expression. These are not segmented aspects of living; they are a part of life and not antithetical to work and kinship. However, because of the influences of industrialization and technology, which have severed family ties by freeing individuals to express their life styles independently of others and divided and weaned out craftsmanship from work, there is an increasing need for recreation and leisure service agencies to improve the quality of human existence by bringing together the fragmented parts of community life and uniting the shredded and disjointed fusion into a whole.

Background of the Recreation and Park Movement

Recreation and leisure service agencies have historically responded to America's changing social conditions and implemented service approaches to meet the needs of youth, elderly, handicapped and deprived. The challenge of a highly urbanized and technological society will require once again that leisure service agencies alter "traditional" service values and approaches and provide meaningful opportunities to citizens. The disruptiveness of community life has had a marked impact on the human condition.

> *"The challenge confronting the recreation movement today involves
> the ability of its leaders to identify and then implement a diversified,
> flexible and comprehensive leisure opportunity system which will
> embrace the needs of people posed by the new frontiers of a
> post-industrial society."*[8]

The recreation and park movement has progressed through
seven stages of professional development. The initial development
of organized recreation in the United States occurred in the latter
part of the nineteenth century by spirited socially concerned
individuals, including Joseph Lee in Boston (considered to be the
"father" of recreation in the United States), Jacob Riis in New York,
and Jane Addams in Chicago (Nobel Peace Prize recipient and
founder of the Hull House). These pioneers of the recreation and
park movement were motivated primarily by deleterious conditions of urban living and the need to provide underprivileged youth
constructive leisure opportunities amidst crowded and impoverished living conditions. According to Neumeyer and
Neumeyer the initiation of the play movement (as it was then
called) in the late nineteenth century grew out of the following
factors impinging upon urban life.

> *"It grew out of a situation of need owing to such factors as
> technological developments, particularly the introduction of modern
> machinery of production with its monotonous and nerve-racking
> work; urbanization, especially the overcrowded living conditions in
> sections of cities; changing home conditions and family disorganiza-
> tion; the speed of living, including increased mobility and daily
> rushing about; and the increase of leisure."*[9]

The efforts of the early pioneers to provide play opportunities
for children and youth came from social and civic workers who
provided funds for the establishment of the first playgrounds,
community centers and settlement houses. The impetus led to the
formation of the YMCA, Boy and Girl Scouts, Boys' Clubs and local
governmentally supported recreation programs. Sessoms states:

> *"Recreation activities were thought of as a means of building
> character, installing values, and providing informal teaching. The
> philosophy and programs of this period were distinctive; recreation
> was a means to an end — the building of better citizens."*[10]

Recreation was thought to be an important wholesome social
and personal outlet for young people exposed in metropolitan slum
and crowded urban areas to undignified and cheap forms of
entertainment and improper delinquent activities. Butler indicates
the several related issues which inevitably led to the formalization
of an organized recreation movement in 1906.

> *"Bad housing conditions resulting from the growth of tenement slum areas, the great influx of immigrants, the rising tide of juvenile delinquency, the increase in factories accompanied by the evils of child labor and unsanitary and unsafe working conditions, the spread of commercialized amusements which were often associated with vice — all helped to create a condition which made the provision of wholesome recreation a necessity."*[11]

At the same time social group workers were initiating urban recreation programs, conservationists and park planners were busy setting aside open spaces and park areas. They were designed as pleasant, passive surroundings in which people could enjoy leisure at their own pace. The construction of Central Park in New York in 1858, Franklin Park in Boston in 1883, Fairmount Park in Philadelphia in 1867 were examples of the establishment of park areas in large cities to provide relief from the tensions of urban living and opportunities for city dwellers to enjoy "country" living and natural landscape without having to travel long distances outside the city. Such early efforts of park professionals were oriented primarily at providing opportunities for peaceful enjoyment and beautiful surrounding of a naturalistic kind.[12]

The third stage emerged following World War I when the importance of recreation as a necessary and fundamental part of community life was increasingly recognized. Local public authorities were pressured to assume responsibility for the provision of recreation.

> *"High governmental officials, prominent organizations, citizens and economists voiced the opinion that public parks and recreation centers were like schools, essential to the health, safety and welfare of the community. State legislatures passed enabling laws empowering municipalities and counties to conduct recreation activities."*[13]

The influence of World War I and the War Camp Community Service is particularly important for the Recreation Movement as over 600 recreation programs were established in communities near military bases. For the first time in many parts of the country recreation activities were conducted for all family members and it was this broadening role of recreation which led to an improved image and the "recreation for all" motto became a symbolic concept as a consequence of wider and more representative recreation opportunities for everyone.

During the 1930's and early 1940's as a result of The Depression and the resulting enforced unemployment, impoverished conditions, and a surplus of free time, recreation became a diversionary instrument of community life for breaking the monotony of poverty. Sessoms comments on its accelerated growth during World War II.

"This movement toward comprehensive organized recreation was accelerated during World War II, when the need to get away from the tragedy of war increased the demand for activities of amusement and diversion for all groups."[14]

The diversionary approach to community recreation service continued into the 1950's with more comprehensive programs being provided all family members, although the emphasis was still on youth, particularly sports oriented activities.

During the 1960's two notable patterns emerged. First, the tumultuous period of the 1960's was marked by a period of civil unrest and social upheaval and stimulated a return by the recreation and park movement to issues of social concern, particularly as influenced by rioting, youth dissent and racial disorders. It is felt by many that it was not until the decade of the 1960's that the recreation and leisure service field began to give special attention to the complex needs of the poor — especially the non-white poor living in urban slum areas. It was only after several riots and "civil disorders" in many of the nation's cities that the needs of inner-city residents were brought forcefully to the attention of the public. Many of the efforts initiated by municipal recreation departments were typically oriented to providing special summer "crash, cooling off" programs and were partially or totally subsidized by the federal government's Office of Economic Opportunity. The role summer enrichment programs played in the development of recreation expanded service profile in the community, although only a temporary stop-gap effort in many instances, did revitalize its service role "as a means of improving the self-concept of participants, of overcoming apathy, and encouraging community involvement."[15]

During this period recreation and leisure service came to be seen as a *threshold* activity which drew participants to other forms of involvement for the purposes of improving community life, organizing neighborhoods for socially constructive activity and an opportunity to actualize their potential for leisure expression. Recreation and leisure service increasingly became equated with the opportunity to improve the quality of life, reduce social disease, nurture constructive human values and generally make communities a better place to live. It became more apparent that recreation experience contributes to individual growth and to social development.

Second, a tremendous increase in outdoor recreation participation occurred which was particularly encouraged through the expansion of state and federal provision for additional camping and water sports opportunities and the promotion of vacation travel.[16]

The development of the Outdoor Recreation Resources Review Commission in 1958 served as a catalyst to this phase of the recreation and park movement in the 1960's. The establishment of the Land and Water Conservation Fund program and the creation of the Bureau of Outdoor Recreation which was precipitated by the Commission's recommendation "led to increased Federal support for conservation and open-space development. State planning and accelerated municipal land acquisition programs were key elements during this period."[17]

The BOR was the first Federal agency established principally for the fostering of recreation opportunities and the first to be identified in title by the word recreation. The Commission made over 50 recommendations with the intent of meeting the burgeoning outdoor recreation needs of Americans.

The most recent phase, beginning in the early 1970's, has been marked by a human developmental concern by the recreation and park movement. This period has been characterized by a concern for the individual and a focusing by the movement to establish a human service field responsive to a person's total needs. This phase was sparked by disenchanted youth who rejected the often impersonal, rigid and desensitizing structure of institutions. Youth have joined with discriminated minorities, oppressed women, disenchanted workers and have expressed a need for flexible and spontaneous framework for realizing personal goals and opportunity for self-fulfillment and meaning in life. What appears to be emerging is a new "social character," an effort by a growing number of people to humanize work, leisure and community life. Maccoby's comments on a new generation of young workers who are seeking alterations of work and life styles is reflective of the whole of American life. He states,

> "[they are seeking] to create an America in which resources are organized optimally to allow each individual to develop himself to the fullest, and in which projects are carried out by free people, none used as an object by another. Progress toward this goal will require that individuals become more self-directed, less competitive, and more responsible. The process of humanizing work [and leisure service] will enrich the lives of many people, and at the same time, move towards a society which needs free and active citizens."[16]

The progression toward a humanistic, ecologically based human service means that the recreation and park movement will increasingly manifest an enabler or catalyst delivery approach in an effort to optimize human growth potential. This phase is an important shift given the technological thrust of the country and the growing recognition that there are several life paths, each of which should be encouraged. Recreation and leisure service agencies increasingly have come to recognize that there is a wide diversity of human values and efforts should be made to allow for divergent life style patterns of behavior and avoid the imposition of unnecessary uniform standards upon all individuals. In a highly technological society it is paramount that leisure service agencies adopt a service model which accents the positive qualities of life experience. Kurtz comments:

> "A significant life which fuses pleasure and creative self-realization is possible . . . and men can again discover ways of enriching experience, actualizing potentialities, and achieving happiness." [19]

Such a task of aiding people to actualize potentialities and creating an environment which promotes self-satisfaction and happiness will increasingly require leisure service agencies to be sensitive to the plurality of human needs and the diverse means that may be required for their satisfaction. Additionally, the recreation and park movement is addressing itself to the totality of an individual's needs. Weiner comments:

> "Now the profession appears to be moving into another phase where the focus seems to be on the individual and in creating a total environment in which the human can flourish according to his own interests and capabilities, to meet his individual needs as he copes with the tensions of a high-density life." [20]

This phase is correspondingly characterized as an *ecologically* based trend, in which recreation and leisure service agencies are concerned with interrelationships among people in their physical and social environments and the ways these relationships contribute or hinder their ability to realize their human potential. This new strategy of service is seen as a more active, responsive approach to human service in an effort to satisfy human needs and minimize problems *before* they occur. Weiner suggests that the community leisure service worker,

> "must view himself as the key recreation strategist in the community using any and all of the following alternative approaches to achieving recreational goals: (1) direct execution of a program; (2) stimulating community interest in a program by offering 'seed' money; (3) guidance, counselling, training and encouraging innovation; (4) providing information services and general support; and (5) determining interests/needs and identifying new resources." [21]

The relationship among family, education, leisure and work has become increasingly fractionalized and disjointed. Human relationships serve as the locus of one's identity and self-concept and it has therefore become a primary responsibility of leisure service agencies to foster habitability by providing a relatively unified and yet diverse stable, personal and enduring basis for community life.

Discussion of Terms

Recreation has several connotations, as it reveals varied attitudes, beliefs, mores, cultural backgrounds, etc. Recreation has a unique meaning for each person. Some people may deny its value, others extoll it. Kraus describes the various views of recreation and indicates the particular elements inherent in the definitions:

> "1. *Recreation is widely regarded as activity (including physical, mental, social or emotional involvement) as contrasted with sheer idleness or complete rest.*
>
> 2. *Recreation may include an extremely wide range of activities, such as sports, games, crafts, performing arts, arts, music, dramatics, travel, hobbies, and social activities.*
>
> 3. *The choice of activity or involvement is completely voluntary rather than because of outside pressures, compulsory, or obligatory.*
>
> 4. *Recreation is prompted by internal motivation and the desire for achieving personal satisfaction, rather than 'ulterior purpose' or other extrinsic goals or rewards.*
>
> 5. *Recreation is heavily dependent on a state of mind or attitude; it is not so much* what *one does as much as the reason for doing it, and the way the individual* feels *about the activity, that makes it recreational.*
>
> 6. *Recreation has potential desirable outcomes; although the primary motivation for participation is personal enjoyment, it may result in intellectual, physical, and social growth.*"[22]

There is a more recent interpretation of recreation, which combines some elements as noted by Kraus and which reflects a humanistic perspective and contemporary assessment of the human condition. David Gray suggests that the recreation experience is characterized by three important elements: aesthetic experience, achievement of a personal goal and positive feedback from others. Gray offers the following definition:

> "*Recreation is an emotional condition within an individual human being that flows from a feeling of well being and satisfaction. It is characterized by feelings of mastery, achievement, exhilaration, success, personal worth and pleasure. It reinforces a positive self-image. Recreation is a response to aesthetic experience, achievement of personal goals or positive feedback from others. It is independent of activity, leisure or social acceptance.*"[23]

According to Gray's definition recreation has considerably greater potential than once conceived. Gray's view provides for a full range of internally motivated pleasurable forms of expression. It is not linked to leisure "time" which is often equated with quantitative outcomes and suggests that each individual is the sole interpreter of one's own recreation experiences. Murphy, et al. state:

> "A definition of recreation which recognizes individual potential and responds to the developmental traits of each participant seeking optimal satisfaction is qualitative and underscores the view articulated by Gray, which seeks to promote the realization of self-worth by each individual participant."[24]

Recreation then represents a wide and complex variety of individual differences which have potentiality for influencing recreation behavior.

> "By viewing recreation as an individual response which may reflect social, physical and emotional behavior, the primary objective of leisure agencies is to provide opportunities for people to optimize and fulfill internal need-drives and represent the total human personality."[25]

It increasingly appears that the activity approach to viewing recreation is becoming an obsolete philosophical perspective. Too often planners and providers of recreation opportunities utilizing this approach focus on supply and give too little attention to why the individual is engaging in the experience, what satisfactions are received from the activity and what other experiences might have been selected if the opportunities existed. Driver and Tocher suggest that a behavioral approach to recreation must be developed. Recreation is not seen as an activity but more appropriately as a psycho-physiological experience. One task to be faced by recreation planning will be to ask the following question.

> "Are we providing those recreational opportunities which will elicit those responses in the user that are most instrumental in satisfactorily meeting his needs and desires?"[26]

It is suggested by this interpretation that a behavioral interpretation of recreation will add another dimension to the traditional activity conceptualization. If recreation is a segment of behavior "we have an unavoidable responsibility to learn as much about the behavior as we possibly can. Only in so doing can we be effective in delivering appropriate leisure services."[27] However the program objectives of leisure service agencies are defined, the basic purpose of any recreation agency is to provide opportunities for people, individually and collectively, to engage in leisure behavior.

Work

There has been a demise of the Protestant Work Ethic in America in which work was viewed as activity ulterior to religious sanctions[28] and that one had to sacrifice individual expression and growth in order to survive. Work justifications were not seen as intrinsic to the activity and experience, but were religious rewards. This perspective contrasted with the Renaissance view of work, which saw it as intrinsically meaningful and the experience centered on technical craftsmanship. The Protestant work perspective, appropriate perhaps to an industrializing nation of immigrant factory workers who found opportunity in America for good pay and improved standard of living gladly accepted a subordinated role at the workplace. However, technological developments, the organization of work and education have altered worker expectations. These developments have increased productivity and consumption of goods. Increasingly young workers seek to be more autonomous and active in their work and wish to be treated with respect by their employer. Maccoby comments.

> *"The average American industrial worker now enjoys a standard of living that seems fabulous to the rest of the world. Once a certain level of affluence is taken for granted, this tends to undermine the attitudes based on the principle of scarcity, that one must sacrifice individual expression and growth in order to survive."*[29]

Work is going through a transformation and its roots lie not just with the industrial worker but with highly skilled craftsmen and engineers too. These individuals feel deep dissatisfaction in jobs which do not demand a fuller use of their skills and desire work which allows initiative and growth.[30] A growing number of contemporary workers are seeking more opportunity for self-expression in their work and their satisfaction in a technological society, as with the craftsman during the Renaissance, may well be determined and enhanced to the degree it becomes infused in the worker's entire life style.

Work does provide an important source of identity and role fulfillment in our society. It does not appear that work as we know it now will be completely eliminated. However, there are several projections which indicate some possible alterations in commitments people may be making to their jobs and conversely to other spheres of their lives. Denis Johnston reveals three such patterns.[31] The three work scenarios for the future provide insight into how people may opt to live.

Johnston's first scenario, the *green* concept visualizes an automated society in which a small elite of cybernetic engineers would be responsible for the production and distribution of goods, and the rest of the population would be limited to consumption. However, a leisure ethic is seen emerging in this configuration and providing intrinsic motivation and satisfaction for people outside of work. This concept is supported by the continually diminishing work day, week and year, increase in length of paid vacations and the corollary reduction in proportion of one's life spent in work.

The second and most characteristic work projection is the *blue* scenario, recognizes a continuation of existing trends with the "realization and maintenance of a full employment economy, together with the progressive removal of remaining barriers to the employment of those groups whose desire for employment has been frustrated by a variety of handicaps or by discrimination."[32] This concept assumes the continuation of the work ethic with a steady flow of trained persons who are desirous and willing to work. Additionally this perspective visualizes an expansion in the number and variety of professional, technical and service occupations geared to the operation of automated machinery. It is expected that efforts to achieve our national goals in a number of areas are likely to generate a high level of demand for labor, thus facilitating the achievement of full employment.

The third work scenario articulated by Johnston, the *turquoise* concept, views a gradual unification of work and leisure into a holistic pattern as was characteristic of most preindustrial societies. Such a reunification process has already occurred in the guise of coffee breaks, informal on-the-job socializing, and increasing concern for amenities of the work setting. However, even more profound have been the various on-the-job training and professional development courses, reflecting "an increasing concern with the need to elicit from workers a greater sense of commitment by increasing their opportunities for growth and fulfillment within the work setting."[33] Such innovations are attempts to humanize the work setting and as several studies have revealed, the work ethic appears to be undergoing a radical transformation. Employees, particularly the younger "new" workers, are taking their work *more* seriously, not less.[34] Workers are concerned about dignity associated with their work and with opportunities for career development. Maccoby states, "they are also increasingly concerned that the work be 'meaningful,' that it involve clearly useful tasks and require sufficient skill to be worthy of respect."[35]

What in fact may be occurring is the movement away from a work ethic to a life ethic in which workers (now representative of approximately 90% of all men and 48% of all women in the country) are seeking to have meaningful lives, both on and off the job. The expansion of this trend recognizes a gradual reduction in average hours worked per year, together with a subtle blending of work and leisure activities.

Play

There are several approaches to viewing play—physiological, psychological, anthropological, sociological, developmental and interactionist. The physiological perspective suggests that play is basic to organic health as it contributes and maintains health. The psychological perspective states that there are certain basic needs, drives and goals that an individual strives to satisfy. The individual has a desire to achieve these through play, to explore and assimilate manageable portions of the environment. One's self-concept may also be enhanced. The anthropological view of play sees it as ultimately a universal activity found in all societies and passed on to each generation and an individual develops play patterns because of contact with others. In the sociological concept, play is viewed according to its relationship with other institutional forms, behaviors and functions. According to developmentalism play is caused by the growth of the child's intellect and conditioned by it. The individual passes through successive stages and play occurs when the individual can impose on reality his conceptions and constraints.[36] The interactionist concept of play combines hereditary (developmental) and environmental (learning) factors. According to Ellis the interactionist arousal-seeking approach to play assumes that:

> "1. *Stimuli vary in their capacity to arouse*
> 2. *There is a need for optimal*
> 3. *Change in arousal towards optimal is pleasant*
> 4. *The organism learns the behaviors that result in that feeling and vice versa*"[37]

This concept views play as a class of behaviors which is concerned with increasing the level of arousal (stimulation) of the human organism. Successful community operations will be ensured to the degree that "they deliver opportunities for their patrons to engage in behavior that optimizes their arousal during nonwork hours."[38] Paul Friedberg, the noted landscape architect believes that to stimulate creativity in children playground designers and recreation and park administrators have to provide children an environment in which to grow, which is itself creatively stimulating. If one believes in the developmental play perspective, then good designers will accommodate the developing needs of children and provide environments and apparatus which can be used in many varied and complex ways. Asher Etkes suggests that children should chart their own course during play and that directed play is not play at all in the creative sense.

> *"Thus, in a model environment, only minimal intervention is needed. Children name and perform their own games. As a game runs its course, a child undertakes play tasks at his own level. When he accomplishes one successfully, he assigns himself another, more difficult one . . . and so it goes."*[39]

The play environment should be one that permits an individual to move from one formation of components to another as a game theme or fantasy is played out and a new one springs up. It is suggested that play environments be established in such a way that they be fully comprehensible to and negotiable, yet challenging to the participant.

Concepts of Leisure

There are several conceptual and theoretical perspectives of leisure. A theory is a set of interrelated principles and definitions that serves conceptually to organize selected aspects of the empirical world in a systematic way. Theories allow intellectual movement to a higher, more generalized, inclusive level of understanding; summarize empirical findings; provide bases for exploration and prediction; suggest the next steps in systematic inquiry; serve as a spur to the scientist's indigenous and acquired curiosity; and are useful in integrating and abstracting the interrelatedness of natural phenomena. Most views of leisure are only at a conceptual level; that is they represent philosophical insights, ideas and general notions of phenomena.

Theories are classified as to their representation of grand theory, which involves a large number of interrelated propositions and provides a major conceptual scheme of terms of which a range of human behavior can be explained or middle-range or mini-theories, which attempt to explain a limited area of human behavior. Whatever the case the propositions that comprise a theory are constantly subject to further empirical testing and revision.

Many of the theoretical explanations used to delineate leisure behavior have dealt with demographic variables of income, age, sex, education, social class, race and occupation. Several theorists believe these variables offer only a partial explanation of the complex components affecting leisure behavior. Havighurst and Feigenbaum[40] have contended that the most fruitful approaches toward understanding leisure behavior lie in the psychological domain (personality needs). Additionally, they stated that there are few cases where one's life style (a reflection of personality, values, attitudes and aspirations) and leisure style are not in close relation. Therefore, leisure expression, is shaped principally by personality traits or basic personality needs rather than social factors.

Burch[41] suggests that the social circles which surround the individual may be the primary determinants of variation in leisure preferences. In his view, the individual interacting with factors in one's environment — such as the occupational milieu, family and particularly friendship settings—predispose the individual toward certain leisure pursuits. His "personal community hypothesis" asserts that an individual is more greatly influenced by social issues and psychological drives that are significantly filtered and redirected by the social circles of workmates, family and friends. He contends that his personal community hypothesis has greater predictive power than either the "compensatory hypothesis" which suggests that whenever an individual is given the opportunity to avoid his regular routine he will seek a directly opposite activity or "familiarity hypothesis" which suggests almost directly the opposite, in that it assumes that individuals have worked out a comfortable routine for social survival and the benefits of security outweigh any possible rewards that may accrue from venturing into uncertain activities or experiences.[42]

Cheek[43] reported a sample of white- and blue-collar male park users and found no significant difference by occupation in park use and that attending a park shares a common social structural characteristic with several other settings. While middle-range theories may provide some limited explanation of leisure behavior, it appears that we must increasingly look to more integrated theoretical perspectives which reflect interrelated, empirically unifiable propositions of human behavior. Leisure expression appears to be interrelated to other social and personal spheres which cannot be isolated by a single variable and must be treated and analyzed within the broader framework of culture.

Burdge and Hendricks[44] argue that there is need for an integrating or holistic leisure theoretical framework to be developed. Such a synthesizing theoretical perspective is recognized as an important conceptual development in understanding leisure behavior as *homo sapien* is seen not as an aggregation of his individual spheres but rather incorporates an interpretation of one's ability to integrate normal occupational demands, educational and family background, value orientations as well as the immediate environmental conditions of facilities and locale. They comment on the need of scholars and researchers to emphasize a holistic approach in the study of leisure.

> "*[they need to] focus on the subjective fusion of work and non-work spheres and attempt to establish the relationship and relevance of leisure in terms of other human behavior. Leisure is not seen simply as activity, but rather includes time and attitudes toward time and non-work activities. Implicit in this orientation is the notion that leisure is not an isolated sphere remaining after obligatory activities have been completed nor do they see leisure, as does the survey group, as an end in itself or as recuperative activity. Leisure, in the holistic orientation is seen as a complex of multiple relationships involving certain choices which indicate societal and individual aspirations as well as life styles.*"[45]

Such a need for a holistic perspective in highly industrialized cultures is echoed by Bacon.

> "*Indeed it is probably that a different conception of leisure will be needed to investigate the nature of social cohesion in sections of society where poverty has largely been eliminated, where prosperity is endemic and where work is declining in importance in favour of non-working or leisure oriented life style.*"[46]

Bacon's suggestions for leisure research correspond to Burdge and Hendrick's who similarly see the multidimensional, unitary essence of leisure in which we can no longer view leisure as an isolated, residual sphere of unobligated behavior. The term leisure has many different connotations and is used in many different ways depending upon the intent of the individual.

There are seven concepts of leisure that have been developed, each with a particular set of precepts about human behavior. It should be indicated that six of these concepts might be viewed as having middle-range theory possibilities, and are seen from a segmentalist perspective (in which leisure is viewed as an isolated and residual sphere of unobligated behavior). The other, the holistic concept previously described has grand theory potential and may be seen from a multidimensional perspective. These concepts have been illustrated in more detail in another volume[47] so only a brief interpretation will be made of each in this text.

The most common approach to conceptualizing leisure views it as that portion of time which remains when work obligations and the basic requirements for existence have been satisfied to do what one wants to do within the range of one's abilities and interests. Leisure is *discretionary* or non-obligatory time. This approach puts emphasis on distinguishing the time of work from the rest of time—especially if the individual is free from all kinds of necessities. According to this perspective time may be viewed as being divided into three categories: time for existence, sleeping, eating (meeting biological requirements); time for subsistence (working at one's job); and leisure (time remaining after the basic necessities of life and work requirements have been accomplished). While this perspective is most commonly understood by the lay public, it is too influenced by economic categories and does not advance our thinking significantly beyond an eroding Protestant Work Ethic or the multidimensional problems of leisure as it is related to family, socio-spiritual/socio-political, and self-fulfillment activities.

The oldest interpretation of leisure, the *classical*-hellenic concept, sees leisure as "an activity which involves pursuit of truth and understanding. It is an act of aesthetic, psychological, religious and philosophical contemplation."[48] Leisure is viewed as a state of being, an attitude of mind. To Pieper[49] leisure is the basis of culture and culture depends for its existence on leisure, and leisure in turn is not possible unless it has a durable and consequently living link with divine worship.

> "*The revitalization of leisure as an appropriate aesthetic, epistomological, and spiritual expression by various religious sects and hip young people has initiated a disciplined form of self-realization and Christian rediscovery based on community cooperation and lack of material concern. Rejuvenated interest in Eastern religious philosophy, yoga, contemplation, and communal living is part of this spiritual movement.*"[50]

The spiritual and religious potential of leisure expression as exhibited in the wave of interest manifested by young people in further investigating the spiritual aspects of the universe outside of "main line"[51] churches underscores the apparent need by society in general and leisure service agencies for fostering ritualistic expression and community celebration.[52] This position is further indicated by Kraus who states that some people believe that leisure should extend opportunities beyond the purely utilitarian, providing opportunity for enrichment of life, for aesthetic involvement, and for personal joy, release and reward.

> "*All such experiences, whether they relate to the need for ritual and celebration, artistic involvement, or education, are part of the need of enriching the total quality of life.*"[53]

Dumazedier[54] has indicated that the decrease in socio-spiritual and socio-political obligations related to the decline in holidays and rites controlled by these traditional institutions has freed time, "now taken up by purely hedonistic activities freely chosen by the

individuals concerned rather than institutionally imposed."[55]
Dumazedier attributes this celebrating, feasting and collective
leisure as part-cult, part-leisure.

Leisure may also be viewed as a *social instrument*. In this
sense it is seen as a means of meeting an individual's social needs
and fulfilling deprived and physically or mentally impaired
person's needs who might require permanent and/or temporary
assistance in non-obligatory areas of self-expression.

> *"Leisure in this view is seen as a means of meeting needs of the poor
> through VISTA and Community Action Programs and as a threshold
> for the disadvantaged to help them actualize social needs and develop
> self-help skills."*[56]

Increasingly more individuals in human service field are
desirous of serving others and to operate in concert for the
achievement of qualitative societal goals. Kraus comments on the
need for recreation and leisure service agencies to be more
responsive to the social needs of urban dwellers and achieve
significant outcomes.

> *"Today it must be recognized that the United States has become
> predominantly an urban society and that it is marked by major
> differences in terms of social class, racial affiliation, economic status,
> and attitudes of morality. Particularly in the cities, the pressure upon
> the tax dollar is tremendous. Within this context, the notion of
> recreation as an experience which, by definition is not designed to
> meet important social needs or achieve 'extrinsic' outcomes can no
> longer be applicable. Every area of service that is provided by
> government and voluntary agencies today* must *be purposeful and
> must achieve significant outcomes."*[57]

This charge has been further articulated by David Gray and
Seymour Greben who have provided a re-definition of leisure
which explicitly holds recreation and leisure service agencies
accountable for their programs.

> *"We must recognize the potential role of recreation in the development
> of people. The goals of organized recreation programs are to provide
> people opportunities for the exercise of their powers, opportunity for
> recreational experience, opportunity for the development of a positive
> self-image. Any program that receives a participant whole and sends
> him back damaged in self-respect, self-esteem, or relationships with
> others is not a recreation program."*[58]

Leisure may also be viewed as non-work *activity*, in which an
individual is free to engage in experiences oriented towards
self-fulfillment as an ultimate end. This perspective has been
advocated by Dumazedier who believes the essence of leisure has
resulted from shorter work-schedules, reduced family duties, and
lessened socio-spiritual and socio-political obligations creating a

new social value of the person which is translated into a new social right to dispose of time for one's own satisfaction. According to Dumazedier leisure fulfills three functions: relaxation, entertainment, and personal development. He states:

> "*Leisure is activity—apart from the obligations of work, family, and society—to which the individual turns at will, for either relaxation, diversion, or broadening his individual and his spontaneous social participation, the free exercise of his creative capacity.*"[59]

Dumazedier indicates that while socio-economic conditioning governs most activities in society, they are increasingly giving way to leisure activities which tend to affect the determining institutions of work, religion and the family as we move toward a post-industrial society. The growing amount of spare time, a result of shortening work weeks, increases in paid vacations, earlier retirement and longer life span, tend to be dominated by the dynamics of leisure.[60]

Greater consideration is being given to the concept of *life style*, a perspective which provides a more complete understanding of the leisure behavior of the individual, as the standard variables of income, age, race, education, social class, occupation and sex as previously mentioned provide only a limited explanation of the extremely diverse behavior possibilities found in leisure. Burch notes that an analysis of the data retrieved in a national survey indicated a "significant" association between level of outdoor recreation activity and such factors as sex, age, race, religion, place of residence, education of head of household, income and life cycle. However, he notes that the survey report suggests that "taken together these factors account for approximately 30 percent of the variance in the measure of outdoor recreation activity."[61]

The typical factors used by recreation and leisure service agencies do not provide a very high level of prediction about leisure behavior. A more comprehensive leisure behavior prediction tool will be explored in more detail later in the text. As research has shown leisure to involve the total self, a fully developed comprehension of the individual's personality, attitudes, aspirations, and racial, cultural and family background is necessary before adequate delivery of leisure service can occur. The life styles reflective of ceramic buffs, skiers, surfers, off-the-road motor vehicle enthusiasts, etc., are indicative of different leisure interests. According to this leisure concept, leisure service agencies must be receptive to a variety of expressions of leisure choices and provide an environment conducive for such people to have an opportunity for growth, relationships and creativity.

> *"The concept of life style is a relatively stable, but flexible concept which must be viewed with greater concern by recreation and leisure agencies in the future as it provides for understanding how and why various subcultures and groups make choices throughout a life span. By using this concept agencies will necessarily alter their service offerings to focus more on enhancing self-development and personal gratification since it springs primarily from within the individual rather from others and provides an acceptance of self-responsibility and identity and self-worth."*[62]

A sixth view of leisure attempts to explain leisure behavior by one's *social class, racial* and/or *occupational* background. A number of studies have indicated that a person's social class position, racial background and/or occupational designation seem to be associated with some forms of leisure activity. Certain activities might be monopolized by members of a particular social class, racial group or occupational group, but it cannot be stated uniformly that people of such groups will exclusively participate in the same activities.

While certain differences may still be found utilizing standard socio-economic-status variables they have become less significant elements in advanced industrial and technological societies. Some reasons for this decline include the following:

> *"(1) the population as a whole is growing more affluent, which will increase the range of activities available to an ever-widening section of the community; (2) growth of mass leisure industries and mass media will spread similar tastes (diffuse culture) and opportunities, resulting in more people using leisure in similar ways; and (3) the volume of free time that people have has expanded, resulting in increased opportunities for people to develop autonomous leisure interests."*[63]

Certain differences in leisure pattern have historically been related to sex, largely because women could not engage in certain "male-oriented" sports and games, either because of cultural constraints or arbitrary discriminatory behavior. Much of the same case might be made for males who were often discouraged from entering arts and crafts type of activities, dance or music oriented programs. With changing sex-role patterns and more egalitarian practices, one would expect "male only" classes and "girl dominated" activities to slowly recede from the scene. Age differences have been linked to leisure activity preferences and pattern, largely through declining physical abilities of older persons resulting in reduced participation in physically arduous activities. However, Schmitz-Scherzer and Strodel, for example, indicate that "chronological age is not necessarily the key variable with regard to leisure-time activities. Rather, social variables, personality traits, and health status seem to influence greatly the use of leisure time."[64] Neulinger indicates that often interpretation of findings relative to leisure activity patterns results in differences arising from social class rather than educational discrepancies in the population being studied. Typically, data reveal that the *more* educated person has a higher affinity for leisure and work, which may only indicate that the more educated person has a longer vacation or reflect the greater meaningfulness of his or her job.[65] Similarly, the higher a person's income the more likely that individual is to be identified through work, perhaps suggesting that such persons have jobs which allow ego satisfaction. Most measurements of social class combine income, education and occupation as an index reflective of leisure activities. However, while these three variables are useful in correlating leisure activity patterns, the desirability of using occupation as an independent variable for distinguishing one's job and his free time activities is diminishing in significance as blue-collar and white-collar classifications become more diffuse. There have been a number of studies attempting to determine whether leisure participation does vary as a function of social class and/or occupation and while there continues to be debate on this question, it does appear that doubts are being increasingly raised, particularly as noted by Burdge[66] and Cunningham, et al.[67] Neulinger offers a suggestion for future consideration relative to neglected aspects when attempts are made to establish relationships between social class and leisure behavior.

> *"The quality of the free time activity, its context, mode and subjective experience, is never taken into account in these investigations. Swimming is coded in the same category whether it takes place on a crowded city beach or at an exclusive private one. Going out for dinner at MacDonald's is equated with going out for dinner at the fanciest restaurant, and traveling on the crowded Long Island Railroad commuter train is taken to be the same as going by parlor car. One cannot find differences that one does not include into one's coding system!"*[68]

A recently described leisure expression, as manifested typically by youthful members of the counter culture and disenchanted white-collar workers, is the *anti-utilitarian* perspective. This concept views leisure as a state of mind that is a worthy end in itself. As noted by Gray this perspective rejects the,

> *"position that every investment of human energy must produce a useful result. It rejects the work ethic as the only source of value and permits the investment of self in pursuits that promise no more than the expression of self. This concept accents joy and seeks pleasure."*[69]

According to this concept, the individual must learn to rejuvenate the inner self and add the dimension of pleasure in order to make sense of technology's antagonistic influences. Unlike the discretionary time concept which is based on a linear-mechanical time perspective or classical view of leisure which is intertwined with natural-biological time, the anti-utilitarian concept reflects a more personal time reference, in which the essence of leisure is seen as self-expression through activities that have no useful end. Dumazedier recognizes the decline in influence in socio-spiritual obligations on free time resulting in the expression of activities which reflect the anti-utilitarian view of leisure, although he suggests, as previously indicated, that the appearance of celebrating, feasting and collective leisure expressions which are religious or pseudo-religious in character are part-cult, part-leisure.

> *"Yet, even when the control of religious institutions on free time recedes, ambiguous activities, religious activities or pseudo-religious in character, often oriental in inspiration and containing elements of idealism and mysticism, of dream and metaphysics, of erotism and of the supernatural etc. . . . appear in some circles and especially among the young. These activities are performed in small groups or in large gatherings during weekends or holidays. . . . It seems difficult to consider them as leisure phenomena which should be viewed as distinct and analysed sometimes by religious sociology, sometimes by the sociology of leisure."*[70]

While each of the foregoing may be helpful in isolating some facet of leisure behavior, none alone appears to be able to fully account for all of the variation. A more holistic orientation may come closest in accounting for explained variance. Social-economic-status profiles provide some insight into explaining leisure behavior patterns and personality variables provide alternative considerations for studying leisure activity[71] and suggest a basis for substitutability among activities which provide an understanding of the underlying meanings and consequences of activities to participants as reported by Ferriss.[72] Hendee and Burdge[73] suggest that various social groupings of leisure participation may serve as a basis for substitutability as activities may be interchangeable depending on who participates with whom. An endemic problem, particularly in resource based recreation areas, is identified by Hendee and Burdge as reflective of the lack of understanding of leisure preferences and which might be overcome through the application of the substitutability concept.

> *"The current concern by recreation managers over excessive crowding, disregard for environmental values, and preference for inappropriate facilities and activities may reflect the selection of outdoor recreation by persons whose leisure interests might reflect other priorities. The popularity and overuse problems in outdoor recreation areas may thus be due in part to the presence of people seeking leisure satisfactions that might be, but are not, met elsewhere."*[74]

Hendee and Burdge indicate that as a result of research they carried out in two independent studies,[75] five activity clusters (cultural hobbies, organized competition, domestic maintenance, social leisure, and outdoor activities) can be identified based on similarity of participation patterns and activity rates of participants. Thus the concept of leisure activity substitutability is defined as the interchangeability of recreation activities in satisfying participants' motives, needs, wishes, and desires.

References

1. Leonard, George B.: *The Transformation: A Guide to the Inevitable Changes in Humankind.* New York, Dell Publishing Company, Inc., 1972, p. 177.
2. Jerome, Judson: Radical Premises in Collegiate Reform, In: *Let the Entire University Community Become Our University.* Edited by Philip C. Ritterbush, Washington, D.C., Acropolis Books, Ltd., 1973, p. 206.
3. Ruitenbeek, Hendrik M.: *The Individual and the Crowd: A Study of Identity in America.* New York, The New American Library, Inc., 1965, p. 24.
4. Kostelanetz, Richard, editor: *The Edge of Adaptation: Man and the Emerging Society.* Englewood Cliffs, New Jersey, Prentice-Hall, Inc., 1973, p. 1.
5. Sessoms, H. Douglas: The Meaning and Significance of Leisure, *Journal of the Medical Association of Georgia* July, 1973, p. 256.
6. Ibid: p. 257.
7. Ruitenbeek: Op. cit., p. 118.
8. Murphy, James F.: *Recreation and Leisure Service: A Humanistic Perspective.* Dubuque, Iowa, William C. Brown & Co., 1975, p. 4.
9. Neumeyer, Martin H. and Neumeyer, Esther S.: *Leisure and Recreation: A Study of Leisure and Recreation in Their Social Aspects.* New York, The Ronald Press Company, 1958, p. 64.
10. Sessoms, H. Douglas: Recreation — Theory and Practice, *The Encyclopedia of Education.* New York, The Macmillan Company, 1971, p. 435.
11. Butler, George D.: *Introduction to Community Recreation.* New York, McGraw-Hill Book Company, 1940, pp. 60–61.
12. See Doell, Charles E. and Twardzik, Louis F.: *Elements of Park and Recreation.* 3rd ed., Minneapolis, Burgess Publishing Co., 1973, p. 54.
13. Murphy: Op. cit., pp. 43–44.
14. Sessoms: Op. cit., p. 435.
15. Richard Kraus: Providing for Recreation and Aesthetic Enjoyment, In: *Governing the City: Challenges and Options for New York.* Edited by Robert H. Connery and Demetrios Caraley, New York, Praeger Publishers, 1969, p. 99.
16. Sessoms: Op. cit., p. 435.
17. Kraus, Richard: *Recreation and Leisure in Modern Society.* New York, Appleton-Century-Crofts, 1971, p. 209.
18. Maccoby, Michael: Introduction, In: *Where Have All the Robots Gone: Worker Dissatisfaction in the 70s.* Harold L. Sheppard and Neal Q. Herrick, New York, The Free Press, 1972, p. xxxiv.
19. Kurtz, Paul: The Moral Revolution, *The Humanist* March/April, 1971, p. 4.
20. Weiner, Myron E.: A Systems Approach to Municipal Recreation, In: *The Municipal Year Book.* Chicago, The International City Manager's Association, 1971, p. 167.
21. Ibid: p. 169.
22. Kraus: Op. cit., pp. 261–62.
23. Gray, David E.: Recreation: An Interpretation, Summary of Research Findings, December 12, 1971, California State University, Long Beach, California.

24. Murphy, James F., Williams, John G., Niepoth, E. William and Brown, Paul D.: *Leisure Service Delivery System: A Modern Perspective.* Philadelphia, Lea & Febiger, 1973, p. 12.
25. Murphy: *Recreation and Leisure Service,* Op. cit., p. 14–15.
26. Driver, B. L., and Tocher, S. Ross: Toward a Behavioral Interpretation of Recreational Engagements, In: *Elements of Outdoor Recreation Planning.* Edited by B. L. Driver, Ann Arbor, University of Michigan Microfilms, 1970, p. 24.
27. Murphy, et al.: *Leisure Service Delivery System,* Op. cit., p. 92.
28. See Mills, C. Wright: *White Collar: The American Middle Class.* New York, Oxford University Press, 1951, pp. 215–23.
29. Maccoby: Op. cit., pp. xxvi–xxvii.
30. Sheppard, Harold L. and Herrick, Neal Q.: *Where Have All the Robots Gone.* New York, The Free Press, 1972, for a report of a survey of contemporary work attitude of the "new" worker who rebels at the lack of variety, autonomy and challenge to his potential that is characteristic of many jobs today.
31. Johnston, Denis: The Future of Work: Three Possible Alternatives, *Monthly Labor Review 95*:3–11, May, 1972.
32. Ibid: p. 5.
33. Ibid: p. 6.
34. "Is the Work Ethic Going Out of Style," *Time* October 30, 1972, pp. 96–97.
35. Maccoby: Op. cit., p. xxv.
36. Ellis, M. J.: Play and Its Theories Re-Examined, *Parks and Recreation 6*:51–55, 89–91, August, 1971.
37. Ibid., p. 55.
38. Ellis, M. J.: *Why People Play.* Englewood Cliffs, New Jersey, Prentice-Hall, Inc., 1973, p. 143.
39. Etkes, Asher B.: Where The Play's the Thing, *Early Years* May, 1972, p. 52.
40. Havighurst, Robert J. and Feigenbaum, Kenneth: Leisure and Life Style, *American Journal of Sociology 64*:396–405, January, 1959.
41. Burch, William R., Jr.: The Social Circles of Leisure: Competing Explanations, *Journal of Leisure Research 1*:125–147, Spring, 1969.
42. Ibid: pp. 127, 132.
43. Cheek, Neil H., Jr.: Toward a Sociology of Not-Work, *Sociology of Leisure 14*:7–20, July, 1971.
44. Burdge, Rabel and Hendricks, Jon: The Nature of Leisure Research: A Reflection and Comment, *Journal of Leisure Research 4*:215–19, Summer, 1972.
45. Ibid: p. 216.
46. Bacon, A. W.: Leisure and Research: A Critical Review of the Main Concepts Employed in Contemporary Research, *Society and Leisure 4*:90, 1972.
47. See Murphy, James F.: *Concepts of Leisure.* Englewood Cliffs, New Jersey, Prentice-Hall, Inc., 1974.
48. Gray, David E.: This Alien Thing Called Leisure. Speech delivered at Oregon State University, Corvallis, Oregon, July 8, 1971.
49. Pieper, Josef: *Leisure: The Basis of Culture.* New York, Pantheon Books, Inc., 1952.
50. Murphy: *Concepts of Leisure,* Op. cit., p. 44.
51. A Comeback for 'Main Line' Religion *U.S. News & World Report* February 25, 1974, pp. 53–55.
52. Murphy, James F.: A Rediscovery of the Spiritual Side of Leisure, *California Parks and Recreation 28*:22, December 1972/January 1973.
53. Kraus: *Recreation and Leisure in Modern Society,* Op. cit., p. 396.
54. Dumazedier, Joffre: *Sociology of Leisure.* Amsterdam, Elsevier, 1974, pp. 69–70.
55. Ibid: p. 70.
56. Murphy, et al.: *Leisure Service Delivery System,* Op. cit., p. 9.
57. Kraus, *Recreation and Leisure in Modern Society,* Op. cit., pp. xii–xiii.

58. Gray, David E. and Greben, Seymour: Future Perspectives: An Action Program for the Recreation and Park Movement, *California Parks and Recreation 30*:16, June/July, 1974.
59. Dumazedier, Joffre: *Toward a Society of Leisure.* New York, The Free Press, 1967, pp. 16–17.
60. Dumazedier: *Sociology of Leisure*, Op. cit., p. 72.
61. Burch: Op. cit., p. 144.
62. Murphy, James F.: Leisure Determinants of Life Style, *Leisure Today* November/December, 1974, p. 5.
63. Murphy: *Concepts of Leisure*, Op. cit., p. 99.
64. Neulinger, John: *The Psychology of Leisure.* Springfield, Charles C Thomas, 1974, p. 96.
65. Ibid: pp. 97–98.
66. Burdge, Rabel J.: Levels of Occupational Prestige and Leisure Activity, *Journal of Leisure Research 3*:262–274, 1969.
67. Cunningham, David A., Montoye, Henry J., Metzner, Helen L., and Keller, Jacob: Active Leisure Activities as Related to Occupation, *Journal of Leisure Research 2*:104–111, 1970.
68. Neulinger: Op. cit., pp. 100–01.
69. Gray: Op. cit.
70. Dumazedier: *Sociology of Leisure*, Op. cit., p. 70.
71. Hendee, John C. and Burdge, Rabel J.: The Substitutability Concept: Implications for Recreation Research and Management, Unpublished research paper, 1974, 13 pp.
72. Ferriss, Abbott L.: The Social and Personality Correlates of Outdoor Recreation, *The Annals 389*:46–55, 1970.
73. Hendee and Burdge: Ibid.
74. Ibid: p. 8.
75. Ibid: pp. 6, 8.

CHAPTER 2

The Nature of the Recreation Experience

"While it is often necessary for recreation and leisure service agencies to program for the "majority culture" in any particular community they cannot continue to ignore the growing number of subcultures which are arising at increasing rates, particularly as they orient their lives around non-work beliefs, values and behavior patterns."

Recreation is viewed alternatively as an attitude, expression, behavioral sequence, emotional response, process, activity and as a life style. Depending upon the interpretation each definition may reflect accurately the experience of the participant. There is little research to refute the validity of any of the descriptions of recreation. However, since there is so little understanding of what is the most accurate interpretation of recreation no one definition should be construed as being the most definitive meaning.

The one view of recreation that has been most commonly accepted is the one which sees recreation as activity. People have often viewed recreation in this context and unfortunately oftentimes the quality of a leisure agency's service is measured by the amount and variety of activities it offers. This has several drawbacks. One, service delivery is typically only measured quantitatively; two, recreation and leisure service agencies ignore or give little attention to the psychological dimensions of recreation experience; three, a small priority is given the social and human developmental potential of recreation experience; and four, only certain activities are accorded as being expressive of human needs.[1] While recreation activity may provide an understanding of what one is doing, it may not provide an understanding of why the person is engaged in the experience nor recognize individual potential and respond to qualitative developmental outcomes derived. It should be the intent of recreation agencies to begin to measure at least indirectly their contribution to personal fulfillment and self-satisfaction.

Howard[2] states that while recreation may be seen as activity, the real value of the act or experience is derived from its ability to satisfy certain underlying needs which exist within the individual. Recreation experience is then recognized as a means to an end, purposeful, goal-directed behavior. Kraus comments:

> *"It is important to recognize that human beings are commonly goal-oriented, purposeful creatures. When they engage in recreational activity, they frequently do so for reasons that go beyond personal enjoyment or satisfaction, such as the need to make friends, to keep fit, to obtain physical release, to become involved in competition, or to gain prestige. There are many purposes for recreational involvement which transcend the search for diversion alone."*[3]

It is suggested that recreation may best be explained in a behavioral context and the experience that results from one's engagement in activities that meet certain needs. Motives for participation vary from individual to individual, and from experience to experience. This necessitates the need for recreation and leisure service agencies to recognize the varied and complex interrelated individual differences which have potentiality for inflencing recreation behavior. *"Individuals are motivated to recreate by internalized needs which are set in motion by a multitude of forces or drives in an attempt to respond and achieve internal consistency."*[4]

The recreation experience is a personal response. Each individual has certain needs or dominant values around which one's personality is organized. Howard indicates that the selection of specific recreation activities is most likely prompted by the desire to satisfy these personal needs. An example illustrates this concept.

> *"Painting, then, may become a free time medium for individual self-expression, recognition or the satisfaction of a host of other needs. The specific need or combination of needs motivating the artist, or any other individual, is dependent upon the individual's own unique personality."*[5]

The primary value of recreation experience, then, is its ability to satisfy needs which exist within the participant. As noted by Mercer[6] recreation need is a highly complex and relativistic concept, constantly changing through time. An individual's felt and expressed needs are often of a short-term nature both at the individual and at the societal level. Because different individuals of the same generation develop different recreation tastes, what may be identified as felt or expressed needs of a particular age group in a particular season or year may be quite irrelevant for planning proposed by recreation and leisure service agencies for this same age group category another season or year.

Recreation As An Emotional Response

Leisure service agencies have focused their attention on the provision of recreation activities designed to fulfill expressed community needs and interests. This approach has tended to limit the goals of the agencies and restrict their services to the delivery of activities with little or no regard for the influence such activities have on the participants. Gray has articulated a definition of recreation expression which provides a contemporary assessment of the human condition:

> "Recreation is an emotional condition within an individual human being that flows from a feeling of well-being and self-satisfaction. It is characterized by feelings of mastery, achievement, exhilaration, acceptance, success, personal worth, and pleasure. It reinforces a positive self-image. Recreation is a response to esthetic experience, achievement of personal goals, or positive feedback from others. It is independent of activity, leisure, or social acceptance."[7]

According to Gray's interpretation of recreation expression, it is *not* activity, but that it is the *result* of activity. Recreation is seen primarily as an internal, individual, pleasurable response to certain needs of the organism. This definition reflects Howard's interpretation and underscores the potential of recreation in building a self-image of personal affection and competence. Gray's definition invites rethinking of leisure service not only in terms of the types of activities and programs typically offered, but also in terms of human experience. Recreation, like education and work, should and can help each individual extend his or her intellectual and emotional reach through opportunities which improve awareness, deepen understanding, stimulate appreciation, develop one's powers, and enlarge the sources of enjoyment. The implications of Gray's definition of recreation include the following points:

"1. We must alter our programs and the way they are conducted to emphasize human development, well-being, and development of a positive self-image.

2. We must enhance the possibility that people can experience the peak experience described in the definition—in short, the opportunity for aesthetic response, achievement of personal goals, and positive feedback from others.

3. We must rethink competition and the way it is used in recreation programs.

4. We must accept responsibility for the human consequences of what we do.

5. We must evaluate everything we do in human terms. The critical questions are not "How many were there?" or "Who won?" The critical question is, "What happened to Jose, Mary, Sam, and Joan in this experience?"[8]

It is suggested that recreation defined, perceived and fostered as an emotional response promotes individual fulfillment and encourages self-discovery through self-realization. It may well be that leisure service agencies will need to reorient the training of their personnel to be cognizant more of individual variation in recreation expression by providing minimal organization and maximum flexibility. Stainbrook states:

"The emerging self must be allowed to define its experience in the very act of creating, and not be coerced by the structure, the value system, or by the preconceptions of those in recreation and leisure planning who expect only certain kinds of self-fulfilling behavior to happen."[9]

The leisure setting should provide opportunities for the individual to engage in a full range of possible experiencing which will allow for spontaneous and direct use of the environment. It must also provide opportunities for diverse expressions to allow each age and life style group as well as subculture the chance to meet its needs through recreation participation which is meaningful to them. Recreation is seen as a personal response, which grows out of personal experience. Leisure service agencies must develop goals and objectives for planning purposes which include a recognition of the worth of the individual. In the future, agencies must make available to the individual the necessary attitudes, knowledge, and skills in which one can make relevant recreation choices to realize personal goals.

Recreation Experience As A Humanistic Expression

Humanism represents a central concern for the dignity of each person and the development of human potentialities. It sees this as the fundamental consideration for all human beings—that the individual should have a measure of choice, autonomy and self-determination. A humanistic approach to life seeks to embrace a person's positive capacities, his or her expressions of joy, freedom and self-fulfillment. The new morality of humanism views the "good life" as a realization of human potential.

A humanistic view of life perceives the fully functioning person as one who is *inwardly* free to move in the direction of his choice. According to Carl Rogers[10] people should not try to create something in an individual which is not there, but rather to provide the conditions which make for growth; growth will come from within. Rogers believes that a fully functioning person is not "happy," "fulfilled," "contented," "actualized," per se. These words imply a fixed state of being, an objective achieved. The full life, is not a state of anything—it is a process, a movement, in a direction which the individual chooses when he is free to move as he wishes, unimpeded and unafraid.

Recreation and leisure service agencies which incorporate a humanistic approach to service would seek to promote the capacity and ability of groups and individuals to make self-determined and responsible choices in light of their needs to grow, to explore new possibilities and progress toward realization of their full potential. A humanistic perspective involves facilitation of growth potentials as well as a concern for eliminating barriers which hinder self-development. Efforts should be made to organize leisure service delivery in a way which fosters individuality and autonomy.

> "Recreation and leisure service agencies are seen as [enablers] . . . of human growth potential and stewards of individual rights of self-expression. *Such agencies recognize that there are a wide diversity of human values and efforts which should be made to allow for divergent life style modes of expression and avoid the imposition of uniform standards upon all individuals.*"[11]

Too often irrelevant standards are established by suppliers of community recreation which do not reflect user needs and goals.[12] Agencies must be sensitive to the plurality of human needs and to the diverse means that may be required for the satisfaction.

Differentiation of Recreation Experience—Minority and Subcultural Expressions

There are a number of individual and group variations as expressed in leisure behavior. A number of studies have revealed the diversity of types of activities as manifested by different social classes, occupational and age groups, races, etc. While the genesis of motivation apparently stems from an internal drive to satisfy certain need/goals, based on one's own unique personality (as indicated previously), there are, nevertheless, some generalizations which can be made regarding the various recreation participation patterns of certain population groupings.

Leisure Preference and Residential Selection

In a study of the Greater Toronto, Canada area, Michelson[13] indicates that people select places of residence based on their own personality and life style characteristics and preferred recreation activities and the degree to which they are consistent with satisfaction of these perceptions. The study found (1) those people becoming high rise apartment dwellers tended to exhibit more passive in-house leisure behavior than those moving to houses, particularly as related to T.V. viewing. An influencing factor is the general lack of space and specialized intra-unit recreation facilities and noise distraction from neighbors by those living in apartments; (2) apartment dwellers spend more time outside of their dwellings and those in downtown areas are concerned with the concentration of leisure opportunities near their place of residence, whereas home owners, because of the amount and diversity of recreation facilities in the house are more likely to spend their leisure in-house; (3) high rise apartment dwellers, because of their isolation from their neighbors, even though in close proximity to many of them, tend to engage in more solitary leisure pursuits, and entertaining in other people's home and those in downtown areas in public establishments, whereas those living in houses in the suburbs tend to engage in more social groups since the suburbs serve as the center of social participation with the various formal and informal groups located there.

Bell[14] indicates that there are three concepts of residential selection which may well have a bearing on the type of recreation activities offered and the setting in which they occur. He posits that people moving to the suburbs value "familism" (an emphasis in childrearing and family life) as a major reason for residential location. Those individuals living in downtown, center-city areas tend to reflect "careerism" (an emphasis in one's job) and "consumerism" (an emphasis in consumption) as the characteristics for choosing to live in this environment.

While there may well be small but regular differences in the choice of living area, nonetheless, the variations in life style by environment may well be reflective of the perceived self-satisfaction of apartment and home dwellers and therefore the necessity to promote certain recreational opportunities to fulfill these needs.

Rural-urban differences have been linked to outdoor recreation participation patterns with urbanites typically being represented disproportionately in many forms of outdoor recreation (principally fishing and hunting). Data from the comprehensive Outdoor Recreation Resources Review Commission's National Recreation Survey showed variation between recreation activities in rural-urban areas. However, Mueller and Gurin[14] indicate that while suburban areas tended to show somewhat higher participation in outdoor recreation than urban communities and other areas, these differences may be disappearing and affected by other combined factors.

> *"Since city and country is part of their day-to-day environment one might expect them (urban and rural residents) to differ in the extent to which their recreational patterns involve outdoor activity . . . Of four categories, (1) the cities themselves, (2) the suburban fringe, (3) adjacent areas to a distance of 50 miles, and (4) outlying areas at least 50 miles from a city of 50,000 . . . Suburban areas show somewhat higher participation in outdoor recreation than cities and other areas . . . However, the relatively high participation by suburbanites is a reflection of their income, education, and occupation . . . although pronounced differences appear in two or three instances, in general the relationships . . . tend to be weak, certainly with respect to . . . age . . . with the increasing homogeneity of our national culture, many value and interest differences between city and country people are disappearing and decreasing differences in outdoor leisure patterns would seem to be part of this trend."*

Hendee suggests that since ORRRC studies and others reveal little and sometimes conflicting variations in outdoor recreation participation by rural versus urban residence the validity of some recreation studies reporting differences is called into question. He offers a few plausible theories for reported differences. One theoretical perspective involves rural versus urban population densities, often referred to the "opportunity theory," which implies that participation in different forms of outdoor recreation depends on their availability. "Since city residents have less opportunity to participate in rural leisure activities, they will be under represented in them. They will be over represented, however, in activities readily available in the city, such as walking for pleasure."[15]

Similar to population density is a concept which suggests that everyone has a desire to get away from it all; "to escape to levels of extraneous social contact less intense than normally experienced in their daily lives. Rural residents would seek, therefore, the more isolated activities such as wilderness camping, while urban residents might find reduced social contact in car camping, walking, or driving for pleasure."[16]

A second theoretical viewpoint involves rural-urban cultural differences. Burdge[17] found rural farm residents to be more work-oriented, provincial, traditionally puritanical and conservative and therefore less inclined toward the "frivolity" represented by outdoor recreation activities. One's attitude toward the natural environment may explain participation in certain outdoor recreation activities and may possibly relate to rural or urban residence. Hendee offers a possible explanation for rural-urban differences arising from varying cultural perspectives.

> *"Since rural occupations such as farming, mining, and logging are typically based on the exploitation and consumption of natural resources, they might encourage an exploitative attitude toward natural resources and thus serve as a retarding influence on outdoor recreation. The view that nature is to be used, not just appreciated, characterized such a utilitarian perspective. Urban occupations ... are typically in manufacturing or service industries far removed from the natural environment. Urban residence may thus allow the development of appreciative attitudes toward nature ... A utilitarian attitude toward nature may thus be associated with "harvesting" recreational activities—fishing, hunting, etc.—whereas an appreciative orientation is more closely linked to the realization of aesthetic and social values in outdoor activities."[18]*

The above mentioned rural-urban theory adds the dimension of occupational differences between city and country. Burch and Wenger[19] have developed three theories, the "familiarity," "new experience," and "pleasant childhood memory" perspectives which may also be linked to rural-urban difference in outdoor recreation activity patterns. The familiarity theory suggests that people seek leisure experiences similar to their everyday lives. The new experience theory indicates that people seek leisure experiences that allow them to escape their everyday lives through sharply contrasting and new experiences. The most promising theory, the pleasant childhood memory perspective, suggests that individuals will tend to participate in outdoor recreation activities that were pleasantly familiar during childhood.

The Impact of Leisure on Family Life Styles

The family exercises an important influence on its members and provides certain norms giving them guidance as to which leisure pursuits are desirable and worthwhile. The socialization process within the family context involves learning by group members to evaluate the various leisure opportunities that are available. It is suggested that different family types will encourage their members to participate in different kinds of leisure pursuits and even provide certain skills and knowledge necessary to participate in them. It is Dumazedier's[20] contention that leisure is shaping the whole style of life of the modern family. His beliefs concerning the desire of the family members for particular types of leisure that exercises the main influence upon decisions such as residential location and the relationships between husbands, wives and their children are coming to be based around the co-operative pursuit of mutual leisure interests. Orthner[21] suggests that within the family the ability of leisure activities to differentially stimulate social interaction should have important consequence for marital relations. He suggests that there are three patterns of leisure activities which characterize families—parallel, joint and individual. Parallel activities are individual expressions which occur in a group setting providing little direct communication, such as television viewing or going to a theater by married couple. Joint activities require a higher degree of interaction for successful completion of the activity, and make the individuals involved more aware of new communication opportunities as expressed in picnics, for example. Individual activities are pursuits in which communication with others is not required and actually may interrupt successful completion of the activity.

Intra-spouse parallel and joint activities will conceivably have a primary impact on marital communication and role patterning as they directly reinforce spouse interaction and influence, in turn, the internal needs and constraints of the marital relationship. Individual activities are more likely to reinforce personal or other needs and are largely external to the marital relationship.

Skinner[22] has observed that workers are developing a fundamentally different ethic about life. He indicates that fewer workers want to work overtime, especially the younger workers who increasingly find their jobs boring and monotonous. What is occurring is that the job is no longer the focal point for many workers. Wolfenstein[23] studied the changing attitudes toward child rearing and observed that while discipline, firmness and obedience had formerly been the basic training of children, it was being replaced by a new fun morality in which parenthood is being characterized by fun and enjoyment. Additionally, Dumazedier[24] notes that for many people religious days and holidays have lost much of their symbolic meaning and commitment and are now utilized more for alternative family leisure activities than they may have been in the past.

Miller and Sjoberg[25] have suggested a theoretical framework for understanding and interpreting the nature of new life style patterns of the middle-class. They characterize two subgroups—straight or traditional, and alternative or non-traditional, as typifying urban middle-class life styles. As noted in Figure 1 straights tend to segment and compartmentalize work, leisure and kinship-friendship, while alternative middle-class groups seek to unify and blend each of these social and institutional forms into a more holistic living style which have formerly been segmented. To a degree, rural communal systems represent an attempt by people who work, live and play together according to a schedule regulated only by nature. Urban collectives follow a similar pattern as friends work together at something they enjoy. "Thus work becomes leisure and leisure becomes work, all intertwined with kinship-friendship."[26]

As technology has increased our ability to produce beyond marginal survival, a vast range of goods, services and life conditions, previously unattainable, have become freely available and accessible to most families in our society.

> *"The commitment of society in the late nineteenth century to a machine-based production economy and more recently in the latter quarter of the twentieth century to automated processes, has removed dependence on day/night and seasonal cycles, as well as freeing individuals from geographically limited life locations, and has resulted in the prospect of the human condition being characterized by a multiplicity of choice possibilities."[27]*

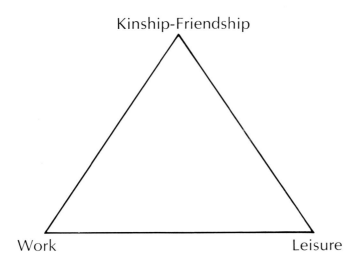

Fig. 1.   Segmentation of work, leisure, kinship-friendship life style pattern.

Miller and Sjoberg indicate that there are a variety of intermediate groups which lie between traditional and alternative middle-class family groups, including *Jesus Freaks* who adhere to traditional activities, but blend work, leisure and friendship through religion; *weekend dropouts* who hold traditionally Monday-through-Friday jobs (and who may even segment their lives during this period), but withdraw to an alternative life style on weekends by blending the main elements of life style that have been delineated; and *play groups* (a way of life associated with "playboy morality") for whom leisure is the chief concern. Members of play groups accept the structure and the value orientation of the straight world, although their emphasis is upon leisure, almost nonstop on weekends. Their friendship ties are rather tenuous and work and binding personal relationships are of secondary importance; leisure is of paramount importance.

There are four major implications indicated by Miller and Sjoberg which have a bearing on the provision of leisure opportunities for urban middle-class groups:

"1.   *The impact of the alternative society upon urban communities as a whole is likely to be far greater than its present number of adherents might suggest. Its effects . . . will continue to be felt in the redefinition of patterns of kinship-friendship, work and leisure by groups who may even reject the alternative social order. Members of the latter have . . . delegitimized many features of the traditional middle-class life style and have intensified the search for new types of differentiation, ones not based upon traditional ethnic or class differences. Conceivably the melding of leisure, kinship-friendship, and work is essential if many groups, such as the elderly, are to attain meaning in life, if they are to avoid viewing themselves as castoffs from a production-oriented society.*

2.   *More directly, the new life styles, especially those espoused by adherents to the alternative social order, are beginning to restructure the urban community in America . . . One solution to working out an effective way of life for persons within the alternative society is for them to map off an area and claim it as their own. In order to integrate kinship-friendship, leisure and work patterns [as noted in Figure 2], a new type of community needs to be formed.*

3.   *The diversification of the urban middle-class life style has important implications for large-scale organizations as well as for specific communities. [The] data . . . indicate that members of the alternative society reject the school system and other service agencies [conceivably recreation and leisure service agencies as well] because these organizations leave little or no room for divergent life styles. School systems typically have reacted to challenges by the nonstraights in a rigid manner.*
       More generally, the client-centered bureaucracies [including recreation and leisure service agencies] have typically failed to grasp certain basic implications of many of the new patterns of living. Legislators and decision makers in government agencies devote

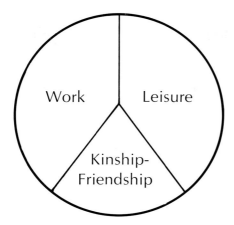

Fig. 2.   Blending of work, leisure, kinship-friendship life style pattern.

> *almost no consideration to changing life styles in their formulation*
> *of urban policy, even though they are concerned with the*
> *accommodation of different groups to one another and with*
> *providing essential services to persons who do not accept the*
> *traditional bureaucratic system. [Client-centered bureaucracies*
> *function in terms of a segmented orientation toward life, which is*
> *sharply opposed to the holistic-integrated pattern of living of the*
> *alternative society. This provides no real congruency to those of an*
> *alternative life style group. Because the integration of activities*
> *may be too difficult within a highly differentiated urban environ-*
> *ment people increasingly may opt to become weekend dropouts in*
> *an attempt to adjust to a different pattern of living. This pattern*
> *may become more widespread with the infusion of the four-day*
> *work week within conventional society.]*
>
> 4.   *... almost all [people participating in this study] respondents were*
> *worried about and were searching for a sense of community.*
> *Almost all were aware that the nature of family life is changing and*
> *they displayed a keen awareness of the transient and often*
> *superficial aspects of friendship ties. The quest for community,*
> *although defined differentially by various subgroups, represents*
> *one common basis for working out an adjustment in urban centers*
> *of the future."*[28]

The alternative life style pattern being established by
middle-class groups is not a myth but in fact a reality in several
cities across America. One such change is being facilitated by the
Outlaw Institute in San Francisco of middle aged people who see
themselves as part of a movement toward greater personal
autonomy, in their work and nonwork lives.

> *"The merging picture is a network of several hundred people helped*
> *toward change in their lives by country workshops and city classes.*

> *Some of them are already living communally, many have dropped from 9-to-5 jobs into more experimental lives, and all of them are served by a newsletter and a recently opened outreach and resource center through which they are coming to know how to support one another by barter, by shared skills and resources, and by collective action of many kinds.*
> *. . . within all of this super-activity framework, it's easy to overlook the real focal point of it all—the many people who merely flow on through . . . and make massive changes in their lives. Sheldon, who moved from a 60-hour week running his own department store to the less structured life of an instructor in stained glass. Don, who has forsaken dental technology to become a weekend janitor; Shirley, who gave up $14,000 a year as an administrative assistant to do massage on her own time; Liz, who sold her employment agency so she could garden, for fun and minimal profit; Aline, who was an architectural secretary until she quit in order to make quilts; Ken who left a high level post with HEW to open his natural food store . . ."*[29]

There are a growing number of people who are deviating from the traditional pattern of urban, suburban and rural living. What is particularly interesting is that the previously described individuals are *not* giving the prime part of each day *nor* the prime years of their lives to work. Work does not dominate their lives, it merely blends harmoniously into their day-to-day living pattern.

Subcultural Group Expressions

There are a number of distinctive styles of leisure expression found in various subcultures. Although there is a common belief that there is one American life style behavior pattern, represented in white middle-income, Anglo-Saxon Protestants, this couldn't be further from reality. In truth, American society embraces many ethnic groups, including blacks, Chicanos, Indians, Chinese Americans, etc., as well as many different interest age group subcultures, each reflective of certain values, beliefs and life style patterns having some particular cultural, ideological or racial meaning and central life interest which pervades their activities and outlook on life.

While there are common elements that are prevalent throughout society, subcultures are found to take the form of variations within a common framework or develop a completely independent and self-contained style of life. With an expected increase in subcultures[30] it is important for leisure service personnel to come to understand the nature of variant subcultures and their application to leisure in American life.[31] This is particularly an important issue as related to minority groups, who, through their subordinated role in society and various cultural traditions and necessary adjustments to discrimination and intolerance, have had to evolve leisure life styles which have been seen as "deviant" and outside mainstream society (including participation in leisure activities within the community).

Most Americans' life styles are governed by the dominant rhythm, and the deviants—hippies, blue-collar worker, blacks and Chicanos, etc.—are cut off from this life rhythm. It is expected that the size and number of these groups of outsiders will increase due to the following:

> *"shift work is expected to become increasingly common, acceptance of divergent subcultural groups is becoming more prevalent, and growing alienation will frustrate people no longer gaining moral strength from the repetitive tasks of assembly-line work. Society must find a way of integrating outsiders into normal leisure activities."*[32]

The rise in subcultures has been heightened with the relative increases in the standard of living and growing amounts of free time available to more and more people. Subcultures operate outside of typical social class norms and provide their adherents a cultural identification separate from class structure orientation and expectation. The patterns of living associated with subcultures increasingly appear to be formulated around leisure aspects, particularly as leisure becomes a central life interest and organizer and contributor to one's life style. While it is often necessary for recreation and leisure service agencies to program for the "majority culture" in any particular community, they cannot continue to ignore the growing number of subcultures which are arising at increasing rates, particularly as they orient their lives around nonwork beliefs, values and behavior patterns. It is also an important concern since leisure is being identified as a system of new human experiences which represents the whole life of a person which an individual wants to live. Life styles are becoming expression of individual taste rather than reflections of economic position or social class.

Sessoms has noted three evolving life styles which provide a basic reference point and understanding of the phenomena of life style emerging as a result of the growing amounts of free time, increasing mobility and technology in our society and declining significance in work.

> *"The first leisure style reflects the traditional value system and attitude toward work and leisure. It manifests itself in two types of people: those who enjoy being entertained, the spectators; and those who pursue recreation with a vengeance, consuming equipment and experiences in the process. For the former, leisure is a time for amusement; these people ... [seek] ... the newer and more spectacular amusement but always somewhat dissatisfied because theirs has been a vicarious experience.*

The latter form of compulsive leisure behavior is seen in those who literally consume recreation environments and experiences. They are always buying new equipment, trying it out, demonstrating it, and abandoning it as newer and better models or newer forms roll off the assembly line. [One concern about this life style perspective is]. . . that if people only pursue these experiences because they are consumers of goods, then the satisfaction must come from the shopping and possessing of the items rather than from the experience which the equipment was designed to facilitate.

The second major leisure life style is exhibited by those who approach their free time leisurely. They acknowledge the time limits of their experience but during the moments when they are at leisure, they act without reference to the clock. They characterize leisure activities as variable, self-directed expressions, and see leisure and work as equal avenues for fulfillment . . . They let the dynamics of the experience dictate their behavior. They appear to be completely free from set routines and schedules, yet their leisure is acknowledged in relationship to other experiences and time obligations.

This second form of leisure behavior is often characteristic of those professionals and craftsmen who have control over their schedules. Their work tasks and leisure expressions may occur simultaneously or be interrelated. For these proponents, the essential elements of both work and leisure are involvement and freedom, not the time nor setting in which the activities are pursued.

The third major form of leisure behavior in our society is exhibited by the counterculture groups. In many ways they exhibit some of the same patterns as those who consume recreation experiences or compulsively wait to be amused or entertained. On the other hand, they seemingly rid themselves of dependency on the clock and are in harmony with the rhythms of nature.

Essentially, they are a product of the same value system [of the larger society]except for one notable exception: the counterculture groups do not honor the traditional time notion and its related concept of organizational interdependency. To the counter-culturist, experiences are to be lived as they occur; they are to be enjoyed now. They are a different breed; they seem to be pre-industrial men living in an advanced industrial society—blending the technology of this generation with the work habits and leisure attitudes of the distant past . . . . their presence does suggest another dominant way to enjoy leisure and its recreational benefits."[33]

It appears appropriate for recreation and leisure service personnel to note the particular life style patterns and attempt to promote, not deter, the particular forms of expressions and plan for the various interests. The informal but governing relationship of the group upon individual attitudes, values, and aspirations is likely to exercise a powerful influence. While there are common elements prevalent throughout society, subcultures are found to either take the form of variations within a common framework, or develop a completely independent and self-sustained style of life. The norms and traditions found within specific ethnic or other homogeneous communities exercise distinct social control over the leisure lives of people, even to some degree when they seek to use the leisure facilities and service offerings provided by the wider society. "The prevalence of a number of subcultures in American society reinforces the necessity for leisure service agencies to provide alternative means through which various groups within the community could realize their goals and ambitions in the leisure setting."[34]

Minority Group Leisure Expressions

Confronted with discriminatory treatment by the dominant white society, minority members in America have shown various patterns of responses. Some have been eager to assimilate (a group wishing to be absorbed or merged into the dominant group) in order to lose their minority stigma and/or original identity. Others have sought equality with separation (accommodation) and still others accept the status of inequality (and an inferior status). There are some minority members who have rejected both the segregated role and inferior image, and have demanded integration.[35] The process of minority adaptation and response to white American society has had its impact in the area of public accommodations, cultural expression and recreation behavior. To a large extent leisure choices, preferences and forms of ethnic and racial expression have been significantly influenced, even dictated, by the dominant society. The following are a few examples of minority group leisure expressions and a discussion of their implication for the delivery of leisure service.

Indians. Native Americans were the host culture when white European explorers ventured from across the Atlantic to establish a "new" nation. Indians were subdued over time and were subsequently banished to reservations in some of the most desolate areas of this country. While Indian culture never diminished, the tribal way of life was not integrated within the larger society. The "new" Indian is one who has attempted to blend the old native culture with a new sense of pride and a rejection of the melting pot idea of assimilation in an attempt to develop a viable, racially visible and tribal way of life.[36] The discretionary time, segmented approach to life, so pervasive in the highly technological, bureaucratic dominant society, is contrary to the more harmonious tribal life in which there is an "Invisibleness" of time. Time is more cyclical and has its own way of repeating. The Indian seeks to live within these continuous circles of harmony as they live within him. The Indian has a reverence for life, not for work per se. Human needs take precedence over commercial and bureaucratic needs and demands.

Recreation as a separate free time opportunity for self-expression has little meaning to the Indian who lives on a marginal subsistence level. However, recreation as intertwined and fused within his total life style affords the Indian an opportunity to preserve the beauty and richness of his culture while living in harmony with the land. Many recreation pursuits fragment time and exploit the land; these forms of expression are alien to the Indian.

Chinese Americans. Unlike the Native Americans, the Chinese were an immigrant population who were welcomed to this country to serve as laborers because of the demands for cheap labor following the discovery of gold in California. Later they were brought into direct competition with whites and other immigrants in the mining industry and a pattern of conflict and hostility developed. As a result the Chinese maintained a sociopsychological separation and withdrew from the larger society and insulated themselves against the full impact of the dominant society's values, norms, attitudes and behavior patterns. The Chinese have often developed voluntary segregation as their way of responding to the challenge of the environment and their segregation in Chinatowns still persists, although not as pervasive in the past, to institutionalize their own way of life distinct from white society.[38]

The Chinese are not a large minority and thus their numbers have not lent themselves to large scale open conflict with the dominant views of society; many Chinese have made a real contribution to the intellectual, professional and business life of American society. The Chinese have been extremely conscious of their own cultural heritage and strong prejudice against them has simply strengthened the "we-feeling" among them.

While the Chinese have engaged in more direct economic competition with the larger society, their cultural adaptation has been less manifest. They have been more conscious of their own identity and many of the "old culture" ways of life are still practiced in their communities. The preservation of the Chinese way of life is an important leisure consideration and to the degree that they do not disperse themselves throughout society in a large scale, requires sensitivity and an appropriate leisure service delivery response to preserve the early customs and folkways that are relative to Chinese cultural heritage. Recreation and park departments must attempt to establish more liaison, utilizing Chinese personnel to support and facilitate Chinese traditions, particularly with the first generation immigrants. While peculiar and different from many European influenced American folkways,

Chinese customs are an important form of identification to a minority largely excluded from public affairs and social activities in the wider society.

Chicanos. Like the Indians, Chicanos were a native indigenous people who held land prior to the colonial conquest and westward expansion. Spanish settlements in New Mexico, California and Texas have been in existence for over 3½ centuries. The Spanish developed distinctive cultural traditions, which have been submerged over the years by the dominant society. Their plight has witnessed an expropriation of their land and resources, negation of native language, and the breakdown to a large measure of the close extended family system and certain other cultural ways of life.

Leisure services, often alien to the Chicano, have the potential to breed intergroup relations and strengthen the Spanish and Mexican cultural heritage for the fulfillment of white and brown mutual expectations. While the average social and economic status of the Chicano has been improving, and many are moving upward on the socio-economic scale, the inevitability that all Chicanos will become an equal partner in the American social system is largely a matter of white acceptance of a different cultural pattern of beliefs, values, and way of life.[38]

The barrio, the center of Chicano family and social life, is a similar form of segregated living, which has inculcated and isolated the Mexican cultural way of life and allowed Chicanos to develop their own life style without the threat of subversion from white society. However, within the larger community, Chicanos like other minority groups have been discriminated against in their access to and opportunity for fulfillment in various types of recreation facilities and services.

While increasing numbers of Mexican-Americans have adopted Anglo beliefs and behavior patterns, many (particularly low-income Chicanos) prefer to retain their native Spanish language, child-rearing and courtship practices, strong extended family and kinship orientation, present time orientation, and various other aspects of their traditional culture (including religious beliefs) which promotes self-identification with their own heritage while allowing them to participate in Anglo-American culture. The isolation of Chicanos contributes positively to their identity, and many have found this an easier course to follow, since they need not strain to learn another language or to change their ways and manners.

Chicanos as an ethnic group subscribe to a different set of beliefs from the dominant white culture and this has carry-over in the leisure domain. Jackson[39] in a study of Anglo and Mexican American teachers and custodians measured the relationship between socio-economic status and ethnic background to leisure values and attitudes. He found that:

1. Mexican American teachers were positively oriented toward vacations and free time.
2. Both Mexican American teachers and custodians had a greater measure of self-definition in leisure than did Anglo teachers and custodians.
3. Mexican-American custodians perceived leisure and the need for it in the most negative light while Mexican-American teachers were most positively inclined.
4. No group favored a strong role for society in leisure planning.

Jackson suggests the following implications for the provision of leisure opportunities as they apply to variant ethnic value orientations and leisure attitudes:

> "1.   An implicit endorsement of the existence and need for cultural uniformity in American society does not provide adequate guidelines for leisure planning.
> 2.   Many of those responsible for lending direction and substance to leisure programs and services are committed to values of the dominant culture–the middle-class."[40]

Jackson's study reflects similar perspectives surfaced by other researchers of leisure behavior patterns of ethnic minorities.[41] There is a common fallacy associated with leisure planning that there is a uniform attitude and value system which exists within any given community, with only a tacit consideration for varying needs, attitudes and values of various social class, age, sex and ethnic subgroups. These studies indicate the imperative need for those designing leisure service programs to recognize and appreciate the values and attitudes of subgroups which do not conform to the dominant middle class expectations. There is more than one cultural norm in leisure which exists within any community. Typically the white middle class image is the one most often portrayed by community leisure service planners, and as the findings in Jackson's study indicate, there are differentiated attitudes such as affinity to leisure, self-definition through leisure, amount of vacation desired and society's role in leisure planning which deviate *qualitatively* from the traditionally held model for leisure consumption (future orientation, doing, mastery-over-nature and individualism), particularly by lower income Mexican-Americans (present, doing, subjugation-to-nature and lineality).

Black Subculture. Blacks represent the largest minority group in America and have been discriminated against in every area of life. However, in spite of this dehumanizing action, blacks have adapted to this situation in which racial oppression placed them. This has not meant that the degree of depredation practiced by whites and others has not had a marked effect on personalities and social life of blacks; and has resulted in the separation of blacks from the social mainstream of white society. As reported by Liebow[42] lower class blacks have fashioned in an imaginative way their own life style within their separate world.

The creativeness and "limited autonomy" of black residents (the distinct black subculture) serve as a source for finding out some of the solutions recurrent human problems. Blacks have a long history of being barred from places of white amusement— theaters, movie houses, amusement parks, swimming pools, bowling alleys, parks and zoos. Even when these are supported by public funds, blacks frequently could not use them. The degree of segregation and application of Jim Crow laws and the "separate but equal" doctrine served to turn blacks inward to develop their own music, dress, life style and sanctions for fun and pleasure.

Recent studies have underscored the amount of neglect and deprivation of ghetto life, and the lack of provision of recreation services and resources for blacks.[43] The dissension and violence emanating from poor slum neighborhoods in the 1960's served to highlight the degree of deprivation, deleterious conditions and the blocking of opportunities to realize human needs in a dignified way. Two studies, one by Kraus[44] of the 5 boroughs of New York City and 24 suburban communities in New York, New Jersey, and Connecticut, and one by the National League of Cities[45] of recreation in 15 major cities, demonstrated that public recreation and leisure service for blacks and other deprived groups was poorly conceived, extremely inadequate, underfinanced and in demand by inner-city residents.

Recreation and leisure service personnel will have to become increasingly more aware and sensitive to ghetto life in order to understand the dilemma of urban living faced by blacks. The melting pot of blackness is a result of slavery, Jim Crowism, Emancipation, Black Codes, Northern immigration and racism. The distinctiveness of the black subculture, particularly low-income blacks, is an important aspect to be considered in the design and delivery of leisure service. There must be an acceptance of black leisure preferences by community recreation officials, aiding blacks to learn skills, develop a positive self-image, and socialize in a manner consistent with their subcultural values unimpeded by the dominant white values and beliefs.

The provision of recreation opportunities is most successful when applied to blacks and other deprived minority groups which incorporate a comprehensive approach to providing needed services. This principle embraces the belief that leisure service is most meaningful when jobs, education, health and welfare and recreation opportunities embodied in a single approach make leisure a positive and constructive reality. This concept is strengthened by decentralizing the control and implementation of recreation in the communities affected by the provision of leisure service.

Successful re-structuring of recreation and leisure service programs aimed at paralleling the new thrust of black pride and dignity have been oriented to local community needs and have been organized and administered substantially by the neighborhood residents affected by service.[46] The development of productive cultural enrichment and self-help programs (acquisition of skills and knowledge which will enable a group to meet many of its own basic needs in terms of food, housing, clothing, education and recreation) oriented to indigenous neighborhood needs has contributed to the democratization of recreation and enhanced the value of such programs.

Because the black minority has in the past been thwarted in the pursuit of values, ideals and interests appropriate to the direction of their lives within the main stream of society, it was socialized to accept the socializing function of recreation in the black community and which has been inappropriate with regard to the real needs and interests of the black community. The recognition of the black subculture and incorporation of the differentiated but relevant values, opportunities for leisure expression and design of programs related to blacks (as with other ethnic minorities, social classes and age groups), appear to be the most meaningful way of serving people within a pluralistic societal framework.

> *"The provision of recreation and leisure service which recognizes the validity of the black subculture and incorporates a program consistent with the life styles and self-determination of black people appears to be the most relevant approach to the elimination of racism and inappropriately designed recreation facilities and activities."*[47]

Blue-Collar Workers

There is a growing interest among working class and lower-middle class blue-collar workers for increased diversionary and personal development opportunities made available to them during their free time. Klausner[48] found contrary to expectations that blue-collar workers he studied at the Kaiser Steel Plant in Fontana, California reported strong, favorable reactions to a 13-week paid vacation of extended leisure and indicated greater personal and family integration as a result. Among his findings were: (1) workers viewed the 13 weeks as leisure and not as an opportunity to improve their financial positions. They typically did not seek additional work to fill in the free time as they used their extended vacations in ways they felt were useful for themselves and their families; (2) the majority of the workers traveled at some time during their vacations, usually as families and in so doing provided themselves with the opportunity for growth; (3) the extended leisure experience revealed strongly the secondary nature of work. When freed of work responsibilities, the respondents immediately, and apparently happily, focused their lives on their homes and families; and (4) the workers reported that the extended vacation was, in relation to their families, a definitely integrating, not disruptive, experience.

From Klausner's study it was generally concluded that the 13-week vacation had a strongly positive effect on the workers and their families. Additionally, it may be conjectured that the nuclear family of the blue-collar worker in America is strongly capable of handling extended leisure, and may well benefit and grow from the increases in leisure.

Workers of all classifications, including blue-collarites have tended to enthusiastically endorse the 4-day workweek. In her study of the 4-day workweek, Poor[49] revealed that there is a growing movement by industry to alter the traditional 5-day, 40 hour workweek by having their employees work 4, 10 hours days, providing 3 days of bunched leisure for workers to enjoy. The larger blocks of leisure apparently are enhancing worker opportunities for increased leisure spending, but they also provide a chance for the worker to engage in more family and personally satisfying experiences. While leisure is traditionally viewed in consumer terms, the new life style of many blue-collar workers operating on 4-day workweeks, is not necessarily one of more generated demand for income, but, if anything, more demand for increased leisure.

While Klausner and Poor report positive impacts of increased leisure on blue-collar workers, it still remains that the majority of Americans earn less than $9,000 a year.[50] Work remains the central life interest of most work class people and leisure still is largely the domain of the middle-class and affluent members of our society. White-collar workers typically receive better incomes and benefits, thereby providing a more secure basis for developing a leisure-centered life style. Part of the blue-collar dilemma in working overtime, moonlighting and living less austere lives stems in part from poor wage benefits. Lasson comments:

> "28 percent of all blue-collar types receive no medical or hospital coverage, 38 percent have no life insurance, 39 percent are not included in a retirement program, and 61 percent do not have available to them employer-sponsored training programs."[51]

The blue-collar worker at leisure is typified as spending much of his time around the house in family-related activities, watching television, working on cars, drinking, bowling, traveling for pleasure and playing cards. While there is strong reason to suggest that blue- and white-collar occupational leisure patterns may be dissimilar,[52] several studies (previously indicated in Chapter 1) have shown that blue-collar workers tend to engage in different types of leisure activities (probably due to available opportunities, discretionary money, and other factors previously discussed). Gordon and Anderson summarize blue-collar leisure expression:

> "It appears to flow quite naturally from what are held to be basic themes of the stable working-class subculture: a desire for stability and security and an unwillingness to take social and economic risks which could disrupt the old security found in a group of solidary familiars, an anti-intellectualism which aspires for the understood result and the concrete, and a person-centeredness."[53]

There is less attention given by the blue-collar worker to civic-wide activities and this combined with fewer, well-equipped neighborhood parks located near working class families tends to decrease the options made available for leisure involvement outside the immediate family and relatively cheap forms of commercial entertainment. Additionally, technological advancements have tended to frustrate the blue-collar worker seeking to adopt the styles of living of lower-middle income groups immediately above them.

> "The hard-working blue-collar workers achieve little beyond providing the basic necessities for the families. For many, this means forfeiting the opportunity to develop and contribute as individuals to improved neighborhood and community life. He is too often the victim of social change and technological advances. This creates an attitude of despair, discouragement and disgust. He needs to feel that he can make a contribution and use his human talents and not be pushed aside in favor of progress and advancement."[54]

Blue-collar workers are striving for a degree of material wealth and convenience afforded so many other members of society and the opportunity to enjoy the resultant small increments of discretionary time (possibly gained as a result of bunching the work week from 5 into 4 days or more flexibility resulting from gliding or flex-time work days) and money, rather than status and power so prevalent among white-collar workers and professional groups. This idea is revealed by Berger and Berger[55] who suggest that America is undergoing a "blueing" process (contrary to Reich's "greening" perspective) of rising blue-collar working classes moving into slots vacated by disenchanted middle-class white-collar workers. Similarly, Johnston has suggested three possible work scenarios for the future and the dominant perspective is a *blue* concept which recognizes the "realization and maintenance of a full employment economy, together with the progressive removal of remaining barriers to the employment of those groups whose desire for employment has been frustrated by a variety of handicaps or by discrimination."[56] This concept assumes the maintenance of the work ethic with a steady flow of appropriately trained persons willing to work—most likely blue-collar personnel stunted in assembly-line and factory work and desiring greater working autonomy and control over their work with the increased salary which accompanies the better paying white-collar jobs.

It has also been noted by LeMasters[57] that a certain segment of skilled blue-collar workers, described as "blue-collar aristocrats," tend to deviate from the normal pattern of working class leisure patterns and desire to spend most of their free time away from their families, frequenting taverns, drinking, playing pool and cards, and talking with their buddies (not their wives). These men offer no apologies for their life style, as they work hard, earn good money and feel they should be able to spend it as they please—in their own country club, the tavern. For most of the blue-collar aristocrats, the center of life is not the job, but the leisure activities made possible by the job. Most of the tavern frequenters (at the Oasis, the working-class tavern which served as the study site) have little faith in the next world and seem determined to get as much enjoyment as they can from their lives and be "where the action is." Where the "action" is, for many of them, is located at drinking pubs like the Oasis, which serve as something more than a tavern.

> *"For those who are its regulars, the Oasis functions much as a country club does for middle- or upper-class persons: it is the center of social life, the major locus for leisure activities. The tavern draws into itself not only the male workers who form the core of its clientele, but their wives and families as well. It is a public drinking place which has become, in many regards, a private club."*[58]

Hippie Subculture

America's highly advanced technological society has thrust it into the forefront as the most affluent nation in the world, but this has not been without a price. Many young people in the 1960's, particularly middle-class youth, heirs to their parents' material wealth and comfort, began to reject the economic, achievement dimension of industrial progress. Many hippies have developed a different value base in contrast with dominant middle-class economic, cognitive and material achievement value patterns. They believe that the utilitarian and instrumental goal-orientation of America's advanced industrial society emphasizes dehumanizing life styles. Hippies, members of a "retreatist-rebellious youth movement which emerged in the mid-sixties in affluent segments of affluent societies,"[59] have tended to develop ideals which stress nonmaterial or spiritual concerns (such as participation in cosmology, mysticism and the occult), a search for love and intimacy in human relationships, religious philosophical interests, and self-expression, affiliation and concern for others.[60]

Contrary to the middle-class value patterns of achievement, occupational status through hard work, rational approach to finding solutions, and material wealth, hippie values stress neglected expressive concerns and deemphasize instrumental concerns. The perceived overemphasis of the middle-class on instrumentalism seems to have been matched by a similar overemphasis by hippies on pure expressivism. However, the hippie concern for focusing on fulfilling neglected personal needs of the individual to be a human being, appears to have had a balancing impact on America's changing value system.

> "... the hippie emphasis on expressive values could be regarded as partially illustrative of a process of widespread balancing in American society as a whole, whereby the social system, being pushed more and more to an instrumental extreme, is reintroducing various modes of expressivism at all levels of its structure ... the society-wide trend toward expressivism, exemplified in its most extreme form by the hip movement, could be seen as part and parcel of other strong trends in contemporary America—civil rights, freedom of speech, representation, life style, and the like. [Although it is not likely that the extreme expressivism found in hippie subcultures will be manifest in all subgroups, it is probable that] ... an expressivism suitable to all age levels and classes of American society will become part of the American ideology. It is in this sense that the hippie movement may have its most profound influence on the character of the American value system."[61]

The hippie movement has pervaded the youth subculture in general and represents an expression and a desire to establish a way of life and philosophy that will fulfill not only a social, but a spiritual (an inner and personal) need. Theodore Roszak[62] symbolized the emergence of a counter culture and an ideology of those opposed to objective consciousness and envisioned the need for the development of a new kind of consciousness, new values, new aspirations and new life styles—a culture based on subjective, aesthetic, symbolic and organic values and experiencing.

America's highly technological society has resulted in an increased number and variety of life styles as well as more opportunities for self-realization. Leisure service agencies have tended to gear their services based on the dominant value pattern of the middle-class, and while this is purposeful for a large number of people, it has restricted those who deviate from this value set, belief system and rhythm of life. In a companion publication the following synthesis of leisure service delivery approach was suggested:

> *"Leisure service personnel need to realize that opportunities should be provided which will not render people psychologically incapable of participating and which will not curtail their own personal life rhythm. The role of leisure service managers must then be not one of maximizing some life styles and values (those associated with the dominant group) and minimizing others (those associated with hippies, housewives, unemployed, physically disabled and retired people) but of achieving an integration of both sets of life styles and values."*[63]

The implication for leisure service personnel to comprehend the expressive nature of hippies and other young people lies in their ability to realize that the goal of the agency's efforts should be to maximize each person's potential, so that the individual can find his own life solution whether it be an instrumental goal (learning a skill, making friends, etc.) or an expressive desire (merely to realize one's potential as a human being).

References

1. Gray, David E.: Recreation: An Interpretation, Op. cit.
2. Howard, Dennis R.: Multivariate Relationships Between Leisure Activities and Personality, Doctoral Thesis, Corvallis, Oregon, Oregon State University, June, 1973, pp. 9–10.
3. Kraus: *Recreation and Leisure in Modern Society*, Op. cit., pp. 262–63.
4. Murphy: *Recreation and Leisure Service*, Op. cit., p. 33.
5. Howard: Op. cit., p. 10.
6. Mercer, David: The Concept of Recreational Need, *Journal of Leisure Research* 5:37–50, Winter, 1973.
7. Gray, David E.: Exploring Inner Space, *Parks and Recreation* 7:19, December, 1972.
8. Gray, David E. and Greben, Seymour: Future Perspectives, *Parks and Recreation* 9:50, July, 1974.

9. Stainbrook, Edward: Man Happening in a Leisure Society, In: *Leisure and the Quality of Life.* Edited by Edwin Staley and Norman Miller, Washington, D.C., American Alliance for Health, Physical Education and Recreation, 1972, p. 169.
10. Rogers, Carl: To Be Fully Alive, *Pennies Forum* Spring/Summer, 1973, p. 3.
11. Murphy: Op. cit., p. 4.
12. Gold, Seymour: *Urban Recreation Planning.* Philadelphia, Lea & Febiger, 1973, p. 108.
13. Michelson, William: Discretionary and Nondiscretionary Aspects of Activity and Social Contact in Residential Selection, *Society and Leisure* 5:29–53, 1973.
14. Mueller, Eva and Gurin, Gerald: Participation in Outdoor Recreation: Factors Affecting Demand Among American Adults, In: *Outdoor Recreation Resources Review Commission Study Report No. 20.* Ann Arbor, University of Michigan Survey Research Center, 1962.
15. Hendee, John C.: Rural-Urban Differences Reflected in Outdoor Recreation Participation, *Journal of Leisure Research* 1:335, Autumn, 1969.
16. Ibid: p. 336.
17. Burdge, Rabel J.: Rural-Urban Differences in Leisure Orientation. Paper read at Rural Sociological Society, Ames, Iowa, 1961.
18. Hendee: Op. cit., p. 337.
19. Burch, William R., Jr., and Wenger, Wiley D., Jr.: The Social Characteristics of Participants in Three Styles of Family Camping, U.S.D.A. Forest Service Research Paper PNW-48, 1967.
20. Dumazedier: *Towards A Society of Leisure.* Op. cit.
21. Orthner, Dennis K.: Toward A Theory of Leisure and Family Interaction. Paper read at Pacific Sociological Association Annual Meeting, March, 1974, 31 pp.
22. Skinner, Wickham: Watching the Clock, *Wall Street Journal 180*:1, 8, August 29, 1972.
23. Wolfenstein, Martha: The Emergence of Fun Morality, In: *Mass Leisure.* Edited by Eric Larrabee and Rolf Meyersohn, Glencoe, Illinois, The Free Press, 1958.
24. Dumazedier, Joffre: Leisure and Post-Industrial Society, In: *Technology, Human Values and Leisure.* Edited by Max Kaplan and Phillip Bosserman, Nashville, Abington Press, 1971.
25. Miller, Paula Jean and Sjoberg, Gideon: Urban Middle-Class Life Styles in Transition, *Journal of Applied Behavioral Science* 9:144–161, 1973.
26. Ibid: p. 152.
27. Murphy: Leisure Determinants of Life Style, Op. cit., p. 5.
28. Miller and Sjoberg: Op. cit., pp. 157–161.
29. Thomas, Irv: The Outlaw Institute, *Black Bart Brigade* 6:25, 29, September, 1973.
30. Toffler, Alvin: *Future Shock.* New York, Bantam Books, 1970.
31. Murphy, James F.: The Outsider: Toward an Understanding of Deviance in Leisure, *Society and Leisure* 5:61–69, 1973.
32. Murphy: *Concepts of Leisure*, Op. cit., p. 115.
33. Sessoms, H. Douglas, Meyer, Harold D., and Brightbill, Charles K.: *Leisure Services: The Organized Recreation and Park System.* 5th ed. Englewood Cliffs, New Jersey, Prentice-Hall, Inc., 1975, pp. 73–75.
34. Murphy: *Recreation and Leisure Service*, Op. cit., p. 105.
35. Kurokawa, Minako: Editor. *Minority Responses: Comparative Views of Reactions to Subordination.* New York, Random House, Inc., 1970, 376 pp.
36. Steiner, Stan: *The New Indians.* New York, Harper & Row Publishers, 1967.
37. Yuan, D. Y.: Voluntary Segregation: A Study of New York Chinatown. In: *Minority Responses.* Op. cit., pp. 134–144.
38. Simmons, Ozzie G.: The Mutual Images and Expectations of Anglo-Americans and Mexican Americans. In: *American Mix: The Minority Experience in America.* Edited by Morris Freedman and Carolyn Banks, Philadelphia, J. B. Lippincott Company, 1972, pp. 59

39. Jackson, Royal G.: A Preliminary Bicultural Study of Value Orientations and Leisure Attitudes, *Journal of Leisure Research* 5:10–22, Fall, 1973.
40. Ibid: p. 20.
41. Murphy, James F.: Egalitarianism and Separatism: A History of Approaches in the Provision of Public Recreation and Leisure Service for Blacks, 1906–1972. Unpublished Doctoral Thesis, Corvallis, Oregon, Oregon State University, 1972; and Heath, Eward H. "A Semantic Differential Study of Attitudes Relating to Recreation as Applied to a Bicultural Setting." Unpublished Doctoral Dissertation, Urbana, Illinois, University of Illinois, 1967.
42. Liebow, Elliott: *Tally's Corner.* Boston, Little, Brown and Company, 1967.
43. See *Report of the National Advisory Commission on Civil Disorders.* New York, Bantam Books, Inc., 1968; Jenkins, Shirley: *Comparative Recreation Needs and Services in New York Neighborhoods.* New York, Community Council of Greater New York, 1963; Kraus, Richard: *Public Recreation and the Negro: A Study of Participation and Administrative Practices.* New York, Center for Urban Education, 1968; *Recreation in the Nation's Cities: Problems and Approaches.* Washington, D.C., Department of Urban Studies, National League of Cities, 1968; Connery, Robert H. Editor: *Urban Riots: Violence and Social Change.* New York, Vintage Books, 1969; and Dunn, Diana R.: Leisure Resources in America's Inner Cities, *Parks and Recreation* 9:34, 36–38, 56–59, March, 1974.
44. Kraus: *Public Recreation and the Negro,* Ibid.
45. *Recreation in the Nation's Cities,* Ibid.
46. Nesbitt, John A., Brown, Paul D., and Murphy, James F.: *Recreation and Leisure Service for the Disadvantaged: Guidelines to Program Development and Related Readings.* Philadelphia, Lea & Febiger, 1970, 593 pp.
47. Murphy, Williams, Niepoth, and Brown: *Leisure Service Delivery System,* Op. cit., p. 45.
48. Klausner, William J.: Extended Leisure and the Family. In: *Educating for the New Leisure.* Edited by Roy Dull, Riverside, California, Conference Proceedings, University of California, Riverside, February 2–5, 1969, pp. 21–44.
49. Poor, Riva: Editor. *4 Days, 40 Hours.* New York, New American Library, 1973, 333 pp.
50. Sexton, Patricia Cayo and Sexton, Brendon: *Blue Collars and Hard Hats.* New York, Vintage Books, 1972, p. 31.
51. Lasson, Kenneth: *The Workers.* New York, Bantam Books, Inc., 1972, p. 6.
52. Cunningham, et al.
53. Gordon, Milton M. and Anderson, Charles A.: The Blue-Collar Worker at Leisure. In: *Blue-Collar World: Studies of the American Worker.* Edited by Arthur S. Shostak and William Gomberg, Englewood Cliffs, New Jersey, Prentice-Hall, Inc., 1964, p. 411.
54. Murphy: *Recreation and Leisure Service,* Op. cit., p. 115.
55. Berger, Peter L. and Berger, Brigitte: The Blueing of America, *New Republic* April 3, 1971. pp. 20–23.
56. Johnston: Op. cit., p. 15.
57. Dishon, Robert L.: Inside the Workers' Tavern, *San Francisco Examiner,* March 21, 1975, p. 23; and LeMasters, E. E. Social Life in a Working-Class Tavern, *Urban Life and Culture* 2::27–52, April, 1973.
58. Dishon: Op. cit., p. 23.
59. Kando, Thomas M.: *Leisure and Popular Culture in Transition.* St. Louis, C. V. Mosby Company, 1975, p. 44.
60. Berger, Bennett: Hippie Morality—More Old than New, *Trans-action* 5:19–27, December, 1967; Davis, Fred. Why All of Us May be Hippies Someday, *Trans-action* 5:10–18, December, 1967; Greeley, A. M.: "There's a New Time Religion on Campus," *New York Times Magazine* June 1, 1969, pp. 14–28; and Yablonsky, Lewis: *The Hippie Trip.* New York, Pegasus, 1968.

61. Levin, Jack and Spatts, James L.: Hippie Values: An Analysis of the Underground Press. In: *Sociology for Pleasure*. Edited by Marcello Truzzi, Englewood Cliffs, New Jersey, Prentice-Hall, Inc., 1974, pp. 115–116.
62. Roszak, Theodore: *The Making of a Counter Culture; Reflections on the Technocratic Society and Its Youthful Opposition*. Garden City, New York, Anchor Books, 1969.
63. Murphy, et al.: *Leisure Service Delivery System*, p. 61.

CHAPTER **3**

The Meaning of Community

"... A new concept of community is suggested by the high degree of impermanence from a nation of rootless people: one which is based on a greater degree of individual flexibility, vocational choice and selectivity, and leisure options within a highly mobile society ... the new sense of community is predicated upon a wider community network, a common life style based on mutual compatibility and shared interests."

Nature of Community Life

The term community has several meanings. Each perspective provides an understanding of the dynamics of the physical, philosophical, spiritual, functional and psycho-cultural aspects of shared living in a given area. Early views of pre-industrial community life defined community more as a small, closely knit web of meaningful relationships of kindred groups. In this sense they were seen as *moral* communities. The main characteristics of a moral community were: (1) a sense of *identification*, members had a deep sense of belonging to a significant, meaningful group; (2) *moral unity*, members had a sense of pursuing common goals and felt a oneness with other community members; (3) *involvement*, members were submerged in various groups and had a compelling need to participate in these groups; and (4) *wholeness*, members regarded each other as whole persons who were of intrinsic significance and worth.

In contrast with this sense of community, the conditions of a highly technological mass society have resulted in community being viewed in a somewhat more illusive, communion of people sharing large spaces with an extension of highly differentiated more impersonal relationships being fused to incorporate a group of people within a given territory. Mass communities have the following characteristics: (1) a sense of *alienation*, members have a deep sense of being "cut off" from meaningful group associations; (2) *moral fragmentation*, members pursue divergent goals and feel no sense of oneness with other members of society; (3) *disengagement*, members have no meaningful group memberships and feel no compulsion to participate in the collective activities of various groups; and (4) *segmentation*, members regard each other as means to ends and assign no intrinsic worth or significance to the individual.[1]

Modern communities in contemporary American society may also be distinguished by virtue of whether they are *rural* or *urban*. Action patterns in rural communities tend to be illustrative of (1) homogeneity of action; (2) familistic organization of activities; and (3) action guided by tradition. In contrast, action patterns in urban communities may be described by (1) heterogeneity of action; (2) nonfamilistic organization of activities; and (3) action guided by rationality and expediency.[2]

Another approach to viewing community is by interpreting the aspect of social relationships. In 1887 the German sociologist, Ferdinand Tonnies[3] developed a typology to aid the study of social relationships in community life. The two concepts which portray these relationships are *Gemeinschaft* and *Geselleschaft*. The key components of these terms are understanding and unity in that a relationship will be promoted when each member is valued for his own sake and that each individual fully understands the other and takes a direct interest in his welfare.

Essentially, Gemeinschaft-like relationships are characterized by mutual aid and helplessness, mutual interdependence, reciprocal and binding sentiment, diffuse obligations, and authority based on age, wisdom and benevolent force. People that are a part of Gemeinschaft-like relationships share sacred traditions and a spirit of brotherhood which grows out of blood, common locality and mind.[4]

In contrast, Geselleschaft relationships are characterized by individual members who are separated rather than united. Individualism becomes a strong force of community life. Additionally, relationships are contractual and functionally specific and frequently involve the exchange of goods, money or credit and obligations. Geselleschaft relationships are based more on rational and scientific laws and exist independently of superstition, faith and tradition.[5]

Other Ways of Viewing Community

Community may also be defined in other ways which refer to its organization and social life. A community may be defined by the degree of manifest *social interaction.* In this sense, a community's strength is recognized by its ability to unite and direct its members' actions well by the degree of interdependence and sentiment generated between members and for the group as a whole.[6] Community may also be defined as a *place,* "the human contacts on which feelings of commitment and identity are built are most likely to occur among people sharing the same piece of ground."[7] An *emotional* or *sentimental* concept of community refers to the state of mind on the part of its members, a sense of interdependence and loyalty which binds a community together.[8] Out of these conditions grow attachments to the social groups, and these attachments form the basis on which people respond to its collective demands. Community may also be portrayed by the degree of *functional specialization,* in which industry, the trade union, leisure services, corporate structure and professions evolve into a community bound together by their interaction through shared function and loyalties, sense of identification, and values conducive to a cohesive structure.[9]

A *political* community is defined as the way of life and thought of a society as it has organized itself for government activities. "Politics is an activity having to do with the 'allocation of values' in society . . . [and] the political process is presumed to be related to a sense of commitment and some degree of common purpose among the citizenry."[10] Part of the process of politics is a problem of creating community, of developing a consensual base on which the political structure can be organized. And finally, there is a *humanistic* concept of community which refers to the condition in which people enjoy meaningful relationships with other people and fulfill human needs for recognition, fellowship and security.[11] A sense of belonging, living and working together through face-to-face association, experiencing together, being together, is fundamental to human desires and is the only way in which a person can fully capture a sense of oneness.

This latter perspective has been generated in light of the great amount of alienation and heightened sense of anxiety so prevalent as a result of urbanization-suburbanization, population explosion-implosion (an in-migration), and the increasing complexity of modern society. Human relationships have become, according to the humanists, non communal in nature and therefore disintegrating to social relationships and damaging to the human condition and the quality of life.

Changing Perspectives of Community

The cities are undergoing a number of changes and urbanism has become synonymous with a contemporary way of life. The large metropolitan areas now number approximately 75% of the total population.[12] Community life is not easily predictable in urban America and the dynamics of living in contemporary society precipitates a lot of challenges, opportunities and dilemmas.

> *"Because cities set the pace for the generation of new ideas and the adoption of new life styles, they are the places where social changes, stresses, and strains acting on millions of individuals and families become visible through confrontations, strikes, demonstrations, vote upsets, and riots."*[13]

The segmentalization of human relationships in contemporary urban society particularly has posed some unique problems and challenges for human service agencies. People are increasingly dependent upon more people for the satisfaction of their life needs than are rural people and thus are associated with a greater number of organized groups. However, people living in urban areas are less dependent upon particular persons and their dependence upon others is confined to a highly fractionalized aspect of the other's day-to-day activities. City life is thus characterized by secondary rather than primary contacts, and while they indeed may be face-to-face, they are nevertheless often impersonal, superficial, transitory and segmental.

The superficiality, the anonymity, and transitory character of urban-social relations has been portrayed vividly by Packard, Toffler, and Wirth among others. Packard[14] notes that mobility is a chief phenomenon of our society, resulting in the fragmentation of families, individual disengagement from commitment to social causes, loneliness and suffering. Between 1970 and 1973 approximately 32% or over 67 million people moved in America, disrupting homes, neighborhoods, industries and businesses, and community life. People, in effect, are becoming strangers to each other. This has implications for recreation and leisure service agencies, where our acquaintances tend to stand only in a relationship of utility to us. Wirth relates:

> *"Whereas . . . the individual gains, on the one hand, a certain degree of emancipation or freedom from the personal and emotional controls of intimate groups, he loses, on the other hand, the spontaneous self-expression, the morale, and the sense of participation that usually comes with living in an integrated society."*[15]

The segmental character and utilitarian accent of interpersonal relations in the city have resulted in the proliferation of specialized tasks occurring within an institutional framework to handle the needs of people. The family has been altered considerably as a unit of social life, and as indicated in Chapter 2, individual members have been emancipated from the larger kinship group characteristic of the nuclear family to pursue their own diverging interests in their work, educational, religious, recreation and political life. The functions of various community services related to health, and methods of alleviating hardships associated with personal and social security, to provisions for education, recreation and cultural advancement and expression have given rise to highly specialized institutions and agencies on a community-wide and even national basis. Because of the relative impotence of the individual in contemporary life, the urban dweller particularly finds himself being exerted to join with others of similar interest into organized groups to meet personal needs. In this sense many recreation agencies serve to provide a means for creative self-expression and spontaneous group association, unavailable within the family milieu.

Toffler[16] similarly believes that contemporary American society has become highly fractionalized by high speed change and disrupted community life. The following paradigm, "Relationships of Concepts of Future Shock and Leisure Service," illustrates Toffler's major themes and their relationship to leisure service agencies. Transience is a pervasive theme of Toffler's, as the rate of turnover of the different kinds of relationships in an individual's life has perpetuated a nation of rootless people reaching for some degree of stability and permanence. Thus community life, particularly in urban centers, has become disintegrating for a large number of people. Our relationships with people and things are increasingly temporary.

A New Concept of Community

While community life has been disrupted, a new concept of community is suggested by the high degree of impermanence resulting from a nation of rootless people; one which is based on a greater degree of individual flexibility, vocational choice and selectivity, and leisure options within a highly mobile society. A *new* sense of community is emerging which transcends kinship ties, geography and social distance. There are no longer any natural geographical boundaries in the land that give a community identity. The traditional sense of community was largely rooted to the land and based on strong kinship affiliation. The new sense of community is predicated upon a wider community network, a common life style based on *mutual compatibility and shared interests.*

If anything is certain about the future of community life, it is not to stereotype what it could be. Community life may actually become centered around people's common leisure life style preferences, meaning that such communities will be distinguished not so much be family composition, ethnicity, or geographical orientation, but oriented around distinctive life styles, including social relationships, environments, dress and mores emanating from avocational interests. Participation in these communities will be voluntary and will continue as long as the member is *motivated* to participate in the community and will terminate when that person is not. Thus, recreation and leisure service conceivably could become the locus of community life and may well serve as the prime generator of values and nucleus for communication participation and involvement.

Community leisure styles of life are seen occurring as a result of the fragmentation of human associations as reflected by (1) the growing secondary nature of work (represented by the growth of the 4-day work week, increased absenteeism and worker dissatisfaction, rise in national "leisure" holidays having no particular symbolic significance, earlier retirements, rise in craft vocations which seemingly integrate work and leisure, etc.); (2) disengagement of nuclear family and traditional kinship groups (represented by a number of experimental living arrangements, including contractual marriages, group marriage, communal families, and rise in specialty villages, including communities for singles, young marrieds and retired people, etc.); and (3) disruption of neighborhood life (representative of over ¼ of America's workers who cross county lines to go to work, transience resulting from approximately 40 million people moving each year).

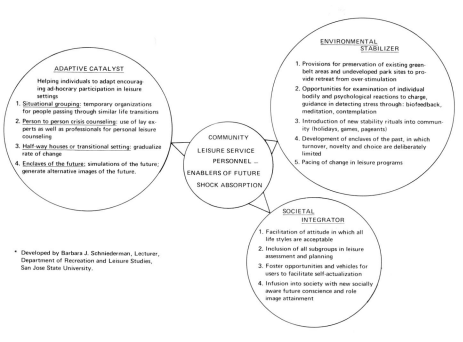

Fig. 3. Relationships of Concepts of Future Shock and Leisure Service.*

Essentially, leisure life styles, as opposed to work or kinship associations and ties, are emerging as the framework for community participation by people who are seeking to preserve individual identity and integrity in the midst of a highly mobile and fractionalized society, which is occurring as a result of an exponentially changing social, cultural, political and economic environment. There is a need to develop such institutions on a human scale which will permit the individual to identify with others of similar orientation on a more accelerated, intense basis.

It will be increasingly necessary for recreation personnel to facilitate human associations in spontaneous settings where people congregate and serve as an enabler of human interactions that are immediate, intense, and without traditional props, rituals and distancing mechanisms.[17] This seems to be a necessary step because by the time the individual arrives at this "where-is-the-real-me" state, he will find himself alone again. There is need for immediate gratification and opportunities to accelerate growth processes in cohesive groups that do not require the duration of chronological, sequential development. Immediacy is the antithesis to the traditional approach of developing social relationships and of the typical approach utilized by recreation and leisure service agencies in serving people.

Leisure Patterns in Urban, Suburban and Rural Communities

People engage in leisure experiences in a variety of settings and it has only been in recent years that more population groupings from other than the upper- and middle-income brackets have had sufficient (a recession notwithstanding) amount of time and financial resources to avail themselves of the leisure opportunities which exist. The setting in which one engages in leisure behavior is an important indicator for potential site development plans, but is only illustrative of what has been made available in the past, not necessarily what a person would do in the future given additional leisure options.

> "A services error persists in much of our recreation-planning of this kind: we are able to judge the demand for recreation facilities solely by observing present recreational habits and multiplying the current participation rates by anticipated future populations. There is serious danger that the resulting magnitudes are completely meaningless. The participation-rate figures observed are those under prevailing conditions of recreation opportunities. This use of facilities is determined not only by what the population in question demands, but also by what has been made available to them."[18]

Suburban communities (there being a greater movement out of central cities to the suburbs than the reverse during the time between 1970–1973, reflective of a trend which started in the 1960's) tend to reflect different leisure patterns, they being particularly influenced by white working and lower-middle-class groups, who have continued their home-centered leisure activities adopted from urban life, including T.V. viewing, going to the movies and having informal gatherings of neighbors. They have added gardening, working around the house and traveling for pleasure to their list of leisure preferences. While a great number of people spend their vacations at home, an increasing number of people, influenced particularly by the ownership of a car and reduced work weeks, are able to take their vacation outside of the community, participating in boating, camping, sightseeing, picnicking and swimming. Of course, this is contrasted with low-income urban residents who because they lack use of a car, are without money or time for trips and vacations, and because their apartment is likely to be small and lack recreational equipment and space, must utilize local neighborhood or community park areas, playgrounds, swimming pools or other recreation areas.[19]

It has been shown that participation in most recreation activities increases as income increases.[20] However, most patterns of non-white leisure participation in outdoor recreation are similar to those of whites, except for bathing, water skiing and camping.[21] The degree of non-participation in these activities may largely be attributed to their high cost and/or unavailability to the individual of suitable facilities. Lindsay and Ogle comment on the reasons why there are differences of income groups in participation rates of outdoor recreation.

> "Specifically, as income increases, the economic availability of some forms of outdoor recreation, such as boating and snow skiing, also increases. Similarly, when a relatively unexpensive activity, such as fishing, is located several hours' driving time from a population center and necessitates an overnight stay, it is no longer inexpensive nor convenient to participate in fishing. In fact, under the above conditions, for much of the population on the lower end of the economic scale, there very likely is, de facto, no opportunity for fishing."[22]

Lindsay and Ogle, in their study of the urban population of Weber County, Utah, concluded that to the extent that they cannot afford public recreation due to the location of opportunities, low income and poorly educated members of society are naturally discriminated against in the allocation of recreation resources. It is their reasoning, as distinguished from the study findings of Mueller and Guerin or by Hauser, which indicate the socioenvironmental factors combine to result in proportionately greater preference for public outdoor recreation to those of higher income or educational groups, that "socioenvironmental factors combine to cause nearly equal preference for public outdoor recreation in all income and education groups, but external factors, such as opportunities, allow higher income and well-educated elements of society to fulfill this preference to a greater extent than the lower income and poorly educated elements."[23]

If the findings of Lindsay and Ogle are correct, it is then paramount that recreation facilities and leisure opportunities be provided closer to urban areas for easy and inexpensive access for all socioeconomic groups.

There appear to be little or no significant differences in the variation of rural-urban resident population patterns. Several studies indicate that urban dwellers represent a disproportionate number of outdoor recreation participants.[24] Contrarily, other authors suggest that there is a preponderance of rural residents participating in various forms of outdoor recreation, particularly in such areas as fishing and hunting.[25] While such additional outdoor activities as ice skating, camping and taking nature walks appear to be common among rural residents, these differences may be more attributable to geographic reasons than place of residence. What appears to be most influential in the determination of outdoor recreation preferences is the participation patterns one had as a youth. Burch and Wenger[26] reported that childhood camping and hiking experiences and adult styles of camping were highly related. Similarly, Hendee[27] found that a high proportion (70%) of wilderness users reported taking their first trip before they were 15 years old.

It was found by Stutz[28] in his study of the Lansing-East Lansing, Michigan metropolitan region, that contrary to expectations, low income, non-white families exhibit a larger proportion of inter-residential social trips in urban areas than did those of higher income, white groups. However, this may be explained by the fact the low income families must substitute inter-residential social interaction for other leisure time activities requiring greater cost. "Lower income individuals have a greater kinship interaction component than higher income individuals and this interaction is usually home-based."[29] It may also be inferred that families from lower income levels substitute in-the-home social activities for the more expensive non-home recreation and entertainment activities.

Nonuse of Urban Neighborhood Parks

It has been suggested by Gold[30] that public parks accommodate only a small proportion (5%) of the total population of a community at any given time, peak use levels seldom exceed 20% of the service area population, public parks now accommodate an insignificant portion of the average leisure budget (.1 hr./day) and both the users and time they spend in urban public parks are decreasing. Gold relates three factors which contribute to nonuse.

> "(1) those who do not use the park may have some significant physical, mental, or cultural differences from those who do; (2) the park's image and facilities do not coincide with the leisure preferences and satisfactions of the majority of users; and (3) some physical, environmental, institutional restraints encourage nonuse."[31]

The major causes of nonuse in neighborhood parks include (a) *behavioral aspects,* (1) user orientation (users commonly are seeking fantasy-oriented recreation as opposed to agency encouraged self-oriented activities), (2) social restraints (a lack of a familiar and comfortable social context—public parks tend to frown upon a public display of pleasure including eating, drinking, dancing, social interaction, and making love); (b) *environmental aspects*, (1) convenient access (the recommended service radius of one-quarter mile for neighborhood parks may deter use and be a significant cause for nonuse), (2) site characteristics (topography, landscaping, lighting, water, shade, shelter from the winds, rain or sun, quiet areas, privacy, identity, and diversity are often lacking in many neighborhood parks); and (c) *institutional aspects*, (1) goal differences (much of the leisure behavior is now marked by spontaneity, choice, and diversity while recreation and park agencies tend to emphasize organization, program leadership, and scheduling of activities which may be at odds with the leisure preferences of most Americans) and (2) personal safety (what the cities and suppliers of leisure service have labeled as "deviant behavior" in public parks, including vandalism, drinking, narcotics, nudity, and civil disorder, reducing normal use levels in many neighborhood parks). The level of nonuse appears to be fairly well equated between upper and middle income families and low income groups, with the former two groups spending more of their leisure in regional resource-oriented parks and private clubs, resorts or second homes, and a significant number of the latter being no longer attracted or relying on neighborhood recreation opportunities.

While Gold's findings appear to be accurate Lick's study[31a] of eight neighborhood parks ranging from 8 to 17 acres in widely dispersed geographical and socioeconomic areas throughout San Jose, California, found that approximately 67% of adult individuals residing within ¼ mile of the surveyed parks use the facilities. The leading reasons for park use were for aesthetic purposes (cleanliness, park design, landscaping and location) relating to the general appearance of the parks. From the data it was found that unsafe conditions, vandalism and illegal behavior were factors of nonuse of the sampled nonusers. It appears that Lick's study correlates with Jacobs' relationships of park design and park use (see "An Exploration of Human and Social Meanings of Parks" later in this chapter).

It appears that there is a need on the part of park planners and designers to take into account the historical and scenic factors of park areas, the socioeconomic characteristics of the surrounding neighborhoods and the provision of diverse landscaping arrangements which allow for a variety of recreation behaviors to be actualized within a defined park in order for such a recreation space to be "successful."[31b]

Developing a Model for Urban Communities

It has become difficult to adequately develop a model which appropriately relates to a given community. In fact, following a series of several studies[32] it has been determined that adequate minimum requirements for open space and recreation facilities cannot be accurately prescribed. Dunn comments:

> *"Cities differ dramatically from one another; each has unique characteristics shaped by such factors as history, climate, economy, and location. Inner city residential areas differ also. Population density, housing, income, education, and family unity vary tremendously. So do the recreation resources provided by public and voluntary agencies such as the Boys' Clubs, the YWCA and YMCA, municipal governments, schools, and churches. To further complicate the issue, inner-city open space and recreation needs cannot necessarily be equated with nor inferred from citywide needs."[33]*

While it is difficult to adequately utilize one socio-economic need and/or resource index to equitably assess local neighborhood desires relative to recreation priorities, several types of measurements of effectiveness have been developed in recent years.[34] Dunn offers three principal techniques for assessing local recreation need stemming from the urban recreation movement. It is increasingly apparent a "sensitive" instrument and a rational basis must be developed which will provide for the allocation of resources to meet variances in need condition across sub-units (neighborhoods and sub-divisions) and respond to the plurality of life styles representative of contemporary American community life.

> *"Grass Roots Technique."* [*Individual citizen assessment of their need for recreation as expressed through voting, e.g., a bond referendum*] *Two pertinent generalizations emerge of recent studies of local referendum elections. First, socio-economic status is directly related to how an individual votes. Second, while it is clear that a vote cast on a local issue is conditioned by a wide range of factors, one of these is the voter's implicit perception of self-interest and need for service.*
> *"Equality Technique."* *Standards, commonly based upon population density, provide the basic measure for the "equality technique" to determine local recreation needs. No general provision is made in any space or facility standard for adapting practice or priority because of the presence or absence of any other factor included in a broad community survey. The primary virtue of this tradition appears to be that the equal distribution of recreation resources based on the distribution of population is easy to compute, and, more appealingly, easy to interpret, defend, and sell.*
> *Although they have been disparaged in recent years, standards still offer the most common approach to comparative need assessment for many public services . . . Regrettably, the efforts of the profession have resulted in but a single undifferentiated set of standards, and community leaders across the Nation have been admonished to 'adjust the standards to fit the local situation.' . . . Despite extensive efforts to*

halt the practice, however, 'standards' have frequently been adopted as the ideal, rather than the minimum.

"Social Concern Technique." A significant part of the public conscience reawakening of the 1960's was the reversal of a quarter of a century of maximizing centralizing in local public service administration. Decentralization, accessibility, and participation became legitimatized goals for the first time since the 1930's—at least in theory at the local level. Subunits of urban areas were brought into focus to create an awareness that the parts which make up the whole city may be quite dissimilar, and more important, that the needs of the parts may be very different.

This [technique]. . . is based largely on precedent which evolved from the social welfare field, where the assessment of need priority among geographic sub-units and among social services has been a part of many metropolitan area social planning studies.

Need variables [most often used in this technique]: age, juvenile delinquency rate, population density, income, housing, population stability, occupation, education, race, mortality rates and percentage of foreign born. Resource variables used, in the order of frequency: acreage, facility, leadership, attendance, costs, and programs." [35]

Need indices provide an overall perspective as to the existing supply of resources on the one hand and the degree to which certain social indicators illuminate which factors are impinging on certain sub-units within a community. There is a growing demand on the part of citizen groups (sometime initiated through class action suits) to gain an equitable share of public services and the traditional measures of local recreation and park services have utilized descriptive indices which only focus on the resources of the agencies. Typically, most effectiveness measures do not account for the "human" factors and ignore the impact of society on the human condition and do not give consideration to individual growth needs. Also, with the increasing proliferation of diverse life styles it is becoming more important for effectiveness measures to be developed which incorporate perspectives accounting for the differences in population groups.

"Every community is unique and it is important that leisure service agencies be cognizant of the significance of the attachment and mutual feeling of belonging of residents of each neighborhood. By properly determining the nature of each neighborhood's composition, resources and other social attributes, leisure service managers can more adequately assess the distinctive aspects and form of leisure opportunity that may be successfully blended into the style of people's lives." [36]

While it still remains that there is no conclusive evidence as to the most effective measure of recreation services (partially attributable to the fact that there is yet to be determined what causes people to engage in leisure behavior and what are the social and environmental determinants that influence and/or modify the experience), it is increasingly necessary that effectiveness measures be tested and applied to the operations of leisure service agencies.

Contributions of the Recreation and Park Movement to Community Development

As indicated earlier in Chapter 1 a sense of community contributes to the integration of people within a geographically defined area or those sharing similar interests. It is within this construct that recreation, both as an institution and vehicle for realizing personal, group and societal goals, very conceivably contributes most beneficially to community development. As previously indicated, community life has undergone vast changes in this country since 1850, highlighted by a movement from an agrarian society and way of life to a highly technological and industrial one; from a rural society of small towns to one of large urban cities and megalopolises which devour vast areas of open space and prime agricultural land; from a relatively illiterate population to a highly educated society; from a farm-based economy to an industrial economy of factories, blue-collar-workers, sweat shops and physically arduous toil to a cybernated, post-industrial economic system characterized by highly trained white-collar technicians, service workers and experts engaged in mentally demanding work; and from a society in which leisure was the domain of only the rich and distant hope or disdained expression of the middle-class and poor to a society increasingly altering its rhythm of life to center around leisure.

Cities are characterized by heterogeneity in people, organizations and services. The urban-suburban community represents people of all races, religions, value orientations and life styles co-mingling within a shared geographical space. The occupational specialization results in a high division of labor, largely unknown in the rural community. The American community has become increasingly metropolitan in character[37] as many of the preceding factors have led a continuous stream of immigrants to move into the sprawling cities. At the same time, there has been a corresponding outward expansion of the city.

The Structure of the Metropolitan Community

The following briefly outlines the structure of the metropolitan community, a composition of the central city area, suburban ring and rural-urban fringe. The metropolitan community absorbs varying members of separate local communities into its economic, political and cultural organization. The metropolitan community is an extensive geographic unit whose social and economic activities form more or less an integrated system centering around a large city.

The Central City. The locus of business and commercial life resides in the central city, which houses large department stores, financial institutions, big corporations, medical specialists, legal firms, advertising agencies, various speciality shops, usually a large park and malls. While the most prominent occupants are usually the various business and commercial organizations, the "other Americans" also reside within the central city, millions of low income, minority, and disenfranchised elderly people.

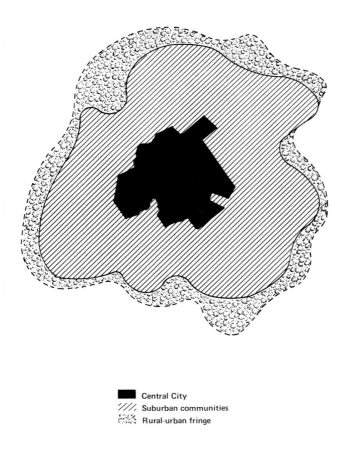

■ Central City
//// Suburban communities
:::: Rural-urban fringe

Fig. 4. Structure of the metropolitan community: ● = central city; ○ = suburban communities; - - - = rural-urban fringe.

The central city has been in a state of flux and change over the past several decades. Once, a focal point of community life, it has declined in most large communities, urban renewal notwithstanding, due to the movement of businesses to suburbia and the outward migration of whites. As a result, the contemporary central city has become a "community that is populated mainly by black Americans, Puerto Ricans, Mexican Americans, and other minority groups."[38]

The Suburban Ring. Typically the suburban ring consists of two components: first, vast tracts of land are devoted to residential users and secondly, the suburban ring is dotted with suburban (residential areas dependent on the central cities for services and facilities) and satellite (centers of production that dot the suburban ring) communities. Residents living in satellite suburban areas may not be particularly dependent on the central cities because of the jobs available there.[39] Usually, the suburb is distinguished from the central city by the physical and political separation from the central city and the economic dependence of the suburb on the central city.

According to Dobriner[40] life in the suburbs differs from life in the city in terms of social relationships and life styles arising out of (1) transportation characteristics, (2) informal relationships at the neighborhood level, and (3) degree of home centered activity reflected in gardening, ease of child-rearing, etc. There appear to be three types of residential suburbs, contrary to the typical image of housing development in suburbia being homogeneous both in architecture and in the characteristics of its inhabitants.[41] (1) The traditional upper-class suburb, composed of long-established, high-status families, where little turnover of the community occurs, (2) stable middle-class families located in the newest sections of the suburban ring, and (3) the "packaged" suburb, comprised of mass-produced suburban housing developments of families who desire to enjoy the amenities of suburban living but who cannot afford residences in the middle-class suburb.[42]

Rural-Urban Fringe. This section of metropolitan community consists of a "belt of land which lies between the rather densely populated suburban fringe and that part of the city's hinterland which is devoted almost entirely to farming."[43] This area is characterized by mixed land use. Usually there are scattered residential developments, small communities, industries and farms and unused lands within the rural-urban fringe. It represents the fusion of rural and urban ways of life on the perimeter of large metropolitan communities.

Impact of Mobility on Community Life

Community life in the suburb is often described as lacking cohesion, involvement and affiliation among its members.

> "*The nature of the normal integrative process in the established suburb implies that unless a family is willing to affiliate with community organizations—unless it is willing to devote both time and energy to community activities—primary group membership in the settlement is hard to achieve.*"[44]

Newcomers tend to be integrated more into suburban life, not through the informal social networks of the immediate neighborhood but through the voluntary associations of the total settlement. There tend to be class differences in the degree of family integration within the suburban community. Gutman relates:

> "*Working class [migrants] are more likely than not to assume only limited initiative for meeting other people, striking up acquaintanceships and making friends and usually it will be the husband rather than the wife who undertakes the job . . . In the middle class, both spouses believe it is up to them to inaugurate the encounter with the community. The wife in particular undertakes exploratory forays into the social activities which are going on in the settlement, or into the cliques and friendship groups which already have started to form on the block or in the neighborhood.*"[45]

In much of the research of community life in the suburbs, there is a general skepticism and reluctance on the part of "established" residents to greet and assimilate newcomers in their neighborhood. Generally, there is not a lot of greeting new residents, exchanging recipes, encouraging personal confidence that occurs. This may be due to the fact that people are themselves lacking in sociability skills and self-confidence to integrate newcomers into the way of life of the community. Recreation and leisure service agencies could ease considerably the transition of new residents who have changed residence by choice or who have been uprooted making available opportunities for people to become acquainted through intimate gatherings, to encourage confidence and familiarity of new residents to community life. Mobility is part of the American way of life and leisure, because of its growing significance to people's consciousness and behavior patterns, may well aid the internalizing of this common phase of existence in contemporary society.

> "*The ability to strike up satisfying conversations with people one has never met before, the willingness to concede the legitimacy of a wide range of behavior patterns, the focus on the family as the primary group which must provide the principal [although not only] source of emotional satisfaction—indeed play a very positive role in easing the transition from one settlement to another.*"[46]

While there is indeed a disruption on the family in its movement from one community to another, Gans[47] indicates there are only minor changes in the way of life of city dwellers who move to the suburb. Those changes that do occur, desire for ownership of a single-family house, availability of more living space, more relaxed way of living, increased social life, greater organizational participation, etc., have had positive effects on the development of the family. Those experiencing negative effects are those who "deviate" culturally from the majority of their neighbors, particularly adolescents who find that the suburb often does not provide many of the equivalent urban entertainment and recreation facilities, working-class people feeling the economic pinch and social isolation from the lack of public transportation which cuts them off from relatives and old friends. However, despite these problems, suburban living tends to be characterized by a fairly private and free way of life, and most behavioral differences are tolerated. It can generally be said then that the central cities are more congested and crowded and have greater cultural and recreation opportunities, while the suburbs are comparatively open and quiet and characterized by private houses.

Need for Community Organization

While there is probably no country in the world in which more people are engaged in voluntary civic activity than in the United States, represented by men's and women's service clubs, youth organizations, chambers of commerce, P.T.A.'s, and a variety of citizen's associations. While much community activity and civic centers continue to grow, urban problems of varied sorts and alienation manifest in all age groups are also present. Traditional community participation has focused on social service or some other limited goal in a specialized area of interest. Community development, as contrasted with these forms of community organization, is concerned about a much deeper and broader type of civic action aimed at gaining the interest of the whole community in a continuous process of growth in the quality of community life.[48] Effects of community development are directed at reaching the essence of the problem affecting the human condition and quality of life. This is seen as a particularly relevant process to be undertaken by human service fields concerned about the impact of the environment on residents.

In community development, the community is visualized as a "social organism or as a human organization which in itself constitutes a major aspect of the environment of its residents, and which therefore exerts a powerful influence upon their habits, their attitudes, their values, their interests, and their patterns of behavior."[49] Problems manifest within the community are seen as an outgrowth of the environment which itself is the community. Any deficiencies occurring in the community are viewed as only symptomatic of the environment as a whole and therefore recreation and leisure service agencies, a part of the community framework, must be conscious of the overall factors which influence the quality of living and provide assistance, direction and support and take necessary steps to meet the needs of community members.

An example of an attempt to assess the "liveability" of a community is expressed in a report[50] of the model cities area of San Diego, California. It utilized a Social Area Analysis technique in an attempt to measure the "quality of life" of San Diego's Model Cities area. The report reduced pertinent variables into three sets or constructs, which account most for differences in residential patterns. They were:

Construct	Census Measures
Socioeconomic Status	Mean House Value + % High School Graduates 25 years and over
Family Status	% Childrearing Families + Mean Household Size
Ethnic Status (Segregation)	% Blacks + % Browns*

*Persons of Spanish language or Spanish surname.

Model Cities programs use a comprehensive planning process to determine the needs of the community, to establish objectives and strategies, and to determine priorities. Such programs address themselves to meet problems of education, health, social services, recreation, law and justice, manpower, economic and business development, communications, housing, and the physical environment. While most recreation and leisure service programs do not by themselves serve in this capacity, there is an increasing mandate that recreation services be tied more closely to allied human service programs in an attempt to facilitate a person's total needs. As indicated in Chapter 5, this approach recognizes the leisure service worker as a "broker," who acts as the interface between various client groups attempting to meet their recreation needs and all the leisure opportunity resources and services available to satisfy them.

Additionally, the recreation worker is moving away from the traditional "direct provider" approach as the only appropriate process for meeting an individual's or group's needs; serving as the organizer, planner and leader of community recreation programs for patrons. The service approach which is increasingly recognized as an important aspect of the delivery system is the "outreach" approach characterized by the agency's efforts to reach out and assist various clientele groups and to promote more active community involvement in the decision making process. The recreation worker is necessarily involved in his constituency's total community concerns. It was found in the 25 city national study of open space and recreation opportunities in core city areas that: "Until the provision of recreation resources is seen as a total subsystem within the overall system of delivery of public services, efforts will remain piecemeal."[51] A prevailing dilemma in the last one-third of the 20th century is that biological communities have largely become more concerned with the environment for the use of tools than for the people themselves. "Where to park the car? How high should a skyscraper be? Where to land the jumbo jets? In some technologies, man has adapted his entire life style to one transportation tool, as with the automobile in Los Angeles; or to one monotonously replicated housing tool, as with four-bedroom houses in suburbia."[52] The community can be hostile to human life. The role of recreation and leisure service personnel, as with all allied human service fields, is to make community living habitable and enriching.

It is suggested by the foregoing that it is *only* in a community which attempts and succeeds in interrelating all of the various functions, life styles, ages, and technical process that a workable and viable linkage can be facilitated between people and governmental and public servants, that will make it possible to realize the full potential of any given community in our society.

There is a strong belief held by many social planners, sociologists, environmentalists, and human service professionals, that there is a need to generate a unified community for purposes of enriching the environment as a whole, and thereby motivating increased civic responsibility and self-reliance. This is seen as an urgent problem and one in which members of society are desirous to see facilitated a more vital sense of community, a more active and meaningful pattern of interpersonal and intergroup relationships and a deeper and more widespread feeling of local responsibility.

Role of Community Recreation Agencies in Facilitating Community Development

There are an increasing number of communities who have developed philosophical statements and operational procedures which embrace the concept of community development and a human service catalyst or enabler perspective. The city of Long Beach, California is an example:

> *"Recreation serves as a catalyst within the community to create a climate for developing leisure time activities that enhance the quality of life and meet the basic needs shared by all human beings—the need to belong, to achieve, to be recognized, to have status, to acquire and use skills, to have a creative outlook. Recreation develops sportsmanship, leadership, physical fitness, appreciation of the cultural arts, conservation of the environment, and education for leisure. Recreation creates opportunities to promote family units and develop understanding and positive interaction among people."*[53]

One of the goals of the city of Long Beach's Recreation Commission is to "be alert and responsive to current and changing recreational needs and interests in the community." Accordingly, the Commission enacted a series of objectives to carry out the content of the goals. In order to fulfill the objectives, the Commission outlines a series of evaluative criteria for the staff of the service area.

> *"A. Establish an advisory council within 6 months of the adoption of these objectives.*
> *B. Identify formal and informal recreation-related interest groups in the area and determine potential relationships with the department program by defining goals and objectives within 6 months of the adoption of these objectives.*
> *C. Identify within 6 months of the adoption of these objectives, socio-economic characteristics through demographic data of the service area with particular reference to those characteristics which have relevance for program planning.*
> *D. Visit with a minimum of three different community/leisure serving agencies within the service area, per quarter, to assess areas of mutual cooperation and accomplishment of similar agency objectives.*
> *E. Visit with a minimum of five homeowners and a manager of at least one business within the service area each month, to discuss and explain the objectives of their recreation programs and to ask for suggestions for providing better service.*
> *F. Visit or communicate with a minimum of one public, private or commercial recreation agency per quarter to assess new, workable, or successful program ideas."*[54]

Similarly, the city of Los Angeles Department of Recreation and Parks has enacted a goals and objectives statement which sees its main purpose to "play a major, leadership role in improving the quality of life for citizens in its community, by productive services to individuals and protection and enhancement of the livability of the urban environment."[55] The stated goals are to:

> *"A. Provide maximum opportunities for positive use of leisure-time for Los Angeles residents.*

> B. *Preserve, enhance and restore our natural environment, and encourage physical development which is vital to the well-being of our residents.*
> C. *Join with the community to create a better society."*[56]

The objectives indicated to fulfill the latter goal are:

> "1. *Help to create a social environment which will tend to reduce anti-social activities, such as vandalism and coordinate with all public and private organizations to accomplish these goals.*
> 2. *Within the limits of the City Charter, utilize selected recreational centers to provide a broad range of community services; recognize the integral relationships of recreational programming to all other types of social programming.*
> 3. *Help to create an awareness and appreciation of our multiple cultural heritage by planning facilities and programs which honor and afford communication between all of our sub-cultures.*
> 4. *Assume the role of community catalyst, causing needed action to occur from within the community."*[57]

The city of Cerritos, California's Department of Human Affairs responsibilities include stimulating and coordinating those aspects of human life which make for a happier and more fulfilling life of the community, including recreation and community participation. Part of the philosophy of the community is related by its director:

> *"Citizens today need more than survival. Even when external conditions permit biological survival, the internal spiritual emptiness of the individual can lead to a personal destruction of that biological existence. Therefore, these aspects of individual and communal living are of no negligible importance even for those functions of the government that are indispensable for the survival of the community."*[58]

Cerritos recognizes the spiritual emptiness replete in urban-suburban community life, which has left many members of our society rootless and lonely to a degree that was not common in former times when people lived in villages and small cities. The Department of Human Affairs seeks to promote and facilitate the active participation of citizens in the political, cultural, environmental and social affairs of the community. The Department seeks to provide environments for the free choice and involvement of the individual citizen. "It assists the involvement of the individual to facilitate personal development and satisfaction, without guiding to the point at which mature development is retarded."[59]

In the growing recognition that community social service programs, including leisure services, youth services, programs for the elderly, cultural activities, etc., are becoming more complex and fragmented through the variety of public and private sponsorship and service delivery, the League of California Cities issued an "Action Plan for Social Responsibilities of Cities."[60] It has been increasingly recognized that existing social services are highly fragmented and suffer from a lack of comprehensive planning and coordination. It is felt that because each community is composed of several sub-units, uniformity in programs will do a disservice to the social service system and to the people of the cities. It is deemed essential that program flexibility, locally determined, is the key to any human service delivery approach, with the recognition that community social services must be elevated to equal status with other city functions, such as public safety, land use control and public works. Additionally, many social problems, because of their interrelationship with the total environment, require area-wide as well as local neighborhood or sub-unit solutions. Accordingly, the "action plan" developed by the California League of Cities suggested a *holistic* coordinated and cooperative social service delivery approach. Among the recommendations are the following:

"1.   Responsibility of Cities. *Each city should assume responsibility for identifying all community social needs, and for planning, coordinating, and evaluating programs to alleviate social problems within its boundaries. Cities should insure the delivery of all essential social services either by serving as an advocate or catalyst to insure the most effective delivery of service by the appropriate public and/or private agencies or by delivering such services themselves.*

2.   City Social Services Planning. *Each city should prepare and adopt a social services element [including dependency avoidance services; health services; individual and family services; justice, rehabilitation and protective services; transportation services; and leisure services]to its general plan, treating it like the other general plan elements, and as part of the overall planning process. The social services element should be a plan for determining city goals and objectives and for establishing standards and priorities to meet community social needs. The social services element should address the needs of all city residents from the youngest to the oldest.*
  The social services element and the social services plan should seek to provide services to meet the total needs of the individual and/or family in a unified rather than a fragmented manner. The social services element and the social services plan should seek to eliminate the overlapping and duplication of services, and to identify service gaps. Social services planning should be related to and coordinated with physical, economic and environmental planning.

3.   Delivery of Social Services by Cities. *Each city shall have the option to deliver within city boundaries any social service provided by the county when the city desires to increase the level or amount of service above the basic level provided by the county ... Extending beyond each city's responsibility for integrating and coordinating its social services through its own planning program is the responsibility to join with other groups in the support of community and/or area social planning bodies. In some communities, cities may be required to take the lead in sponsoring such planning bodies; in others they may wish to participate in and strengthen existing citizen based community planning bodies.*"[61]

Earlier in the chapter in the discussion of community life it was suggested that the foundations of society are being eroded by high speed change and the individual increasingly is finding himself becoming alienated and anxiety-ridden. There has been a suggestion that human beings function to their fullest when they are able to determine and participate in the decision-making affairs and contribute to the functioning of community life. The relationship between family, education, leisure and work has become increasingly fractionalized and disjointed. There is a need to build and facilitate human relationships through an effective human-social service delivery system; one which recognizes the need that people have to attach a personal, socially significant meaning to programs and services. Such an approach is more likely to result in people feeling a part of their community and enhancing the quality of life.

The Park As Community

Since 1965, the American urban park has undergone many changes, particularly as influenced by the innovations in New York City's Central Park. This has included the closing of Central Park to automobiles on weekends (a policy extended to other New York parks) and the hiring out of bicycles which had healthy effects not only on the park and its users, but to the rest of the city, as bicycling became an alternative to the car. This revolution launched in New York parks, served to heighten public awareness of the relationship of parks to the total way of life of the community.

> *"In short, one of the many lessons of the American experience in the 1960's was that open spaces—however visually attractive in themselves—are not separated slices of urban tissue; rather, they are inextricably related to the total life of the city."*[62]

Parks were originally conceived as important contributions to the total meaning of open space planning to city life, offering multiple recreation opportunities as well as visual pleasure. Essentially, there have been three periods in the provision of urban open spaces in America.[63]

> 1. *1850–1878. A flowering of the comprehensive Anglo-American environmental tradition. During this period various park planners and environmentalist's were responsible for creating many of the open spaces presently available in cities.*
> 2. *1878–1920. A period characterized by a more aesthetically aggressive, but socially and ecologically impoverished, concern with the comprehensive conditions for urban life. The era saw a heavy influx of immigrants from abroad, an increased movement of blacks from the South into urban centers, and introduction of the automobile into society.*

3. *1920–1964. A period in which white middle-class citizens began moving in increasing numbers from the central city to surrounding suburbs. During this era there was a lack of park acquisition, planning, and maintenance which became increasingly detached from comprehensive urban needs and from the awareness of the various social and ecological processes with which they intersect and on which their preservation and maintenance depend.*

The revolution in urban parks, reflective of a movement since 1965 toward historic recognition of homes and open spaces to which they are tied physically and functionally, is highlighted by the New York experience as previously mentioned. Whitaker and Browne describe what took place to make the park system a more meaningful part of the community.

"*In 1965 a successful revolution was launched in the parks of New York City. It was a peaceful coup, led with style and flair by Tom Hoving . . . As had happened in other cities, parks were ceasing to play any part in people's lives; visitors to Brooklyn's neglected Prospect Park had fallen by two-thirds in 15 years. Mugging and vandalism had made Central Park—once the world's cynosure—unsafe by day and lethal by night. Working from Jane Jacob's belief that popular use of the parks is the best policeman, Hoving set out to show that it is possible to make a centre for the lives of New Yorkers. Communities were consulted as to what they needed. A target was set of at least some form of park being provided for every eight blocks. Vacant building-lots were put to use with portable mini-parks and children's playgrounds. Rooftops in business and commercial districts were made into daytime oases for workers. Hoving banned all cars from Central Park on weekends and hired out bicycles instead—with the result that crime fell and families from all segments of New York took to meeting there. Since 1965 the numbers using Central Park have been increasing by some ten percent annually.*
Together with his successor August Heckscher, 'Hip Hip' Hoving built new parks and sixty children's pools in the crowded slum areas. Design competitions were held; architects such as Marcel Brewer, Felix Candela and Philip Johnson produced new recreational structures, and work was started on restoring Central and Prospect Parks to their original plans. In 1967 for the first time the Metropolitan Opera gave free open-air performances in parks throughout the city. Poets gave readings without being—as they had been previously—prosecuted. Crowded costume parties, kite-flying competitions and fashion parades were held. Artists designed a kinetic environment, with a Rain Tree, a Smell Tree, a Bubble Machine, and an aluminum pond and a string of helium balloons. The Parks Department provided chalk for contests in sidewalk pavement decoration; five thousand members of the public took advantage of an open invitation to come and paint on a canvas a hundred yards long.
The change in the parks had subtle effects on New Yorkers. They interrupted their apologies for their city, and almost began to take pride in it. Some people even started to talk to each other. No miracle occurred and New York did not become a paradise. But a new dimension had been added to urban life."[64]

City life, particularly, as evidenced in most urban communities, is slowly being eroded by mechanistic living, swallowed up by cars, and polluted by industrial waste and automobile fumes. At the same time demand for recreation is growing each year and unless there is a concerted effort to improve our parks and open spaces, beautiful and attractive park areas may be destroyed paradoxically through over-use on the one hand, and nonuse by local residents because of a lack of imaginative and meaningful design on the other.

An Exploration of Human and Social Meanings of Parks

Contemporary city life is characterized by human interactions which are comprised mainly by secondary groups, seeking common interests, not bounded by memberships in the primary groups of families and friends. City spaces for secondary group interaction typically are facilitated in areas ordered by social heterogeneity. City parks are areas which provide opportunities for such interaction and tend to epitomize city life.

> *"Such parks, especially the squares, parklets and vestpocket parks in neighborhoods of mixed commercial and residential use, and in downtown cores, contribute to city life by providing opportunities for people to remain in the public purview throughout the day. If they receive such continuous use, the parks can compliment the loci and temporal rhythms of business activity . . . The physical character of such parks, their capacity for concentrating different types of people in the same small space, and the activities they stimulate, together augment the lively diversity that makes up a city."* [65]

There is a relationship between park design and park use. Jacobs[66] indicates there are four elements which a park must have to attract people of various types found in an urban population. These include: *intricacy* (the degree to which a park is capable of satisfying a variety of reasons for visiting it such as relaxation, play, the contemplation of scenery that contrasts with the surrounding buildings and cars, keeping an appointment, or the entertainment provided by watching other people); *centering* (a park's design contains a centripetal focal point or climax that draws people to it, thus becoming the high point of activity); *enclosure* (the way in which a park's surroundings shape and define its space); *sun* (the warmth and light provided by the sun). These elements motivate people to visit a park. Park design may be the most important aspect in attracting people to a park, as it must compete with other community attractions. This was not the case historically, particularly in Western Europe, where a,

> *"central city open space or plaza served as a common pasture, a parade ground for the militia, a stage for religious ceremonies, a platform for politicians, as an arena for the display of deviants, goods,*

nature, status and fashion, and as a place for 'wholesome' exercise, recreation, courtship, and secondary leisure activities that were integrated into community life."[67]

To a large degree, community life in pre-industrial times was reflected by the use of park areas for various rituals. Prior to 1965 it can be stated that a sense of community was declining through a combination of factors, particularly unimaginative design, shifting population migration in and out of the city and the decline in "we-feeling" among community members eager to gain status and acquire wealth. In a study of two urban parks in an urban renewal area of Portland, Oregon, with fountains serving as their focal point, Love[68] found three main factors which contributed to their popularity and use: (1) the element of centering made possible by the pools and walls of the fountains, which centralize people around and in the water, providing settings for people watchers, (2) the complexity of the fountains' design stimulates visitors to participate in a variety of pastimes, and (3) the fountains' management rules contribute to their versatility. The minimal rules that exist are concerned about littering, disorderly conduct and health measures for waders. Beyond this, rules do not limit participation and enhance people watching. The fountains offer a range of choice to which visitors respond in a variety of ways, providing sufficient versatility to a heterogeneous population characteristic of the surrounding community. A medium for social interaction is made possible by attractive and differentiated design, allowing for varied corresponding behavior implicit in the wide range of needs of community members.

What is the function of a park? Is it to serve one type of visitor or all types? Is the park to satisfy an entire spectrum of goals, from solitude and tranquility to sociability and action? It appears that urban-suburban parks must be designed in such a way as to attract all potential users, and in this sense we may continue to see a revitalization of urban parks and therefore in community life. Love comments:

> *"This means that if central city parks are [going] to contribute to the revitalization of city life, park designers must work much more specifically than they have at the interplay between design features and how people use parks. For designing purposes, it is insufficient to say that a certain type of park design in a certain location will attract a large number and variety of people. One must also consider how a park design allows visitors to relate to each other both spatially and functionally."*[69]

Parks, open spaces, greenbelts, etc., serve as a legitimate part of urban life and urban land use.[70] The current legitimacy resides on having urban parks scaled on "human" terms, that lend aesthetic diversity to the city, that can be enjoyed for their own sake, that offer people reasons for remaining outdoors in central city core areas, and that offer free and interesting sources of rest, relaxation and other tension-releasing, affecting purposes.

Parks afford individuals an opportunity for social interaction and identification and contribute to a community's integration, particularly to the extent to which diverse groups come into contact with one another.

> "A city whose diverse inhabitants confine their work, play, residence and shopping to their respective neighborhood boundaries are to be crossed and recrossed, there must be an acceptance of, and tolerance for diversity ... Neutral territory such as central city parks, then might function as places whose people can become familiar with diverse social types, especially their manner of dress and their pleasures. In this process, visitors might become more accepting of diversity in other areas of at least secondary group interaction."[71]

Parks serve as important contributors to the human meaning of communities. There are different interpretations of streets and residential areas, however, as reflected by middle-class and working class perspectives of their neighborhoods. Middle-income groups, because of their mobile life styles, tend not to be bounded by their living space. Friends are usually widely dispersed and it is characteristic of one out of every four workers to cross county lines to go to work.

> "Space outside the dwelling unit, including hallways, streets and open space, is public and anonymous. It is perceived as belonging to everyone, and as such belongs to no one."[72]

Working class residential areas of cities are typically viewed in a different light, where boundaries between dwelling units and public spaces are highly permeable and the people often at home on the streets. Streets are not just parks but have become bounded places to which people feel they belong.[73] As such a park is a subsystem within a community. Gray comments on the functions of a park in an urban locale:

> "A downtown park may be viewed as a physical environment, an institution, a society, an ecology, or as a system with subsystems and interfaces with the surrounding city. From one point of view, a downtown park is an island in the paved urban world; it is conditioned by the physical environment and the social system of the surrounding territory. The park society of the neighborhood and the neighborhood is a subsociety of the community and so on."[74]

In a study of an urban downtown park in Long Beach, California, Gray observed a dynamic relationship between a park and the surrounding neighborhood. He found that the relationship may be friendly, where people move with ease from their social roles in the park society to ones they maintain in the neighborhood or it may be hostile, with park people and neighborhood dwellers harboring deep mutual suspicion with little exchange of social interaction. Lincoln Park, the site of Gray's investigation, revealed a well-developed social system with a mixture of cliques, class and groups of various kinds.

> *"The lower class, made up largely of indigent men—the homeless, "winos" and the like—occupy the older section of the park. They are more argumentative and more radical in their politics. Their conversations may erupt into oratory. They have a well-defined territory which is seldom visited by any of the other regulars. Here some pass the time of day, look for a handout and sleep in the bushes at night. For a few, the park is 'home' between visits to jail. They look to the park for satisfaction of their biological as well as their social needs.*
> *The upper class—composed for the most part of elderly retired middle-class men and women—belong to the recreation clubs and occupy the redeveloped section of the park. They play cards, shuffleboard and roque, sit on the benches in the sun and carry on endless discussions. They avoid contact with the lower-class individuals whenever possible. Generally people of their class are clean, well dressed and orderly. They look to the park primarily as a source of satisfaction for their social needs."*[75]

It is suggested from studies of urban parks that they are successful open space areas when they provide for a variety of people diversity of opportunity, attractive physical and aesthetic environment, and a design which facilitates amenable social groupings. It is suggested by Gold that recreation behavior in urban parks is typically frustrated because local codes of conduct are not in concert with changing life styles of a growing number of people.

> *"The idea that urban parks are for 'all' people and established for the 'pleasurable' use of leisure time is in contradiction with the lifestyle and leisure behavior of a growing number of people. Although the Puritan Ethic is slowly fading, many parks and recreation professionals still cling to ideas of user behavior that label or exclude some types of leisure behavior as 'deviant,' e.g. nude sunbathing or rock music festivals. The notion that urban parks should be used by only 'normal' people for the 'constructive' use of their leisure time, as defined by others, may be inappropriate or an infringement on civil rights . . . It does not acknowledge that urban parks are one changing reflection of society and an appropriate place to see life as it is, lose some of the pretensions of an anxious world or express many normal human feelings.*
> *For example, if eating, drinking, dancing and social interaction are considered normal leisure behavior, most urban parks do not adequately provide for these activities in the same sense as they do for Little League, tennis or crafts. In a polarized, private and impersonal society, there are few public places left that allow people to gather, participate or watch others express these basic leisure desires."*[76]

It is suggested by Gold that one reason for the increasing wave of vandalism in urban parks is the result of people being frustrated with the visual and functional character of these areas. One response to tension and anxiety has been the conversion of some park areas or specifically created gardens for people to engage in "horticulture therapy," by having an opportunity to grow plants or vegetables. An increasing number of cities and park districts are setting aside plots of land for the public to grow vegetables, a reflection of the need by people for beauty and peace.[77]

The Future of Community

The predominant form of urban open space has been the provision of traditional parks located in sporadic fashion throughout a community. There is now a vision of cities in which these lands could play a far more significant role by providing a continuous green thread of nature interwoven throughout the entire fabric of our urban environment. "It would be a component that separated neighborhoods, gave a structure to individual subdivisions as well as the community as a whole and provided an intimate connection with the natural environment to all the people of the town."[78] While city planners and recreation officials have different views of open space development, the former perceiving open space as mitigating the excesses of urbanization through the design and the latter viewing it as opportunities for healthful, self-satisfying experiences, there is an increasing concern that ecological perspectives be taken into consideration. In this sense, open space is viewed as a necessity to maintain natural processes in a relatively stable equilibrium, providing many benefits to community life, including financial and spiritual. The best recreation land is the best conservation is the best amenity land. "When more than one function is served, priority is automatically established. The lowest priority is where only one function is served; the highest where all three functions are served."[79]

The task is to design park and recreation lands which unify communities and serve to provide an integrated human/plant community that makes up a self-sufficient ecological interrelationship. The image one has for community is an essential part of a person's development of a proper self-identity. We form images of our surroundings (such as the park settings previously discussed), the area we occupy and from these images we place ourselves in both space and in a social unit. "From this develops a sense of place and belonging which the individual uses to aid in his identification with his surroundings. The characteristics of the image of the city that the person forms depends on the qualities of the setting."[80] This means that a small neighborhood which has distinctive qualities and is easily defined allows for stronger feelings of identification (something fast disappearing from contemporary urban life), and hence, a more integrated self-identity on the part of residents than does the "packaged" suburb with its vast areas of sameness. Therefore, park areas that take into account life styles, cultural preferences, user needs, and aesthetic values, are more likely to lend a sense of variety and uniqueness to a given neighborhood and lead to clearer images and a stronger sense of belonging and self-identification by community residents.

References

1. Poplin, Dennis E.: *Communities: A Survey of Theories and Methods of Research.* New York, The Macmillan Co., 1972, p. 6.
2. Ibid: p. 112.
3. Tonnies, Ferdinand: Gemeinschaft and Gesellschaft. In: *Community and Society.* Edited by Charles F. Loomis, New York, Harper & Row, Publishers, 1963.
4. Poplin: Op. cit., pp. 116–17.
5. Ibid: pp. 117–19.
6. Minar, David W. and Greer, Scott, Editors: *The Concept of Community.* Chicago, Aldine Publishing Co., 1969, p. 3.
7. Ibid: p. 47.
8. Ibid: p. 60.
9. Ibid: p. 140.
10. Ibid: p. 222.
11. Nisbet, Robert A.: *Community and Power: A Study in the Ethics of Order and Freedom.* New York, Oxford University, 1962.
12. United States Bureau of the Census. *Statistical Abstract of the United States: 1971.* 92nd ed., Washington, D.C., 1971, p. 17.
13. Birnbaum, Max and Mogey, John, Editors: *Social Change in Urban America.* New York, Harper & Row, Publishers, 1972, p. 4.
14. Packard, Vance: *A Nation of Strangers.* New York, David McKay Co., Inc., 1972.
15. Wirth, Louis: Urbanism As A Way of Life. In: *Social Change in Urban America.* Op. cit., p. 41.
16. Toffler: Op. cit.
17. Bennis, Warren: The Temporary Society. In: *Reflections on the Recreation and Park Movement.* Edited by David E. Gray and Don Pelegrino, Dubuque, Iowa, William C. Brown Company, Publishers, 1973, pp. 112–121.
18. Krutilla, John V. and Knetsch, Jack L.: Outdoor Recreation Economics, *The Annals* 389:69, May, 1970.
19. Gans, Herbert J.: Outdoor Recreation and Mental Health. In: *Trends in American Living and Outdoor Recreation Study Report No. 22.* Washington, D.C., U.S. Government Printing Office, 1962, pp. 233–42.
20. Mueller and Gurin: Op. cit., pp. 10–29.
21. Hauser, Philip M.: Demographic and Ecological Changes as Factors in Outdoor Recreation. *Trends in American Living and Outdoor Recreation Study Report No. 22.* Op. cit., pp. 27–59.
22. Lindsay, John J. and Ogle, Richard A.: Socioeconomic Patterns of Outdoor Recreation Use Near Urban Areas, *Journal of Leisure Research* 4:20, Winter, 1972.
23. Ibid: pp. 23–24.

24. McCurdy, Dwight R. and Mischon, Raymond M.: *A Look at the Private Campground User.* U.S.D.A. Forest Research Paper CS-18, 1965; King, David A.: *Characteristics of Family Camping Using the Huron-Manistee National Forests.* U.S.D.A. Forest Research Paper LS-19, 1965; and Lucas, Robert: *The Recreational Use of the Quetico-Superior Area.* U.S.D.A. Forest Research Paper LS-8, 1964.
25. Maddock, Stephen J., Gehrken, and Guthrie, Alan W.: *Rural Male Residents' Participation in Outdoor Recreation.* U.S.D.A. Forest Research Note SE-49, 1965; Etzkorn, Peter K.: Leisure and Camping: The Social Meaning of a Form of Public Recreation, *Sociology and Social Research* 49:17–89, October, 1964; Peterle, Tony J.: Characteristics of Some Ohio Hunters, *Journal of Wildlife Management 31*:375–389, January, 1967; and Sessoms, H. Douglas: An Analysis of Selected Variables Affecting Outdoor Recreation Patterns, *Social Forces* 42:112–115, October, 1963.
26. Burch and Wenger: Op. cit.
27. Hendee, John C., et al.: *Wilderness Users in the Pacific Northwest—Their Characteristics, Values and Management Preferences.* U.S.D.A. Forest Research Paper PNW-61, 1968.
28. Stutz, Fredrick P.: Intra-Urban Social Visiting and Leisure Behavior, *Journal of Leisure Research* 5:6–15, Winter, 1973.
29. Ibid: p. 12.
30. Gold, Seymour: Nonuse of Neighborhood Parks, *Journal of the American Institute of Planners* 38:369–378, November, 1972.
31. Ibid: p. 372.
31a. Lick, Fred A.: *Factors Relating to Use and Nonuse of Neighborhood Parks in San Jose, California.* San Jose, California, San Jose State University, Master's Project, May, 1975.
31b. Byerts, Thomas O. and Teaff, Joseph D.: Social Research As A Design Tool. *Parks and Recreation* 10:34–36, 62–64, January, 1975.
32. Dunn, Diana R. 1970: Urban Recreation and Park Data Bench Mark Year, *Parks and Recreation*, February, 1971; *Modernizing Urban Recreation and Park Systems.* Proceedings of the National Forum, National Recreation and Park Association, Houston, Texas, 1972, 20 pp.; and *Open Space and Recreation Opportunities in America's Inner Cities.* Washington, D.C., U.S. Government Printing Office, 1974.
33. Dunn: Leisure Resources in America's Inner Cities, Op. cit., p. 36.
34. Hatry, Harry and Dunn, Diana: *Measuring the Effectiveness of Local Services: Recreation.* Washington, D.C., The Urban Institute, 1971.
35. *Open Space and Recreation Opportunities in America's Inner Cities:* Op. cit., pp. 87–89, 98, 103.
36. Murphy, et al.: *Leisure Service Delivery System.* Op. cit., p. 63.
37. Banfield, Edward C.: *The Unheavenly City: The Nature and Future of Our Urban Crisis.* Boston, Little, Brown and Company, 1970.
38. Poplin: Op. cit., p. 54.
39. Poplin: Ibid., p. 55; Dobriner, William: *Class in Suburbia.* Englewood Cliffs, New Jersey, Prentice-Hall, Inc., p. 162; Schnore, Leo F.: Satellites and Suburbs, *Social Forces* 36:121–29, December, 1957; and Boskoff, Alvin: *The Sociology of Urban Regions.* 2nd ed., New York, Appleton-Century-Crofts, 1970, p. 109.
40. Dobriner: Op. cit.
41. Boskoff: Op. cit., pp. 34–35.
42. Berger, Bennett M.: *Working Class Suburb: A Study of Auto Workers in Suburbia.* Berkeley, University of California Press, 1960.
43. Poplin: Op. cit., p. 57; also refer to Pryor, Robin J.: Defining the Rural-Urban Fringe, *Social Force* 47:202–210, December, 1968.
44. Gutman, Robert: Population Mobility in the American Middle Class. In: *The Urban Condition: People and Policy in the Metropolis.* Edited by Leonard J. Duhl, New York, Simon and Schuster, 1963, p. 176.

45. Gutman: Ibid., p. 177.
46. Ibid: p. 182.
47. Gans, Herbert J.: Effects of the Move from City to Suburb. In: *The Urban Condition*, Ibid., p. 185.
48. Poston, Richard: Comparative Community Organization. In: *The Urban Condition*. Op. cit., p. 314.
49. Ibid: p. 314.
50. Erickson, Rosemary J.: *Social Profiles of San Diego: The Model Cities Area*. La Jolla, California, Western Behavioral Sciences Institute, 1974.
51. *Open Space and Recreation Opportunities:* Op. cit., p. 13.
52. *The City as a Biological Community:* Washington, D.C., U.S. Government Printing Office, 1973, p. 2.
53. Statement of Philosophy, The Coordinated Plan of Municipal and School Recreation, Recreation Commission, Long Beach, California, June 11, 1970.
54. Proposed Statement of Objectives, Coordinated Municipal and School Recreation, Recreation Commission, Long Beach, California, N.D.
55. Goals and Objectives, Department of Parks and Recreation, City of Los Angeles, California, January 23, 1973.
56. Ibid: p. 1.
57. Ibid: p. 3.
58. Gabriel, Fred: New Organization Patterns and Structures in Parks and Recreation at the Local Level, *Proceedings*. National Congress for Recreation and Parks, Anaheim, California, 1973, p. 193.
59. Ibid: p. 194.
60. Action Plan for Social Responsibilities of Cities, League of California Cities Annual Conference, October, 1973, San Francisco, California, 6 pp.
61. Ibid: pp. 2–3.
62. Whitaker, Ben and Browne, Kenneth: *Parks for People*. New York, Schocken Books, Inc., 1973, p. vii.
63. Ibid: pp. viii-ix.
64. Ibid: p. 1.
65. Love, Ruth Leeds: The Fountains of Urban Life, *Urban Life and Culture* 2:162, July, 1973.
66. Jacobs, Jane: *The Death and Life of Great American Cities*. New York, Random House, Inc., 1961.
67. Love: Op. cit., p. 163.
68. Ibid: p. 194.
69. Ibid: p. 203.
70. Beauchamp, T. E.: Renewed Acclaim for the Father of American Landscape Architecture, *Smithsonian* 3:68–75, December, 1972.
71. Love: Op. cit., pp. 205–06.
72. Murphy, Williams, Niepoth and Brown: Op. cit., p. 47.
73. Lee, Robert G.: The Social Definition of Outdoor Recreational Places. In: *Social Behavior, Natural Resources and the Environment*. Edited by William Burch, Jr., Neil H. Cheek, Jr. and Lee Taylor, New York, Harper & Row, Publishers, 1972, p. 76.
74. Gray, David E.: The Un-hostile Park. *Reflections on the Recreation and Park Movement*. Op. cit., p. 235.
75. Ibid: p. 236.
76. Gold, Seymour M.: The Titanic Effect on Parks and Recreation. Paper read at the California Park and Recreation Society Conference, Student Section, San Diego, California, March 2, 1975, p. 4.
77. Skelton, Nancy: Peace From Plants—Tension-filled Americans Turn to Leafy Things, *The Sacramento Bee* Sunday, April 20, 1975, p. B1.
78. Little, Charles: *Challenge of the Land: Open Space Preservation at the Local Level*. New York, Pergamon Press, Inc., 1969, p. 13.
79. Ibid: p. 17.

80. Johnson, Per K.: Social Aspects of Environmental Impact, In: *Environmental Impact Analysis: Philosophy and Methods.* Edited by Robert Ditton and Thomas I. Goodale, Madison, University of Wisconsin Sea Grant Program, Sea Grant Publication Office, 1972, p. 87.

CHAPTER **4**

Human Development as the Primary Goal of Recreation and Leisure Service

"A humanistic approach to recreation and leisure recognizes a total concern for human beings
and the environment. The recognition increases the
field's responsibility for facilitating an individual's
total needs. This is a marked change from the activity centered philosophy of most agencies."

A New Concept of the Good Life

America has experienced unprecedented growth in recent decades, becoming the unquestioned economic power of the international community. Most Americans have all the possessions they
need and may have all they desire. However, is it all worthwhile?
Does American prosperity shield an inner poverty? What do the
challenges by the young to conformity, materialism, individualism,
bureaucracy and other traditional ways of life mean? Are we in the
midst of a cultural revolution which is in the process of drastically
altering life styles, mores and community standards and codes of
conduct. Is there going to be an easing of the Protestant Work Ethic
and loosening of the strict application of "law and order" and
movement to a more relaxed sense of "do your own thing" with

relative freedom? The mosaic of American life is no longer seen as a monolithic whole but as a collection of identifiable separate identities, each reflecting various ethnic, sexual, racial and age group values, beliefs and concerns.

What is the good life? Is it something that can be achieved through the acquisition of things? Or is it the fulfillment of an individual's inner experiences? Various people and groups have different interpretations of the good life. Some individuals seek self-respect, affection, security and peace of mind, comfort, status, involvement, good health, freedom, or to accomplish something. Many of these imply a *fixed* state—whether a state of happiness or wealth, or self-understanding. However, there appears to be a growing movement of people desiring to be identified as a *process* in which they are continually moving to the essence of a goal. This latter approach to the good life has been particularly accentuated by an ever-accelerating change in our society brought about by technology.

Increasingly people, according to Carl Rogers,[1] are becoming distrustful of institutions and lack confidence in their ability to provide direction and meaning in life. Thus, the guide of conduct for a growing number of people in America is the ever changing flow of inner experience. The good life is defined in this sense as a process of becoming. It also involves a quest for a sense of community, a thrust toward deeper communication and intimacy with other people. Traditional values of competition and individualism have tended to erode community life and combined with various vehicular forms of mobility, have dissipated social interaction and alienated people from one another. The good life, appears to once again, be increasingly reflective of engagement, interaction, community and interdependence. Recreation and leisure service agencies have an important role to play in fostering a qualitative life for all people. Whether a fixed state or a process, the responsibility for all agencies must be to assure people in their neighborhoods that leisure opportunities will be reflective of goals aiding personal and community development.

Values That Divide/Unite Us

Values are important guides to action. They represent people's general preferences and standards of behavior. They are any phenomena which reflect some degree of worth to members of a given group. America has been characterized as being in the midst of a cultural revolution similar to the period of the emergence of Martin Luther and the Protestant Reformation. There are essentially two general cultural divisions in this country, not one which is representative of a gap between liberal-conservative actions or young and old. It is more a reflection of a clash between traditional "bedrock" values and those who make up "cosmopolitan" America.[2] The traditional cultural perspective is made up of people whose symbols and desires are the flag, home and family, church, law and order, productive work, increased affluence, and education as a means of social mobility. On the other side are people who desire greater spontaneity in life, are sympathetic and support civil and human rights activities and other forms of social action, were against the Vietnam War, and who register varying degrees of sympathy or identification with the sex and drug counterculture, and who are generally critical of traditional modes of life and institutions.

The clash over values has played a major role in various local, state and national elections. And it is expected that it will continue. Additionally, many local community park and recreation departments have found themselves involved in some of these differences; nude sunbathing in public parks, use of drugs and alcohol, and changing life styles reflective of disenchantment with community mores and standards of conduct.

The local scene serves as a microcosm of national trends. Our Puritan values, ideas and behavior patterns have typically served as guides for leisure expression. However, there is growing resistance and the Puritan Ethic is slowly fading with the "greening of America." Many leisure service professionals have for years clung to this conventional approach and in recent years there have been confrontations and even clashes over "deviant" leisure behavior by people whose life styles have been labeled inappropriate. Sessoms notes that for the first time since the ancient days of Greece and Rome, people have the freedom to enjoy their own pursuits, at their own pace. He states:

> *"The arbitrariness of the clock and the work day is giving way to individual rhythm. Each of us is being given the opportunity to escape the clock without feelings of guilt, to engage in personal pleasure without the compulsion to produce some object or render some service. . . ."*[3]

What has occurred is our social policies have not caught up with the changing of people's behavior. There is no question that alternative or variant leisure behavioral expressions require legal precedent and administrative interpretation and are difficult to generalize because of the polarization, rapidly changing values and population of many communities. Thus, it appears that each com-

Table 1. Taxonomy of Deviant Leisure Behavior*

Normal leisure behavior occasionally marginally deviant	Less conventional and more controversial	Controversial/illegal	Totally unacceptable and illegal
Eating	Rock music festivals	Gambling	Vandalism
Drinking	Social protest meetings	Drugs	Prostitution
Dancing	Streaking	Littering	Rape
Social interaction	Nude sunbathing	Vagrancy	Robbery
	Homosexuality		Murder
	Hitchhiking		Suicide
			Theft
			Arson
			Assault
			Civil disorder
			Social perversion

*Refer to Seymour Gold, Deviant Behavior in Urban Parks? *Leisure Today* November/December, 1974, p. 18.

munity will have to define or continually redefine "deviance" as it relates to recreation setting usage and urban-suburban-rural living. Gold comments on the levels of hard and soft deviance:

> "*If eating, drinking, dancing and social interaction are considered normal leisure behavior, most urban parks do not adequately provide for these activities as they do for Little League, tennis or arts and crafts. Beyond these basic activities is a range of less conventional and more controversial leisure activities commonly labeled "deviant" such as rock music festivals, social protest meetings, streaking, nude sunbathing, homosexuality and hitchhiking. An even more controversial, and usually illegal, set of activities include gambling, drugs, littering and vagrancy. Finally, there is a set of totally unacceptable and illegal activities to include: vandalism, prostitution, rape, robbery, murder, suicide, theft, arson, assault, civil disorder and sexual perversion.*"[4]

While the hardcore activities described by Gold are clearly unacceptable and illegal, the others are a matter of degree and some or all could gain public acceptance over time. In some cases, it depends on the local community and who is in the majority. Public nudity is an example. There are several optional swim suit zones or free beaches in several California cities and counties and the California Department of Parks and Recreation has even experimented with the installation of unisex toilets in state parks.

The focus of the recreation and park movement has traditionally been on activities rather than what an individual derives from the experience. A number of things may be attributable to this approach, many of which have hindered the movement from adequately determining the benefits and outcomes of leisure experience and more clearly understanding why different people draw different meaning while engaging in the same experience. People are seeking a deeper participation in life, often with self-discovery as a goal. Since most definitions of recreation and leisure are couched in an activity context, they ignore or give little attention to the psychological implications. Gray and Greben comment:

> "*Definition [of recreation] in terms of activities is unsatisfactory because a given activity may provide recreation for one individual and not for another; worse yet, it may provide recreation for a person at one time but not at another.*"[5]

This false perspective of recreation has distorted our understanding of why people engage in certain leisure pursuits and even appear to display deviant leisure life styles. Gray and Greben suggest that the recreation experience contributes significantly to one's self-fulfillment and lends meaning to life. They state:

> *"We must reorient our approach to service to think not only in terms of activities and programs but also in terms of human experience. The recreation program should help each individual extend his or her intellectual and emotional reach. The three-dimensional person is the person who is the participant in the creative process, one who has something to say, a way to say it, and someone to listen. Recreation improves awareness, deepens understanding, stimulates appreciation, develops one's powers, and enlarges the sources of enjoyment. It promotes individual fulfillment. It encourages self-discovery. It helps give meaning to life."*[6]

Since different people experience physical and social conditions in different ways, it is imperative that facilities and programs be designed with particular clientele and particular reference groups in mind. This is fundamental to the blending of variant values and life styles reflective in community life. As human needs are fulfilled through experiences, leisure service personnel must provide the opportunities which will facilitate wide and divergent forms of expression, thereby aiding the possibility that individuals and groups will achieve personal and collective goals and not turn to negative and "deviant" behavior because of frustration of human needs. However, Sessoms comments on the nature of life style choices and the evaluation of their potential worth to society.

> *"In themselves, life styles are neither good nor bad. Society judges their worth and potential according to their support and maintenance of the social system. Because of this, some life styles are seen as highly desirable and virtuous while others are considered destructive or pathological."*[7]

It is expected that leisure oriented life styles should increase in the years ahead, as people begin to attach a leisure-centeredness to their total life rhythm. It is also expected that they will become more varied and diverse resulting in more public display of different ways of life. Recreation and leisure service agencies must broaden their base of delivery by incorporating a pluralistic, multidimensional approach that will preserve and facilitate the uniqueness of various life styles. "Leisure service agencies must be receptive to a variety of expressions of leisure choices and provide an environment conducive for people who manifest varying life styles to have an opportunity for growth, relationships, and creativity."[8] According to Gold deviance is a social label and there is a need on the part of recreation and leisure service agency officials to attempt to understand and provide for some unconventional forms of behavior instead of doing the usually more expedient: to stereotype individuals by some visible characteristic, enforce the law differentially, or establish arbitrary policies to cope with the deviants. The consequences of the latter type of action often involve the majority's attempt to impose its will or values on a minority segment which can be unnecessary, inappropriate, or illegal. It is felt by Gold that we need to begin to ask the right questions about deviant behavior as it is expressed or displayed in urban parks, including an attempt to understand "normal" much less "deviant" behavior and the behavioral aspects of the recreation experience that can be applied to the planning and design of facilities. He suggests the following areas for research and action as applied to understanding the dimensions of deviant behavior in urban parks.

> "1. *Rationalization and revision of existing policies and regulations that discourage or prohibit some types of behavior now labeled deviant.*
> 2. *Public hearing and widespread publicity of existing and proposed policies and regulations to prompt a community to re-examine its values and leisure life styles.*
> 3. *Citizen involvement on a sustained basis in the planning, design, management, and decision making processes.*
> 4. *Positive law enforcement and preventive action to minimize the impact of objectionable and illegal behavior when and where it occurs.*
> 5. *Development of goals, objectives, and management standards that relate to each planning area and the potential users of each park.*
> 6. *Renewal or relocation of existing parks that do not meet user objectives and encourage nonuse or totally unacceptable and illegal deviant behavior.*
> 7. *Encouragement of advocacy planning for self-generated parks, voluntary program leadership, and self-maintenance wherever possible.*
> 8. *Development of adventure play areas, water features, sitting areas, adequate shelter, landscaping, lighting, circulation, and access that will encourage people to use urban parks.*
> 9. *Encouragement of special activities in some community or neighborhood parks that might be undesirable in other parks but are victimless and not illegal, e.g., nude sunbathing. (The concept of zoning or concentrating certain types of deviant behavior where it may be less objectionable to some park users is one constructive possibility.)*
> 10. *Experimentation by demonstration to find ways to accommodate selected forms of behavior labeled deviant in order to determine and increase levels of park user and community tolerance to these activities.*"[9]

It is deemed important that all individuals be allowed to express themselves and where a minority is not allowed to engage in victimless, deviant behavior a danger of blocking creativity and realization of human potential is possible. With the changing values and types of leisure expression in our society it is important that local park and recreation departments continually re-examine their standards and rules of conduct to see whether or not they mesh with or are representative of community values and behavior norms.

Values of the Recreation Movement

Recreation and leisure service agencies, through the auspice of enabling legislation, are responsible to make available and facilitate the leisure needs of all community residents. Agencies typically embraced middle-class values in establishing standards of conduct, program categories and delivery models. While there have been inroads into the American white-male, middle-class standard as a way of life for community activities (largely stimulated by youth, racial and cultural minorities and women), American moral rhetoric is still rooted in the Protestant Ethic. It is an affirmation of the virtues of hard work and occupational achievement (rather than a commitment to leisure, contemplation and self-expression); in the belief that planning ahead is morally more important than living for the present moment; and in preferring order and predictability to spontaneity.[10]

Bennett Berger notes that there has been documentation of the growing shift and defection from the Protestant morality of the middle-class to a way of life emphasizing divergent forms of leisure and consumption patterns by expressive minorities and subcultures.

> *"From Leo Lowenthal's work studying shifts from 'idols of production' to 'idols of consumption' in the character of biographies to popular magazines, to David Riesman's documentation of the shift from 'inner-directedness' to 'other-directedness,' to William Whyte's work on the triumph of Organization Man over the old Protestant Ethic, to John Kenneth Galbraith's anatomy of private affluence, to the latest reports on family discussion over whether to get a third car or a boat, a cabin in the mountains or a house at the beach, the more prosperous sectors of American society have been learning to give up the asceticism of their ancestors to become consumers, players, and vacationers."*[11]

While there have been changes and defections of support for Protestant asceticism, the corresponding ideology which justifies the substitution of comfort and fun for piety and thrift has not accompanied it. The weakening of the Protestant Ethic has helped pave the way for the leisure demands and life styles of hippies, various cults, racial and ethnic groups and others claiming legitimacy for their expressive subcultures.

The prevailing dominant value system has had a profound effect on and influenced the organization of recreation and park departments, leadership and management styles and the philosophy and delivery system. A portrait of American National Character since roughly the turn of the century provides some insight into the impact it has had on the organization of work, family life and leisure.

At the turn of the century, Frederick Jackson Turner, hypothesized that the rugged frontier conditions created the toughness, resourcefulness, individualism and versatility that characterized American national character up to the early 1900's.[12] Similarly, David Riesman, et al., noted that 19th century social and economic conditions in this country led to *inner-directedness,* and its success.[13] The rugged individualist, the self-made man, the Horatio Alger, the strong and self-determined individual and above all the hard worker typified the inner directed person. Thomas Kando[14] indicates that more recently, Charles Reich[15] portrayed the 19th century American as representative of *Consciousness I*—which centered on truth and individual effort. America would prosper if people proved energetic and hard working. It was the American Dream shared by the colonists and the immigrants, by Jefferson, Emerson, the Puritan preachers, and the Western Cowboy. Thus, historically, America has been a work society, in which individuals were characterized by a spirit of competitiveness and daring, while being ambitious, and forthright. The genesis of the work ethic in America owes to the role of Calvinism in fostering the capitalist mentality[16] and even today "work continues to function, for most [disregarding social class], as foundation of psychological stability and motivation."[17]

Since World War II, it was Riesman's thesis that the inner-directed person had been replaced by the *other-directed* individual. As a result of technological and socioeconomic changes, the mid-twentieth century, urban, middle-class American has become soft, pliant, shapeless, he (in general) is no longer imbued with a purely private ambition but is group oriented. This parallels Reich's theory of *Consciousness II* in which such individuals are concerned with one another's comparative status and the satisfaction, the joy of life are to be found in power, success, status, acceptance, popularity, achievements, rewards.[18] Reich indicates that Consciousness II "came into existence as a response to the realities of organization and technology."[19] As a result, "the consciousness II man thus adopts as his personal values the structure and standards and rewards set by his organization."[20]

William Whyte, in the *Organization Man,* similarly articulated the management process as represented in a changing social ethic by the organizational employee who he felt responded to group pressure, was conforming, had a belief in belongingness and the need to achieve collective goals over individual effort.[21] This bureaucratic ethic, *"makes morally legitimate the pressures of society against the individual. Its major propositions are three: a belief in the group as a source of creativity; a belief in belongingness as the ultimate need of the individual; and a belief in the application of science to achieve the belongingness."*[22]

Kando comments that while our culture and national character brought about by industrialization, urbanization, bureaucratization, technology and affluence, have remained firmly sensate, empirical, materialistic and egotistical, exhibiting very little change in these respects since the advent of the Industrial Revolution, certain important changes have occurred, stimulated primarily by two fundamental economic developments:

"scarcity was replaced by affluence, and the vast increase in scale totally bureaucratized an economic structure formerly based on individual or small-group entrepreneurship. As a consequence, man's modus operandi has, of necessity, become more social, less individual."[23]

Jacques Ellul[24] went further in his treatise on the ills of technocracy, when he wrote in *The Technology Society*, "that the application of technical criteria to all areas of human life, including education, leisure and sports, will result in a 'biocracy' in which man-the-machine becomes an adaptable organism devoid of conscience and virtue. Man thus becomes totally integrated in the group, truly a mass man. He lives in a state of technical anesthesia in which values, religion, love, and emotions are no longer felt. As a final integration, all feelings have become rationalized, everyone is 'happy' in the Huxleyan sense of the term."[25]

To some degree recreation and leisure service agencies have reflected the bureaucratic ethic—a philosophy of sameness—in which managers and workers are concerned about the organization as an end, the scheduling of facilities, tournaments and master plans, compliance with standards and rules, and maintenance and upkeep of grounds. Conformity defined for recreation and leisure organizations the rules of play. Deviance and spontaneity were questioned.

Since the middle 1960's a new cultural ideology has been suggested as emerging in American society, *Consciousness III*, a radical departure from the work ethic, one in which would come close to being labeled as a leisure configuration. Additionally, a more humanistic philosophy has gained increasing acceptance. It is an attempt to view the whole person and the interrelationships of the human experience. Leisure service agencies assume a new societal and community role through the recognition of the whole person, not just *homo ludens* (man the player), and the provision of opportunities and services to facilitate an individual's total needs, either as an enabler or catalyst, broker or leader. The organization is viewed not as an'end or merely as a means, it becomes interwoven into the fabric of community life and serves to meet the total needs of the individual and/or family and coordinates its operation with other social, physical, economic and environmental services.[26]

Changing Values—The Emergence of Humanism

The Protestant Ethic as a set of value orientations, while still pervasive throughout society, has declined in recent years as a major source of direction in people's lives due to two major social developments:

(1) *Technology.*—The infusion of scientific advancements through technology has meant that people have acquired more specialized skills as a result of longer periods of academic work. Additionally, it has given people more free time away from work, and through the medium of telecommunications, more exposure to alternative life styles;

(2) *Affluence.*—Increases in wealth and abundance have lessened the need for greater numbers of people to concentrate on economic pursuits and given them the monetary means for pursuing other goals to a greater degree than ever before. Affluence in a technological society has altered the significance of the central importance of a strictly occupationally oriented concern and has shifted attention to those aspects of individual concerns related to the dignity and worth of each human being as paramount as they relate to social institutions. As noted by Lystad, "incentives to the achievement of status or material advantage are relatively ineffective in the case of an individual who already has solid middle-class status and affluence by virtue of his family of birth."[27]

While automation has resulted in change in the occupational structure, displacing various categories of lower-skilled labor, it has not significantly reduced the number of people required to keep a technological society going. According to the Berger's[28] it has increased the requirements for scientific, technological and bureaucratic personnel. They state that while upper-middle-class individuals may opt for alternative life paths outside the technological work force, their places will be taken by lower-middle and working-class groups.

It is expected, however, that as our abundance continues to expand, increasing members of our society will more easily realize materialistic goals and satisfy "lower" level needs. Therefore, greater numbers of people will tend to seek "higher" level needs—

personal growth, self-esteem and self-actualization—whether it be at work or leisure. Technology has enlarged the options of choice for more and more people and increasingly they are pursuing options which satisfy non-material needs rather than continuing to acquire traditional economic wealth. As more people in American society move to the point of satisfying security and material needs, it is reasonable to "expect not only a widespread tendency to give up additional material goods in favor of non-material goals, but also a desire to integrate and balance our lives."[29] It is expected that people will attempt to avoid the compartmentalization of their lives evidenced by the impact that industrialization had on the dichotomizing of work and free time.

Some people may be expected to adopt a more holistic style of life which will involve the integration of work, leisure and family life to fulfill the needs and aspirations of our total existence rather than solely our economic concerns. The emergence of a "growth" society (one in which the concern for living up to one's potential through full expression is a dominant characteristic and value) will create new goals and options for future human endeavor. Recreation and leisure service agencies will have to provide opportunities which focus on the *totality* of human needs. Through such a process people will be able to integrate their needs in a way which will conceivably give their lives balance, completeness and purpose.[30]

Leisure Service Delivery

Traditionally leisure service agencies have assumed a relatively high recreation literacy and sophistication among community residents. Typically, agencies have utilized a direct service approach, which involves a department's commitment to provide leadership, facilities, and equipment for participants (additional reference is provided in Chapter 7). This delivery model provides opportunities for people so that they can participate directly with a minimum amount of guidance, skill instruction or assistance (see Table 2). The agency assumes responsibility for determining programs, initiating services, scheduling areas and facilities, and developing organizational priorities. The agency's resources are organized and managed with the intent to meet its goals and objectives which the agency has for its various service areas, facilities or programs. According to this perspective, the agency establishes the overall basis for determining and implementing a complex of opportunities which it anticipates will facilitate recreation behavior. "The philosophical commitment of the agency, articulated or not

Table 2. Changing Values and Approaches in Recreation and Leisure Service*

Present Leisure Service Delivery Model (Instrumental Approach)	Shifting (Alternative) Leisure Service Delivery Model (Expressive Approach)	A Possible Future Leisure Service Delivery Model (Interactionist Approach)
Extrinsic-Environmental Stimulation	Intrinsic Motivation	Self-Determinism
Measurement Assessed in terms of Attendance	Individualization of Activities	Agency nurtured individual potentialities,
Standardized Recreation Programs	Diversification of Programs	allowing each individual to find own life solution
Facility Orientation	Serving People	—in work and leisure
Discretionary Time	"Where They Are"	Fused time reference
Recreation is Expression of earned, unobligated time; a relief from dissatisfaction	Psychological-Personal Time Recreation is an Expression of Self; positive, reaffirmation of internal needs,	Recreation occurs when one feels it exists Fused life experience Fostering of Spontaneity, autonomy
Leader directed and organized activities and programs	inner satisfaction Self-initiated activities and programs	Synergistic recreation

DIRECT SERVICE   ENABLER-
LEADERSHIP   COMMUNITY CATALYST

*Chart taken from *Recreation & Leisure Service: A Humanistic Perspective*, by James F. Murphy, Dubuque, Iowa: William C. Brown, Publishers Co., 1975, p. 95.

and planned or unplanned, influences the nature of the opportunities which are provided."[31]

The direct service approach has served as the dominant delivery method by recreation and park departments. It typically has resulted in the operation of leisure service programs on a "chainlink fence" philosophy.[32] This facility oriented concept views leisure service personnel to be primarily concerned with surveillance of the grounds or operation of the recreation center, community center, or playground; developing a master program plan for the facility; assuring superiors and the community that compliance with rules, safety and proper use of facilities is being met; and coordination of maintenance activities of the facilities.

Along the other end of the service delivery continuum is the enabling, referral-coordinated approach. The enabling service approach recognizes the agency's commitment to serve as a catalyst and assist people to implement their desires and interests through programs and facilitate their needs through a comprehensive service offering. This service approach incorporates a broadened conceptualization of programming, as it emphasizes the agency's role as a facilitator or enabler of leisure opportunities rather than an exclusive provider of pre-determined or "packaged" activities. This approach recognizes the necessity to serve the *total* individual and meet one's varied and complex human needs. It concentrates on providing a service environment which will enable individuals and organizations to develop their own leisure opportunities and assume responsibility for the outcomes.

Gray[33] suggests that there is a contemporary view of the deployment of leisure service personnel—community figure concept—which corresponds to the enabling service delivery approach. It identifies leisure service personnel as *encouragers of human and community development* concerned about what happens to people, human interaction and preservation of the quality of neighborhood life. The enabling approach is seen as a helping process which is oriented toward aiding a community to solve problems, and fostering personal growth, self-fulfillment and satisfaction of basic human needs. The approach is a reflection of contemporary post-industrial society in which the complexities of urban life, technological development and growing egalitarian policies have meant that people of all racial, income, sex, ethnic, ability and age groups potentially have equal need for recreation expression. At the same time people of diversified backgrounds require a differentiated approach to service. This approach recognizes that people are at different levels of personal development and that each neighborhood requires varied programs and services. The direct service model has tended to be most commonly structured as part of a centralized operation. However, the centralized system has proved itself incapable of responding effectively to the diverse needs of the population. This has resulted for the most part in recreation and leisure service agencies being organized along a direct service approach to have fostered standardization instead of the diversity representative of a pluralistic society.

Dunn comments on the enabler-community catalyst service approach which includes a provision to encourage and facilitate recreation independence among citizens:

> *"This condition is characterized by sufficient knowledge, skills, and resources to permit an individual or group to engage in experiences of their own choice during free or discretionary time without external direction or intervention."*[34]

According to Dunn, the enabling role serves three primary advantages which make it particularly relevant and functional for organizations strapped with fiscally and philosophically untenable superstructures and destined for irrelevance and obsolescence in the 1970's.

> "First, this dynamic, imaginative approach has great appeal to in-
> novative citizens and professionals, especially those bored with the
> reruns of life. When agency programs are not expanding—even when
> they are cut back severely—the new interests of citizens need not be
> wasted nor the creative ingenuity of staff inhibited. For as profession-
> als 'work themselves out of a job,' they have the opportunity to begin
> new challenges in new program spheres.
> Another virtue ... is that when citizen participants perform the opera-
> tional details, professional personnel productivity becomes impres-
> sive. Output per man hour ratios can achieve incredible levels.
> Stretching scarce public dollars has long been an accepted objective of
> over-extended, under-financed local recreation professionals, and it is
> more necessary today than ever before. 'Helping people help them-
> selves' toward recreational independence is one way of doing it in
> these austere times.
> Finally, more of ... these agencies ... are inexorably committed to the
> continuation of these programs or events if interest wanes or new
> opportunities emerge ... If demand languishes, fads do not become
> white elephants awaiting retirements or demolition for a decent bur-
> ial. Even where new facilities [are] built ... they are sufficiently mul-
> tifunctional to be available for a wide variety of program alterna-
> tives."[35]

It is suggested by Dunn that the enabling approach offers a
dynamic supplement, an alternative to the traditional leisure service approach and deserves greater priority by public agencies.
There may be drawbacks to the sudden inclusion of the enabling
approach by an organization, particularly with respect to program
evaluation. Ordinarily, agencies have conditioned their staff,
elected officials and constituency to measure success and productivity in terms of attendance numbers. Now it appears that
agencies are going to have to change their expectations and a more
"pertinent accountability number for agency enabler-efforts becomes not 'how many do we directly serve,' but rather, 'how many
no longer need us to be served?' "[36]

The direct service approach determines or makes some assumptions about people's recreation needs, desires and interests,
and accordingly makes available ready-to-use agency resources to
them. The enabling approach recognizes a broader commitment
and serves as a catalyst, and helps people to implement their desires and interests. The agency assists people in planning and ob-
taining needed services and resources and is cognizant of the
whole network of human activity and sociopolitical conditioning
factors which exist in community settings. *"The continuum, then, is
from providing opportunities which permit direct and immediate
participation to providing services which enable people to develop
their own opportunities."*[37]

Some agencies tend to operate almost exclusively at one end of
leisure service delivery continuum or the other. Most agencies

have deployed the direct service approach but now there is considerable weight given to varying the approach, depending upon the specific program, participants involved, determined need, etc. Each agency makes a commitment to encourage and facilitate certain kinds of behavior according to their goals and objectives and philosophy of service. It is important for each agency to recognize the interests and desires of users and nonusers and to orient its service approach to meet the needs of citizens in a way which invites involvement, participation, feedback and a realization of individual and group goals.

Human Development As The Goal of Recreation

There is increasing attention being devoted by human service agencies to the recognition that their main goal should be the fostering of human development; each agency would have a primary purpose of promoting each individual's capacities and potentialities as a whole and unique person. David Gray, an articulate spokesman for the humanistic perspective, comments on its relationship to recreation expression.

> "We must recognize the potential role of recreation in the development of people. The goal of organized recreation programs is to provide people opportunity for the development of a positive self-image. Any program that receives a participant whole and sends him back damaged in self-respect, self-esteem, or relationships with others is not a recreation program. The fact that it may be a basketball program with games played during leisure is irrelevant. Such a program is not a recreational program unless the response of the participants is positive."[38]

The leisure setting, as all environments, should provide opportunities for the individual to engage in a full range of possible experiencing which will allow for spontaneous and direct use of the environment. The leisure milieu must be perceived in its totality, in which the individual can explore and take advantage of all possible opportunities for human growth and self-fulfillment.

Typically, recreation and leisure service agencies have focused their approach on meeting the more immediate needs of their constituents, ranging from the desire for skill instruction in basketball, tennis or field hockey; the opportunity to make social contacts, a chaise lounge in the sun in a neighborhood park; or participate in a special holiday program. While all of these experiences offer the individual an opportunity for feedback from others, a chance to master a skill and realize personal goals; leisure service delivery approaches traditionally have not focused on the whole person, leaving such tasks to the school, the church or family. However, it has become increasingly apparent that with each agency serving only a segment of the whole person and growing fusion of life roles, there is a need for each human service agency to comprehend the interrelationships of human beings and the environment.

The individual has certain fundamental human needs that must be fulfilled if one is to sustain life and survive. The way they are met determines our physical and mental health and how one is to develop and function as a total person. The individual's needs are arranged into two overall categories: (1) the need for physical security and love, and (2) the need to meet self-esteem and accommodate the drive toward growth and self-fulfillment. These categories of basic human needs are encompassed by five aspects of living: the emotional, intellectual, physical, social and spiritual (Fig. 5). Brill comments on the interrelationship of these areas:

> *"Theirs is a dynamic interrelationship in which each is continuously affecting and being affected by others, and there is no real and complete understanding of what is happening in one without understanding what is happening in the other."*[39]

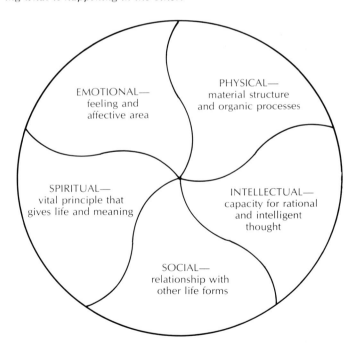

Fig. 5. Total Man—The Continuous, Dynamic Interaction of Five Vital Areas. (Brill, *Working With People: The Helping Process,* courtesy of J. P. Lippincott Company, 1973.)

Basic Human Needs. The individual's basic needs are arranged in a hierarchy of prepotency. Maslow[40] developed a theory of human motivation in which he stated that every drive is related to the state of satisfaction or dissatisfaction of other drives. He arranged his need-hierarchy in an ascending order, with the initial need level being more concerned with material needs to sustain life, including physiological needs (food, rest, exercise, shelter, etc.); safety needs (protection against danger, threat, deprivation); to less concrete ones for loving and being loved, social needs (need for belonging, for association, for acceptance by one's peers, for giving and receiving love and friendship); to more personally enhancing and enriching needs, ego needs (self-esteem, self-confidence, independence, achievement, competence, status, recognition); and self-fulfillment and self-actualization (needs for realizing one's own potentialities, for continued self-development, for being creative). The self-actualizing person is not an individual who has stopped growing. Indeed, growth is a continuous and essential concomitant of the life process. Each individual receives at conception an imprint with a maximum potential for developing in every area of self and if given favorable external conditions will mature throughout his lifetime toward the level of his maximum capability.

Recreation and leisure service personnel must be aware of the total individual and give full consideration to how each person can be satisfied at his level of development. Brill provides an understanding of things which can be done to assist in the development in all areas of an individual to enable him to function as a total individual.

> "In general we could say that in the physical area we need a basic minimum of material supplied, stimulation, opportunity for physical development at crucial points in the developmental timetable, and basic medical services that are one of the benefits of our modern society. In the area of intellectual development, we need stimulation and the opportunity to acquire and master knowledge, each according to his own capacity; in the area of emotional development, we need fulfilling relationships with significant other people and ability to accept and be at peace with ourselves; in the area of social growth, we need the opportunity to become socialized on an increasing wider scale with increasing capacity to relate meaningfully and effectively with people who are different from ourselves; in the area of spiritual development, we need the stimulation and opportunity to find a meaning in life that transcends the mere satisfaction of needs and gives purpose and direction to the total experience."[41]

Figure 6 shows how one's development is related to fulfillment of basic needs. It is vitally important that recreation and leisure

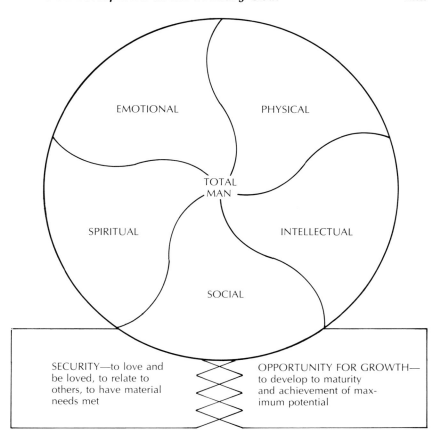

EMOTIONAL

PHYSICAL

TOTAL
MAN

SPIRITUAL

INTELLECTUAL

SOCIAL

SECURITY—to love and
be loved, to relate to
others, to have material
needs met

OPPORTUNITY FOR GROWTH—
to develop to maturity
and achievement of max-
imum potential

Fig. 6. The Development of Man Rests Upon Fulfillment of Basic Needs. (Brill, *Working With People: The Helping Process*, courtesy of J. P. Lippincott Company, 1973.)

service personnel recognize that each individual has a need for security and dependency and contrarily also has a need for growth and independence. Each individual is unique and unique potential for development in each of his living areas. Each aspect of an individual's potential must be seen in a dynamic interrelationship that constitutes the whole.

Life is a dynamic process. The individual moves in life through a series of developmental stages as he develops by adaptation to the changing demands of both his own inherent potential and of the environment in which he lives. This progression is not a uniform state within the person nor uniform among individuals, but it occurs at a steady and continuous pace. In working with people, recreation and leisure service personnel must be flexible in their concept of considering a norm for development at any particular stage. The workers must consider what is normal for the individual, with his particular heredity and his particular environment at the particular time in his development.

Leisure and Human Development

A person's base of support is widened each time one feels competent about a particular motor skill, fitness activity, successful social interaction, etc., and the capability of one's intellectual, social, or physical abilities. The task of the recreator in relation to human development is to help people identify and facilitate specific physical, social and intellectual abilities in line with their potentialities. For one person, it might be embroidering; for another, participating in a play; and for a third, the successful mastering of a dance step.

Self-actualization encompasses what Maslow has labeled peak experiences, those moments of *total* involvement in an experience to which the person attaches his own meaning. Recreation contains the capacity for total involvement, and the meanings that are derived from a particular activity experience range from joy and fun to ascetic notion of pain and the courage to persevere under trying conditions. According to this view, the *process* is all important; the product—e.g., winning—plays a secondary role. These dimensions of self-actualization are anchored in positive feelings about the self so that the participant is free to become totally involved or to express oneself without fear.

The needs that affect a person's feelings of competence, the potential abilities that one possesses, the meaning that recreation activity could hold, the desire to express oneself through recreation experience, the relationship of all these things to each other and to past, present, and future behavior—answers to these kinds of questions, constitute the essence of self-understanding in recreation education.

Humanism is often acused of being mystical, anti-scientific, or, at best, philosophical in nature and therefore not amenable to proof or discreditation by "hard data" research. However, research in recreation has focused on some of the social-emotional outcomes of the recreation experience and the results shed some light on the feasibility of humanistic goals. The results of recreation related research as applied to the sociopsychological-developmental implications of the leisure experience have recently been documented by Ellis,[42] Dumazedier,[43] Howard,[44] Neulinger,[45] and van der Smissen.[46]

To be sure, humanistic goals have been achieved for some individuals both intentionally and accidentally within the current program and activity patterns; but a concerted effort to help everyone reach these goals has not been characteristic of the recreation and leisure service field or American society as a whole. The culture's influence is most apparent here, especially cultural value orientations such as competitive achievement and sex role characteristics which are perpetuated by the recreation field, the family, and schools. As a result, some of the American people are denied full access to whatever behavior development can be gained by taking part in recreation programs as they now exist.

Humanistic methodology is based on the assumption that each participant is a unique person with unique talents and capacities who is potentially better able than anyone else to discern what is most meaningful for him or her and how one best learns. To bring these potentialities to function, the individual must be provided a wide range of opportunities within a non-threatening environment and must progressively move from a structured style of leading to a self-directed individualized approach, slowly shifting the responsibility for initiating recreation activity from the leader to the participant on an individual basis.

The goals of humanistic education serve as an important precursor to the steps which would be helpful in facilitating human development through the auspices of recreation and leisure service agencies. The following adapted goals of humanistic education appear useful to leisure studies curricula as defined by Hellison:

> "*The first goal—self-esteem—refers to those feelings of competence or incompetence which derive from a person's subjective perceptions of his own experiences. An individual's self-esteem is an important beginning, because it forms the base of support for further behavioral development.*
> *. . . the second goal [is] self-actualization—that is, growth toward fulfillment of his special potentialities and talents. Any individual's potentialities span a wide range of abilities . . . Growth toward self-actualization may take place relatively early in life and become part of the individual's special memories and feelings, or it may be an ongoing process which the individual experiences throughout life.*
> *[The] third humanistic goal [is] self-understanding. If an individual's feelings and abilities are unique to him, he is in a better position, at least hypothetically, to determine what and how to learn. To profitably engage in this kind of introspection, however, requires considerable attention to the question "who Am I?" beyond those early efforts to establish a base of self-esteem ("Am I competent?"). He must be able to identify his needs and their sources (such as cultural values), his abilities, his interests, and the interrelationships among these vari-*

ables. By understanding these components on the self, he can more readily integrate them into a meaningful life-style which will bring him closer to social and emotional well-being.

The fourth and final humanistic goal moves beyond the self to social considerations ... the adoption of such values as sensitivity toward others and cooperation should further upgrade the quality of interpersonal relations, especially if the first three goals have already been met." [47]

The traditional teacher becomes a learning facilitator or discovery facilitator, allowing and aiding students to discover things and *themselves,* through humanistic education. The idea is not to *make* students know something. This approach only conditions individuals to be dependent and passive learners and recreationists. Education and recreation experiences should engage an individual *totally.* The following are some suggested guidelines in facilitating a humanistic approach to human development in recreation and leisure service.

(1) Self-esteem can be facilitated in a number of ways: the behavior of the recreation service worker can communicate the unique and special qualities of each participant; recreation activities can be determined which provide ample opportunities for success; the area or facility can be arranged so that there are private places to try things out; and rules and regulations concerning bicycle riding on playgrounds, use of playground apparatus, and alternating fixed lined courts, fields or areas, among others suited to individual needs.

(2) To assist the self-actualization process, very careful program planning is necessary, including needs assessment of social, psychological and physical aspects affecting users and potential participants; individual help; a wide variety of experiences, specialization; a measurement program designed to help participants identify their potentialities; and a knowledge base to facilitate self-development.

(3) The development of self-understanding, extremely important if participants are to eventually plan their own programs, can be encouraged both by staff group meetings (teens, young adults, physically handicapped, elderly, for example) aimed at typical needs, interests, and the integration of these into a life style; and by individual guidance sessions tailored to the uniqueness of the individual.

(4) Sensitivity toward others and cooperation, as values central to interpersonal relations, are often derived naturally as a result of group interaction in arts and crafts classes, sports programs, informal games, community problem-solving meetings, etc., but intentional planning either using

problem-solving or by directly emulating or exposing these values holds more promise for facilitating participant awareness of these values and their connection to peer relationships, neighborhood and community life, and to society as a whole.[48]

The humanistic perspective of the recreation and park movement received its major impetus from David E. Gray and Seymour Greben, when in 1973 they prepared an action plan for the national professional leisure service association's (National Recreation and Park Association) National Council to chart a new perspective for the movement.[49] They felt that there was a need for improving the outmoded approaches of human interaction, redefining satisfaction, achievement and mastery in intrinsic terms, and building a viable community base founded upon a concern for human development, the quality of the environment, mutual compatibility and shared interest.

Gray comments on the role of the recreation experience in relation to human development.

> *"We must recognize the potential role of recreation in the development of people. The goal of organized recreation programs is to provide people opportunities for the exercise of their powers, opportunity for recreational experience, opportunity for the development of a positive self-image. Any program that receives a person whole and sends him back damaged in self-respect, self-esteem, or relationships with others is not a recreation program. The fact that it may be a basketball program with games played during leisure is irrelevant. Such program is is not a recreational program unless the response of the participants is positive."*[50]

Recreation and leisure service agencies must be conscious of the impact of its programs on people and the environment. Agencies must perceive all elements of the social and physical environment as complementary and essential to growth. "The direction of all human service fields would have a common goal and direction: *growth would be toward greater consciousness of our wholeness and uniqueness.*"[51] Agencies must attempt to provide a full range of opportunities which will create an environment conducive to self-development. It is suggested by a humanistic perspective that not only should agencies be aware of how to promote growth through self-development experiences, they must also recognize barriers which inhibit growth potential. "The rigidity of response and seemingly endless specifications, rules, and regulations often required of participants, only serves to frustrate individuals from realizing their potential through recreation."[52]

The individual participates as a totality in the leisure environment, similar to any setting. One's social, emotional, physical, intellectual and spiritual functions are affected through the experience of recreation. It is therefore important for recreation and leisure service personnel to have some understanding how these factors are influenced and motivated by recreation behavior. Individual needs vary according to particular socioeconomic, cultural, ethnic, environmental and personality aspects of the person. There are many possible outcomes derived from the recreation experience which will aid human development and provide a satisfying response. Some of the potential recreation outcomes include:

Physical
relief of tension
relaxation
exercise
motor skill development
rehabilitation
fitness
coordination
physical growth
muscle tone
rejuvenation
testing of body
    capabilities

Intellectual-Educational
mastery
discovery
learning
insight
intensified skills
new experience
develop avocations
cultural awareness
learning about one's self
evaluation
synthesis
problem-solving

Psychological
anticipation
reflection
challenge
accomplishment
excitement
achievement
aesthetic appreciation
self-image
introspection
security
pleasure
self-confidence
self-actualization
enjoyment
exhilaration
self-expression

Spiritual
ecstasy
mind expansion
transcendence
revelation
release
contemplation
meditation
wonderment

Social
interpersonal relation-
    ships
friendships
trust
companionship
involvement
fellowship
communication
group and family unity
develop sense of com-
    munity
compatibility
appreciation
cultural sharing
concern for others
belonging
interaction

The taxonomy of outcomes above lists but a few of the possibilities for individual expression in a recreation experience. They provide a way of viewing how the potential of recreation expression may occur—by providing an environment in which the *full* range of expression may be facilitated from mere relief of tension and relaxation to enhancing communication and developing a sense of community to introspection and self-expression to discovery and learning about one's self to ecstasy and transcendence. Programs which focus on only one "category" of outcomes, or one "level" of human interaction, will not succeed in realizing the *maximum* possibilities for self-fulfillment.

Michaelis has developed a paradigm (Table 3) which illustrates the difference between a human developmental recreation approach (process) and an activity approach (product).[53] It serves to aid recreation and leisure service personnel in establishing an environment which is responsive to the individual and underscores the linkage between the social and physical environment, people who are served through recreation opportunities and the agencies who provide programs and services.

Table 3. Leisure Service Delivery Orientations*

Obviously there is not a black and white situation presented here, but many "gray" areas, many overlaps and interchanges between the two categories. HOWEVER, in analyzing any program or activity it would be wise to utilize this dichotomy in asking to what *DEGREE* does it satisfy one orientation vs. the other.

PROCESS	PRODUCT
1. Individual goals	1. Group goals
2. Locus of control is internal; (individual) constraints	2. Locus of control is external; (societal) constraints
3. Self motivations	3. Motivation for the prize, "the Gipper"
4. Individuals determine their own levels of MASTERY and success	4. People are eliminated or not "successful" by not achieving
5. People start and end at various different skill levels during varying lengths of time	5. Primary concern is with uniform skill development within set segmented periods of time
6. Many solutions or several ways to arrive at "success" (variety and flexibility of opportunities)	6. One solution or one way to arrive at success (fewer and less flexible opportunities)
7. Primary concern with the interactions and growth that occur among *people*	7. Primary concern is one the development of a "master" project or the attainment of a final goal (winning)
8. Cooperations, explorations	8. Competitions
9. Participation is paramount	9. Winning or "achievement" is paramount
10. Playful attitude	10. Often becomes "work??"
11. Less hierarchy	11. More hierarchy
12. Rewards, payoffs for all (all winners)	12. Rewards, payoffs achieved by some denied others
13. Encourage, develop greater levels of risk taking & arousal (continual realistic challenges and stimulation)	13. Many are denied continual "risk taking" opportunities and arousal is diminished (bored, scared away, outmatched)
14. Concern with progressive development	14. Terminal satisfactions
15. Development of "attitudes for lifetime pursuits, and sensitivities to new experiences"	15. Short term gains, more immediate pursuits
16. Maximum numbers	16. Less concern with everyone being involved
17. Participant input, "people concerns"	17. "Leader" of agency predetermined programs, administrative & facility concerns (chain link fence mentality)

*Developed by William Michaelis, Dept. of Recreation Administration, California State Polytechnic University, Pomona, California.

The direct service delivery model incorporated into park and recreation programs has commonly utilized the *product-oriented* approach which has concerned itself with providing people with compensatory relief opportunities through recreation. This is in contrast to the humanistic *process-oriented* recreation approach which utilizes a motivational base for helping people to come closer to meeting their basic psychological needs, with being able to live holistically, to be connected with life. According to the process-oriented approach, recreation is seen as fused within the total community environment, the entire city is a comprehensive park system. One cannot in a sense plan explicitly for recreation. This, according to Williams will yield less satisfying results.

> *"The reason this is a social imperative is that under the definition the better we are at providing special places and special programs for people, the more long-range harm we may be doing. If recreation can and should be a part of the total scene, then the backbone of the individual growth experience in the comprehensive system will be human resources. Recreation directors and their volunteers will act as facilitators to the individual in his quest toward total immersion in something. They will no longer be trying to bring 'balance' back into living, vainly attempting to compensate for voids in the real world by providing impersonal directed programs. People caused to fit programs rather than programs to people."*[54]

Ecology of Leisure Service

A humanistic approach to recreation and leisure recognizes a total concern for human beings and the environment. This recognition increases the field's responsibility for facilitating an individual's total needs. This is a marked change from the activity centered philosophy of most agencies. H. Douglas Sessoms, in his presentation of a position paper on human resources, developed for the National Recreation and Park Association, makes reference to the need for change in the role of the professional recreator.

> *"Individuals are increasingly demanding reform in recreation services and programs. Often these demands are valid and have resulted from the increasing bureaucracy and institutional deafness of organized services to human needs and desires. On occasion they reflect shifts in the system of values. In nearly every instance these changes and charges trap the professional between the demands of the public, his own value system, and the pressures of traditions and structures within his agency.*
> *It is proposed that the organized recreation service take a stand; specify its basic beliefs, philosophy, and values; and give the professional the support necessary to act on the basis of his professional judgment as well as upon the expressed wishes of those he serves. Not only must individual needs and interests be understood if the recreation service is to be valid, but a constant professional evaluation of these services is necessary. As a professional, the*

recreation and park specialist should express his opinion on matters that enslave mankind or which prevent those he serves from attaining their fullest potential. It is his responsibility and the responsibility of the profession to act in the best interest of the total community in matters pertaining to the expression of recreation even when the decision negatively affects immediate participation in and support of the recreation and park service."[55]

The field has a responsibility to the whole person and can meet it only by recognizing the interrelationships among people in their physical and social environment, and the way these relationships influence, or are influenced by, various social and organizational processes. This refers to the concept known as the "ecology" of the leisure service delivery system.[56] The elements of the delivery system, physical environment, social environment, people and leisure service organization must be viewed in a holistic way.

"It is holistic in the sense that any change in the population being served will affect the nature of the programming and vice versa. Each component is an integral part of the overall delivery system and each influences another segment of the unit. All the elements mutually modify one another."[57]

The following table serves to illustrate aspects of each component of the leisure service delivery system and provide some insight into the overall dynamics and range of concern, influence and impact the provision of recreation opportunity has in contemporary society.

A Systems View. The incorporation of a systems approach to understanding leisure services is seen as an appropriate development in the park and recreation field as system implies wholeness and integration—terms which typify interrelationships and synergy. A systems theoretical approach is based on the concept that there exist similarities and organization, variety of different entities, be they physical, biological or social.

Banathy defines systems in the following way.

"Systems are assemblages of parts that are designed and built by man into organized wholes for the attainment of specific purposes. The purpose of a system is realized through processes in which interacting components of the system engage in order to produce a predetermined output. Purpose determines the process required and the process will imply the kind of components that will make up the system. A system receives its purpose, its inputs, its resources, and its constraints from its suprasystem. In order to maintain itself, a system has to produce an output which satisfies the suprasystem."[58]

A system therefore represents a series of interrelated and integrated components which reflect the whole. In order to understand the respective components of the system one must understand the interrelationship of the elements, called subsystems, and how they are integrated. A system serves both as an analytical and as a practical conceptualization of function. The leisure service delivery system can be identified as a larger system (suprasystem) and it contains subsystems (park services, therapeutic services, community and neighborhood center services, older adult services, etc.).

> "As such, each system contributes to overall purpose of the total system in some distinct and yet overall way. The subsystem can be viewed as having its own lesser purpose and separate set of objectives and its own processes. Each subsystem can be separated and analyzed in detail . . . Subsystems do not exist in isolation."[59]

The effectiveness of the overall leisure service delivery system depends on how well all of the subsystems are integrated and interfunction. The components making up the leisure service delivery system are the participant, social environment, physical environment and the agency (Table 4). Each subsystem of the delivery system must be analyzed separately and requires a corollary understanding of the relationships of each component of the delivery system.

Participants. The provision of recreation opportunities will yield a variety of individual behavioral response patterns. A program must be expected to meet a wide range and complexly interrelated diversity of individual differences which occur in a recreation setting. Recreation behavior is influenced by a number of *internal* conditioning factors, including individual differences such as age, sex, life style, motivation and self-concept and by an *external* opportunity system such as laws, mores and folkways, norms, geography, income level, etc. These factors operate in an interrelated fashion.[60] Perloff and Wingo[61] indicate that certain population criteria can be determined which will result in an effective predictor of patterns of recreation behavior. For example, one's position in the life cycle, socioeconomic status, subjective preference patterns, and location are influential factors in recreation behavior. They illustrate the influence of these participant criteria.

1. *Family or Life Cycle.* One's position in the family or life cycle has a substantial influence on certain recreation behavior patterns. For example, families with small children will tend to take advantage of recreation opportunities in which the entire family can jointly participate. Young, single males are likely to engage in more active, competitive activities.

2. *Socioeconomic Status.* The more affluent members of the population can afford more expensive forms of recreation than the

Table 4. Components (Ecology Design) of the Leisure Service Delivery System

Social Components	Physical Components	Participant Components	Agency Components
Ethnicity	Climate	Human needs	Goals
Cultural heritage	Transportation system	Motivation	Objectives
Social class	Topography	Individual self-concept	Philosophy
Race	Business and industry	Age	Organizational structure
Family	Schools	Sex	Leadership
Mores/folkways	Churches	Experience	Recreation areas and
Religion	Environmental quality	Attitudes	facilities
Health	Population density/	Interests	Open space
Sanitation	crowdedness	Desires	Locality
Education		Goals	Priorities
Allied humor		Competencies	Financial support and
Service resources		Capabilities	distribution
Justice/courts			Equipment

poor and the higher social class status of certain groups often results in more prestigious recreation behavior patterns.

3. *Subjective Preference.* Each individual has certain tastes and personal proclivities, ranging from certain psychological predispositions to physical abilities. Obviously, one's personal experience affects what one can do well, so that awareness, training and skills are determining factors in personal preferences for recreation expression. This point is also made by Jensen:

> *"Participation in many cultural programs by persons of low economic status is often limited by low self-image. This psychological factor is evidenced by concern over lack of proper clothing and lack of knowledge about where the activity is being held, what the activity actually is, and what relationship it has to their lives."*[61]

4. *Location.* Certain regions provide unique leisure opportunities (partly stemming from tradition) which are largely climatic and geographical, that influence recreation behavior (e.g., skiing in the Northwest and East). Also, the influence of location results from conditions of accessibility.[62]

Social Environment. The complexity of urban-suburban life affects one's ability to engage in certain recreation activities. Community life is made up of the interaction of housing, transportation and mobility and industrial patterns; health and sanitation; distribution of income among the population; level of education of citizens, etc. This would be the same but on a lesser scale in rural areas. The differential impact of these social aspects will result in varied conditioning circumstances for members of the community. For example, Jensen comments on the distinctions in the values of social and ethnic classes that account for many of the program differences among community members.

> *"For example, the amount of income available to a family is a primary determinant of ability to buy services. A higher income is indicative of discretionary income and can be interpreted to reflect the availability of private transportation, participation in programs which require fees, and the availability of individuals who have uncommitted time and are willing to serve as volunteers. The income level is also considered an index of educational achievement. The higher the educational level, the greater the number of recreational experiences these persons have had, and the more mobility there is of these individuals wishing to pursue them further. In contrast, low income areas are generally related to high density population areas, limited space for recreation, fewer personal cars, and limited education. The limited education of persons in low income areas, therefore, can mean that the opportunity to participate in recreational activities is restricted to recreational sites within walking distance. The service radius in a low income area is generally less than the service radius in higher income neighborhoods.*
> *Socioeconomic data are important to the direction, intensity, and*

quality of recreation and park goals and objectives. For example, substantial increase in the number of families receiving welfare payments, correlated with rapidly deteriorating housing, are indicators to alert officials of a potential trouble spot in the community. Park and recreation departments should react to such implicit dangers by goal reformation to maximize services to this sector of the community at little or no cost to the participants. It would be well to consider these new goals as possessing a high priority for capital improvement projects."[63]

Physical Environment. The provision and quality of and accessibility to open space, park lands and recreation areas and facilities no doubt have an influence on their use by various segments of the population. Increasing population density, accelerating economic growth (although temporarily set back from the recession in the mid-1970's), expanding technological developments, transportation dilemmas and increasing amounts of free time have combined to place a premium on urban park space.[64]

Topography, areas and facilities, transportation patterns, housing patterns, etc. have several characteristics which influence the manner in which people exhibit recreation behavior. A facility, for example, may be so highly specialized in use that only a few types of activities can be carried on in it. Multi-purpose facilities or areas may permit a variety of specialized and unspecialized activities to be carried on simultaneously. The concept of land use carries two important aspects which have unique consequences for recreation use: space and the resource endowment that accompanies it. Perloff and Wingo comment:

"Space as the effective quantity of the land input frequently involves some complex dimensions: length more than area is important in the recreation capacity of a public beach, and similarly, of streams for canoeing and fishing; unobstructed area is crucial for space-extensive games, and other spatial features may influence the way in which we measure the input of space into a facility ... Resources endowment– all of those features which especially suit an area for specific kinds of outdoor recreation–is the qualitative dimension of the space input. Scenic qualities, availability of bodies of water, or of game and fish, all relate to activities for which the land might be used."[65]

Certainly location—where facilities, areas, settings of leisure opportunities are located—affects the performance of a facility because distance influences the recreation decisions of the participant. Normally, given several comparable facilities, a recreationist will frequent the nearer facility to the exclusion of the more remote.[66]

In order for people to enjoy certain opportunities, the users must overcome this barrier and be transported to the facility and this involves cost calculations. It costs money and time to make a trip to a recreation area. Since the supply of both is limited, the recreation user must always evaluate the satisfaction of an anticipated experience against the values of other experience which alternative uses of time and money would have made possible.

Leisure Service Agencies. Organizations establish goals and objectives, policy, employ a work force to carry out these and deliver service. Leisure service agencies, then exist to provide opportunities for people, individually and collectively to engage in leisure behavior in order that certain personal and/or social goals can be satisfied. Agencies structure opportunities which elicit various kinds of recreation behavior through the manipulation of the human and physical environments that are a part of their organization's operation.

> *"The human environment includes agency staff and participants, and the physical environment includes natural resources, developed land and water areas, facilities, equipment and supplies. These two environments, physical and human are inseparable. One affects the other, and they act upon the participant as a combined influence."*[67]

The leisure service delivery system is based on the agency's commitment to provide opportunities which encourage and facilitate selected kinds of recreation behaviors; the specific nature of these behaviors depends upon the goals and objectives and delivery approach of the particular agency and the human and physical resources which are available. The agency which is effective is one which recognizes the needs, interests and characteristics of the public within the particular social context it seeks to serve.

References

1. Rogers, Carl: 'Good Life' is Being Redefined, *San Jose Mercury-News* November 25, 1973, p. 30.
2. Dickerson, James R.: The Two Americas: Bedrocks, Cosmopolitans Clash Over Nation's Goals, *The National Observer* March 10, 1973, p. 1.
3. Sessoms, H. Douglas: Recreation. In: *Recreation in Modern Society.* Edited by Marion N. and Carroll R. Hormachea, Boston, Holbrook Press, Inc., 1972, p. 311.
4. Gold, Seymour M.: Deviant Behavior in Urban Parks? *Leisure Today* November/December, 1974, p. 18.
5. Gray, David E. and Greben, Seymour: Future Perspectives, *Parks and Recreation* 9:49, July, 1974.
6. Ibid: p. 50.
7. Sessoms, H. Douglas: Alcoholism as a Separate Life Style, *Leisure Today* Op. cit., p. 27.
8. Murphy, James F.: Leisure Determinants of Life Style, *Leisure Today* Op. cit., p. 5.
9. Gold: Op. cit., p. 20.

10. Berger, Bennett M.: *Looking for America.* Englewood Cliffs, New Jersey, Prentice-Hall, Inc., 1971, p. 220.
11. Berger, Ibid., p. 226.
12. Turner, Frederick Jackson: *The Significance of the Frontier in American History.* New York, Henry Holt & Company, Inc., 1920.
13. Riesman, David, Glazer, Nathan, and Reuel, Denney: *The Lonely Crowd.* New Haven, Connecticut, Yale University Press, 1950.
14. Kando, Thomas M: *Leisure and Popular Culture in Transition.* Op. cit.
15. Reich, Charles: *The Greening of America.* New York, Random House, Inc., 1970, p. 21.
16. Weber, Max: *The Protestant Ethic and the Spirit of Capitalism.* New York, Charles Scribner's Sons, 1958.
17. Kando: Op. cit., p. 73.
18. Reich: Op. cit., pp. 76, 90.
19. Ibid: p. 90.
20. Ibid: p. 77.
21. Whyte, William H., Jr.: *Organization Man.* New York, Simon & Schuster, Inc., 1957.
22. Martindale, Don: *The Nature and Types of Sociological Theory.* Boston, Houghton Mifflin Company, 1960, p. 428.
23. Kando: Op. cit.; pp. 75–76.
24. Ellul, Jacques: *The Technological Society.* New York, Alfred A. Knopf, Inc., 1964.
25. Kando: Op. cit., p. 11.
26. Pendleton, Clarence M., Jr.: A Rationale for Budgetary Support for Human Care Services in the City, Position Paper, Model Cities Department, February, 1975.
27. Lystad, Mary: *As They See It.* Cambridge, Massachusetts, Schenkman Publishing Company, Inc., 1973, p. 3.
28. Berger, Peter, and Berger, Brigitte: The Blueing of America, Op. cit.
29. Best, Fred. Editor: *The Future of Work.* Englewood Cliffs, New Jersey, Prentice-Hall, Inc., 1973, p. 3.
30. Ibid: p. 16.
31. Murphy, Williams, Niepoth and Brown: *Leisure Service Delivery System,* p. 71.
32. Gray, David E.: The Tyranny of the Chain-Link Fence, *California Parks and Recreation 10*:10, August, 1968.
33. Ibid.
34. Dunn, Diana R.: Dynamic Programming: Enabling Recreational Independence, *Leisure Today* November/December, 1973, p. 35.
35. Ibid: p. 38.
36. Ibid: p. 38.
37. Murphy, Williams, Niepoth and Brown: Op. cit., p. 71.
38. Gray, David E.: Exploring Inner Space, Op. cit., p. 18.
39. Brill, Naomi: *Working With People: The Helping Process.* Philadelphia, J. B. Lippincott Company, 1973, p. 6.
40. Maslow, Abraham H.: A Theory of Human Motivation, *Psychological Review 50*:370–396, July, 1943.
41. Brill: Op. cit., p. 9.
42. Ellis: *Why People Play.* Op. cit.
43. Dumazedier: *Sociology of Leisure.* Op. cit.
44. Howard: "Multivariate Relationships Between Leisure Activities and Personality," Op. cit.
45. Neulinger: *The Psychology of Leisure,* Op. cit.
46. van der Smissen, Betty. Editor: *Indicators of Change in the Recreation Environment—A National Research Symposium.* College of Health, Physical Education and Recreation, Pennsylvania State University, 1975, 471 pp.
47. Hellison, Donald R.: *Humanistic Physical Education.* Englewood Cliffs, New Jersey, Prentice-Hall, Inc., 1973, pp. 110–12.

48. Ibid: refer to p. 114 for similar guidelines related to physical education.
49. Gray, David E. and Greben, Seymor: *Redefining Leisure: An Action Plan for the Recreation and Park Movement.* Washington, D.C., National Recreation and Park Association, 1973.
50. Gray, David E.: Exploring Inner Space, Op. cit., p. 19.
51. Murphy: *Recreation and Leisure Service,* Op. cit., p. 64.
52. Ibid: p. 65.
53. Michaelis, William: Orientations, Paper prepared for California State Polytechnic University, Pomona.
54. Williams, Wayne R.: Social Imperatives and Leisure Planning. In: *Serving More With Less; Financing Park and Recreation Services.* Davis, California, University of California, Davis, 1973, p. 93.
55. Sessoms, H. Douglas: The Role of Recreation in Developing and Nurturing Human Resources, *Parks and Recreation* 9:32–33, February, 1974.
56. Murphy, Williams, Niepoth and Brown: The Ecology of Leisure Service. *Leisure Service Delivery System.* Op. cit., pp. 1–5.
57. Ibid, p. 1.
58. Banathy, Bela: *Instructional Systems.* Palo Alto, California, Farron Publishers, 1968, p. 12.
59. Peterson, Carol Ann: *A Systems Approach to Therapeutic Recreation Program Planning.* New York, Teacher's College, Columbia University, N.D.
60. Murphy, Williams, Niepoth and Brown: Op. cit., pp. 1–2.
61. Perloff, Harvey S. and Wingo, Lowden, Jr.: Urban Growth and the Planning of Outdoor Recreation. In: *Land and Leisure: Concepts and Methods in Outdoor Recreation.* Edited by David W. Fischer, John E. Lewis and George B. Priddle, Chicago, Maaroufa Press, Inc., 1974, pp. 25–44.
62. Ibid: pp. 32–33.
63. Jensen, Marilyn A.: Information Systems. In: *Modernizing Urban Park and Recreation Systems.* Arlington, Va.: National Recreation and Park Association, 1972, p. 23.
64. Byerts, Thomas O. and Teaff, Joseph D.: Social Research As a Design Tool, *Parks and Recreation* 10:34, January, 1975.
65. Perloff and Wingo: Op. cit., p. 35.
66. Thompson, Bryan: Recreational Travel: A Review and Pilot Study, *Traffic Quarterly* October, 1967, pp. 527–42; and Lentnek, Barry, Van Doren, Carlton, and Trail, James R.: Spatial Behavior in Recreational Boating, *Journal of Leisure Research* 1:103–24, Spring, 1969.
67. Murphy, Williams, Niepoth, and Brown: Op. cit., p. 78.

SECTION II

The Dynamics of Managing a Community Recreation and Leisure Service Agency

CHAPTER 5

The Setting: The Community as a System

"It should be clear that recreation organizations are all part of a broad arena of social interaction. The organization and provision of recreation services do not take place in a vacuum. Leisure service organizations whether they be public, private non-profit or commercial are all linked in some form to the larger community system."

In this chapter, the organization of community recreation services will be viewed as a system comprised of three subsystems (public, private non-profit and commercial) which are at the same time part of the larger community social system. The idea of a system is commonplace. The human body is a good example of a biological system. The body is composed of several separate but interdependent parts. While each part or organ works independently, the condition of one affects the condition and behavior of the others. All must work in relative harmony if the human system is to continue to operate effectively. Much like this illustration of a biological organism, the community can be viewed as a social organism comprised of a variety of separate organizations and institutions tied together in a widespread interrelated social network. The prominent components of a community social system have been commonly identified by sociologists as business and/or economic, religious, government, education, social-welfare (of which some consider recreation to be a part), health and recreation.[1-3] Each of these systems came into existence in response to meeting some basic human need. Commenting on this point Sessoms states that:

> *The major social systems reflect the major aspects of living. Man's need to learn and cope with the environment in which he lives gave rise to the educational system. His dependency on others shapes his systems of control (government). His need to play demands a recreation system. It may have the accompanying subsystems of land preservation and development (parks), organized activities and time scheduling (rec. depts.), membership associations and social groupings (YMCA's, country clubs).*[4]

It is essential to realize that the presence of any social system whether it be recreation, education or any of the others will have some effect, directly or indirectly, on the other members of the over-all community system. This interrelationship is illustrated in Figure 7.

For example, the decision of the city council (government) under pressure from the business community (economic) to allow the development of a new industrial park will have a significant impact on the recreation system. Increased industrial development would mean increased population, soaring land prices, reordered land-use priorities, heightened competition for tax dollars and so on. We can see, then, how the desires of people (economic system) are manifested through a subsystem (industrial development) which in turn affects a variety of related processes (urban expansion, land-use planning) and systems, including parks and recreation.

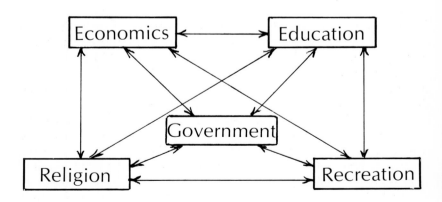

Fig. 7.   The community system.

It should be clear that the recreation organizations are all part of an arena of social interaction. The organization and provision of recreation services do not take place in a vacuum. Leisure service organizations whether they be public, private or commercial are all linked in some form to the larger community system. Due to this fact, the public recreation administrator for example, always has to be cognizant of the ramifications of his decisions. For example, will the offering of a Belly Dancing class alienate certain members of the religious system, or will the sponsorship of an auto mechanics class for teens be viewed as an infringement on the school's vocational training program, or will an increase in fees and charges for recreation programs anger certain members of the City Council? These questions and many others should be analyzed within the context of the dynamic community social system. The challenge confronting recreators is to identify the interdependencies that do exist and to understand how the various units of the social system affect each other and fit together to form the community structure.

The Community Recreation System

The recreation movement was born out of an expression of concern for the underprivileged, particularly youth, in our nation's rapidly industrializing cities. Ushered in during the reform era of the latter 19th century, organized recreation was initially conceived as a vehicle for ameliorating the deplorable social conditions confronting youth in our cities' slums.

Private, voluntary membership organizations such as the YW and YMCA's, Boy Scouts, and Girl Scouts quickly grew into prominence shortly after the turn of the century. Financed from private, philanthropic sources these organizations dominated the recreation movement for a number of years.

A significant transition in the provision of community recreation services occurred during the 30's. The depression years signaled the end of the private organization domination of the recreation movement. During this period local government began to assume a greatly increased responsibility for recreation services. The necessity of providing relief from the tedium of unemployment and poverty coupled with the growing acceptance of recreation as a universal need of *all* people regardless of economic need, age, race or sex stimulated the widespread establishment of recreation as a government function. Acceptance of recreation as a responsibility of local government resulted in the creation of hundreds of city recreation commissions or boards across the country.

Commercial recreation enterprises in the form of taverns,

dance halls and theaters have always been a conspicuous part of the urban recreation scene. In fact, the flourishing nature of these establishments gave impetus to the creation of what is now often considered to be the cornerstone of many municipal recreation department, the neighborhood recreation "Center." Many concerned citizens urged the establishment of government supervised recreation centers on the grounds that they would provide "morally superior and healthier" alternatives for community residents. In spite of such efforts, the commercial recreation sector has continued to flourish and diversify as evidenced by the tremendous growth of such enterprises as bowling centers, skating rinks, movie theaters, resorts and taverns.

Today, a variety of representatives from all three sectors; private non-profit, public and commercial, can be found in most communities across the country. Collectively, they comprise the community recreation system. While all three are involved in the provision of formal, organized leisure activities, each is sufficiently different from the other, with respect to philosophy, objectives and financing to allow for their independent classification as shown in the following Table 5.

Table 5. Comparison and Contrast Study of Public, Private (Voluntary Agencies), and Commercial Recreation[5]

Philosophy of Recreation

Public   Enrichment of the life of the total community by providing opportunities for the worthy use of leisure. Nonprofit in nature.

Private   Enrichment of the life of participating members by offering opportunities for worthy use of leisure, frequently with emphasis on the group and the individual. Nonprofit in nature.

Commercial   Attempt to satisfy public demands in an effort to produce profit. Dollars from, as well as for, recreation.

Objectives of Recreation

Public   To provide leisure opportunities which contribute to the social, physical, educational, cultural, and general well-being of the community and its people.

Private   Similar to public, but limited by membership, race, religion, age, and the like. To provide opportunities for close group association with emphasis on citizenship, behavior, and life philosophy values. To provide activities that appeal to members.

Commercial   To provide activities or programs which will appeal to customers. To meet competition. To net profit. To serve the public.

Administrative Organization

Public	Governmental agencies (federal, state, county, and local).
Private	Boy Scouts, settlements, Girl Scouts, Camp Fire Girls, "Y" organizations, and others.
Commercial	Corporations, syndicates, partnerships, private ownerships. Examples: motion picture, television, and radio companies, resorts, bowling centers, skating rinks.

Finance

Public	Primarily by taxes. Also by gifts, grants, trust funds, small charges, and fees to defray cost.
Private	By gifts, grants, endowments, donations, drives, and membership fees.
Commercial	By the owner or promoters.
	By the users: admission and charges.

Facilities

Public	Community buildings, parks (national, state, local), athletic fields, playgrounds, playfields, stadiums, camps, beaches, museums, zoos, golf courses, school facilities, etc.
Private	Settlement houses, youth centers, churches, play areas, clubs, camps, and others.
Commercial	Theaters, clubs, taverns, night clubs, lounges, race tracks, bowling lanes, stadiums, and others.

Leadership

Public	Professionally prepared to provide extensive recreation programs for large numbers of people.
	Frequently subject to Civil Service regulations.
	Volunteers as well as professionals.
	College training facilities growing.
Private	Professionally prepared to provide programs on a social group-work basis.
	Employed at discretion of managing agency.
	Volunteers as well as professionals.
Commercial	Frequently trained by employing agency.
	Employed to secure greatest financial returns.
	Employed and retained at the discretion of the employers.
	No volunteers.

Program

Public	Designed to provide a wide variety of activities, year-round, for all groups, regardless of age, sex, race, creed, social or economic status.
Private	Designed to provide programs of a specialized nature for groups and in keeping with the aims and objectives of the agency.
Commercial	Program designed to tap spending power in compliance with state and local laws.

Membership

Public	Unlimited—open to all.
Private	Limited by organizational restrictions, such as age, sex, religion, and the like.
Commercial	Limited by:
	Law (local, state, and federal).
	Social conception regarding status and strata in some places.
	Economics—limited to those who have the price to pay.

COMMUNITY RECREATION SYSTEM

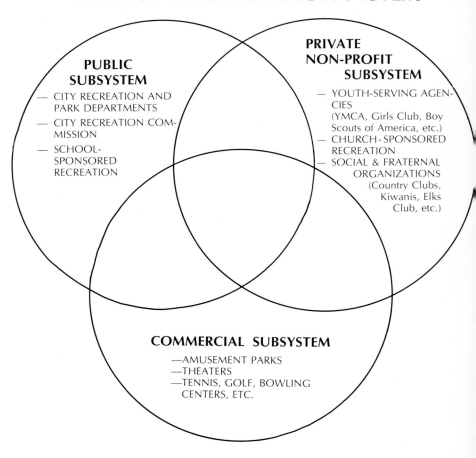

Fig. 8. Community recreation system.

1. The Public Subsystem

The administration of recreation services by local governments is characterized by a great deal of diversity. Unlike public education in this country public recreation does not conform to a common pattern. While public schools are administered with few exceptions by local boards of education, the administrative authority for recreation can vary tremendously from state to state and from city to city. State enabling laws have allowed community

Table 6. Type of Local Government Authorized to Conduct Local Park and Recreation Programs[6]

State	Munici-palities	Counties	Special Districts	Other
Alabama	x	x	—	x
Alaska	x	—	—	—
Arizona	x	x	—	—
Arkansas	x	x	x	x
California	x	x	x	x
Colorado	x	x	x	x
Connecticut	x	—	—	x
Delaware	—	x	—	x
Florida	—	x	x	—
Georgia	x	—	x	—
Hawaii	—	x	—	—
Idaho	x	—	—	x
Illinois	x	x	x	—
Indiana	x	x	x	—
Iowa	x	—	—	—
Kansas	x	x	x	x
Kentucky	x	x	x	x
Louisiana	x	—	x	x
Maine	x	—	x	—
Maryland	x	x	—	—
Massachusetts	x	—	—	x
Michigan	x	x	—	x
Minnesota	x	x	x	—
Mississippi	x	x	—	—
Missouri	x	x	—	x
Montana	x	x	—	x
Nebraska	x	x	—	x
Nevada	—	—	x	—
New Hampshire	x	—	—	x
New Jersey	x	x	—	x
New Mexico	x	x	—	x
New York	x	x	—	x
North Carolina	x	x	x	x
North Dakota	x	—	x	—
Ohio	—	—	x	—
Oklahoma	x	x	—	x
Oregon	—	—	x	—
Pennsylvania	x	x	x	x
Rhode Island	x	—	x	x
South Carolina	—	—	x	—
South Dakota	x	x	—	—
Tennessee	x	x	—	x
Texas	x	x	x	x
Utah	x	x	x	x
Vermont	x	—	—	x
Virginia	x	x	x	—
Washington	x	x	x	x
West Virginia	x	x	x	—
Wisconsin	x	x	x	x
Wyoming	x	x	—	x
	42	33	25	30

recreation services to be administered by a variety of units of local government: city, county, township or special district. These local governments receive their authority for providing services through state enabling legislation. State enabling laws generally provide units of local government with authority to acquire, develop and maintain property for park and recreation purposes and to provide a variety of recreation programs and facilities under the direction of a professional staff. As Table 6 indicates every state has enacted legislation authorizing at least one or more of its units of local governments to establish recreation services. It is not uncommon, therefore, to find in the same community two and sometimes three legally authorized public sponsored recreation agencies. In some cases, the school district, county and the city may all be actively involved in provision of leisure services to community residents.

In addition, the actual body (commission, board or department) charged with the legal responsibility for overseeing recreation services within these various units of government may also vary. In fact, there are as many as five different types of governmental managing authorities for recreation:

1. Recreation as an independent unit of local government organized as either a separate department or as an independent board or commission.
2. Recreation placed under the authority of an independent park department or park board or commission.
3. Recreation administered under the authority of the local school district.
4. Recreation combined into a consolidated park and recreation department or board commission.
5. Recreation under the auspices of an autonomous special purpose district such as a metropolitan recreation district or a county park and recreation district.

Some appreciation for the variety and rate of growth of these major managing authorities for recreation can be derived from Table 7.

Recreation as a Separate Function. Recreation administered as an independent unit or department of a city or county government, separate from the parks department, is a common form for organizing local leisure services. Under this organizational arrangement, the provision of recreation programs and facilities is the sole and exclusive function of the agency. The administrative separation of recreation and parks in many local governments can be attributed primarily to divergent historical development of these two functions. Park authorities' traditional concern with

Table 7. Type of Managing Authority[7]

	1940	1950	1961	1966	1971
Authorities administering recreation as a single function (recreation commissions, boards, departments, etc.)	324	702	949	818	14%
Authorities administering recreation in conjunction with parks.	293	532	549	423	6%
Parks only.					7%
Combined parks and recreation.			466	1,304	66%
Authorities administering recreation in conjunction with schools.	186	287	274	102	2%
Authorities administering recreation under other jurisdictions such as welfare, public works, etc.	179	303	530		5%

horticulture, landscaping and gardening activities was often viewed as incompatible with the later emerging play movement identity of recreation. Hence, in many communities recreation departments were established separate from already existing park departments. The service organization of separate recreation agencies naturally emphasizes the provision of programs and leadership rather than the maintenance and acquisition of open space.

The legal responsibility for managing a separate recreation department is commonly placed in the hands of either (a) an independent or semi-independent board or commission or (b) the city's chief-executive officer, the city manager or mayor, who is in turn directly responsible to the city council. The latter arrangement is very prevalent in communities which have adopted the council-manager form of government. The recreation department operating under this organizational pattern is subject to the administrative direction and supervision of the city manager. In most cases, the recreation administrator is selected by the city manager and held directly accountable to him. The city manager in turn is directly responsible to the city council which serves as the legislative arm of the city, legally charged with ultimate fiscal and policy-making authority. Normally, the recreation administrator, as a department head, is granted a great deal of discretion and latitude in administering the day to day affairs of the recreation department. With respect to major policy questions, however, such as determining the size of the annual operating budget for recreation, the recreation administrator is limited to making recommendations, authority for budget adoption lies with the city manager and ultimately with the city council. Formal lay citizen involvement under this type of arrangement is often provided by the establishment of recreation board whose authority is confined to making recommendations regarding policy and administrative matters to both the recreation department staff and city council. Examples of communities which have separate recreation and park departments operating under this organization pattern are: Washington, D.C., Oak Park and Evanston, Illinois.

In a number of cities the administrative and sometimes exclusive policy-making authority for recreation is placed in an independent or semi-independent recreation commission. A commission is usually comprised of 5 to 9 members, duly elected or appointed by the mayor and/or city council. In those communities with recreation commissions, the degree of authority vested in the commission varies from one city to another based upon local charter provisions and state enabling laws. Some cities with recreation commissions give final policy-making and administrative authority for recreation department operations to the commissioners. Other cities allow the commission to have managing authority over the administrative affairs of the recreation agency subject, however, to final approval by the mayor and/or city council. Cincinnati, Ohio and Topeka, Kansas provide examples of where recreation services have been successfully directed under the authority of a separate city commission.

A number of arguments have been advanced for and against the administration of recreation as a separate responsibility of government. The important points have been summarized by Kraus as follows:

> For: (1) It is a unique function and should be given visibility by having its own department;
> (2) If made independent, it would receive the undivided attention it requires and would not be lost in the general concern of a larger agency; and
> (3) An independent recreation department would be in a better position to coordinate total community efforts in recreation and to be given an adequate budget.
> Against: (1) Having recreation as a separate agency unnecessarily creates another governmental operation whose function could be carried out by existing ones;
> (2) This would add to governmental overhead and the burden of administrative operations; and

(3) Since recreation departments must depend on park departments and school districts for the use of their facilities, it would be better to assign *them* the recreation function rather than to establish a new and unnecessary department.[8]

Park Administration of Recreation. This type of managing authority arrangement finds the provision of recreation services as just one part of an agency's traditional and primary function of providing and maintaining parks.

In most cases park department responsibility for recreation emerged as a product of historical precedent and the natural association that exists between park lands and recreation use. Many cities had formed municipal park departments prior to the turn of the century. Recreation services, on the other hand, did not emerge as a wide-spread concern of municipal government until the 1930's and '40's. Many communities, while recognizing the need for a recreation program, determined that rather than creating another city department, the responsibility for recreation could be most naturally assumed by the established existing park department. By 1961, over 500 recreation programs were administered by park agencies.

Detractors of this organizational arrangement have argued that park administrators are more concerned with such things as floriculture, horticulture, maintenance and "keeping people off the grass" than with providing recreation opportunities and programs. Therefore, recreation more often than not receives secondary consideration with respect to staff time and financial support.

While perhaps some of these claims can be substantiated, most park administrators today recognize the value and need for recreation. The characteristic attitude that now prevails, is that parks are for people and exist primarily for people's leisure enjoyment. This sentiment has contributed to a much closer alliance between the administrators of park and recreation agencies. Currently, with the trend toward the integration of park and recreation services, and the growing recognition of recreation as valuable in its own right, the administration of recreation services under the auspices of park departments has diminished significantly.

Consolidated Recreation and Park Departments. The post World War II period was a time of tremendous growth for government sponsored recreation. By 1950, there were more than twice the number of municipal recreation agencies than had existed at the start of the previous decade. With the increased visibility of recreation, it became evident to many government officials that it made little sense administratively or economically to have separate recreation and park departments existing side by side each other in the same community. George Hjelte, a prominent leader in the park and recreation movement stated as early as 1940 that the merging of parks and recreation ". . . offers an opportunity for the development of a more comprehensive and at the same time more diversified program ... It is conducive to economical administration and enhance the services of the city in recreation."[9] At the urging of Hjelte, George Butler, Charles Doell and many other important figures in the fields of parks and recreation, a strong trend was established toward the merging of recreation and park agencies into one consolidated department. Serena Arnold[10] provides an excellent summary of the reasons which have prompted and sustained this trend toward consolidation.

1. Stimulation of long-range planning and concerted effort toward the development of more adequate areas and facilities.
2. A reduction in the complexities of government.
3. Simplification of operating procedures.
4. Improved coordination between facilities, maintenance, and program scheduling.
5. Reduced overlapping or duplication of services.
6. An increase in the prestige of the service and a clearer interpretation of the program for the public.
7. Budget savings in some cases.
8. Improved services at all levels, including equipment, personnel, and the maintenance and appearance of facilities.
9. Centralization of responsibility and authority, with improved efficiency overall.

While resistance to merger still exists in some communities, it is evident that the combining of park and recreation functions will continue to expand as the most common pattern of administrative organization.

School Administration of Recreation. A number of states, through the passage of enabling laws, have provided local school boards with the authority to administer recreation services. Prominent examples of school administered municipal recreation programs can be found in Milwaukee, Wisconsin, Pasadena, California and Flint, Michigan. The role schools play in providing community recreation opportunities varies from one state and community to the next. In some instances, the board of education accepts major responsibility for conducting recreation programs. In other communities, the school authorities confine their contribution to cooperating with other public and private agencies generally through the enactment of joint-use agreements which allow for shared use of school facilities and equipment.

Rodney[11] cites a number of conditions which affect the degree to which schools become involved in the provision of recreation:

1. The availability of progressive educational leadership that gives full play to the role of recreation in developing "worthy use of leisure" as an educational objective.
2. The legal provisions that permit educational systems to become involved in community recreation programs and services.
3. The community tradition as the role of education and its relation to recreation.
4. The financial status of school districts.
5. The adequacy and availability of school buildings and facilities that can be used for community purposes.

There are many who argue that recreation should logically be the responsibility of school authorities. Proponents of this point of view feel that the schools already possess the necessary facilities and trained leadership for the administration of an effective community recreation program. Hence, the establishment of a separate recreation department would result in an unnecessary duplication of services. In addition, the schools generally enjoy the respect of the community and therefore can more readily obtain the financial support and public backing essential for sustaining a comprehensive public recreation program.

On the other hand, those who oppose the management of community recreation services by boards of education argue that the schools are inadequate to the task of meeting the community's educational needs. With most school districts currently under severe financial pressure, opponents fear that recreation as a secondary function is in an extremely vulnerable position. Invariably it is the first to be cut in an economic crisis.

While school districts do operate many of the facilities necessary for recreation (gyms, swimming pool, auditoriums, etc.), critics also point out that schools do not have jurisdiction over *all* recreation resources such as parks, playfields, golf courses, beaches and marinas. Other claims *against* the school-centered administration of recreation are:

1. That the skilled classroom teacher may not necessarily be an effective leader in the more informal atmosphere of a recreation setting; and
2. That only the leisure needs of school-age children will be served by the schools at the neglect of pre-schoolers, adults and senior citizens.

As most school systems have struggled with financial and social problems (busing, decentralization of authority, etc.) the role of the school in directly managing the community's recreation program has declined significantly. Currently, school authority for recreation is found in less than 2% of the cities and counties in the country.

While the school's role as the primary agency for the direction of community recreation has diminished significantly, an educational movement which is currently sweeping the country may allow the schools to eventually play an even more prominent role in the community's recreation system. The *Community Education concept* is now operating in 464 school districts across the U.S. Community education's general objective is to make the schools the centers of neighborhoods by providing educational, recreational, cultural, and social programs and services selected to meet the interests and needs of all community members. Subsumed under the umbrella heading of community education is the "community-school concept." This concept views the neighborhood school as the community center, open days and evenings year round, operating in partnership with other community groups (YMCA's, Recreation and Park Departments, Police Departments, Health Officials, etc.) to meet the area's educational, social, health and recreational needs.

The concept of expanding the role and extending the use of schools through community education is attractive to school officials for a number of reasons. First, it provides a high return for every dollar invested. On the average, community school programs cost 2 to 8% of the net cost of the regular K-12 program, yet with the community school program, the school plant facilities are used approximately three times as many hours as before—and by many times the size of the total K-12 school age population.[12] In addition, school administrators recognize that community education is a great vehicle for expanding their school system's base of public support. Evidence suggests that people are more likely to vote favorably for school bond issues in communities where community schools have been established.

The community education model was established in Flint, Michigan through the efforts of philanthropist Charles Stewart Mott and Frank Manley, the Flint public school director of health and physical education. Since its inception in 1936, the concept has broadened to presently include close to 500 school districts. Projected growth of the concept through 1978 anticipates an expansion to 2,600 school districts with 7,846 community schools.[13] Federal and state legislation providing substantial funding and operational assistance to local school districts has provided tremendous impetus for the sustained growth of community school concept. In addition, largely through the efforts of the C. S. Mott

Foundation, training and research on community education are taking place in fifteen Regional University Training Centers across the country. The expectation is that eventually every school district in the U.S. will be involved to some extent in community education.

The rapid emergence of community education has created concern among many established members of the community recreation system. Across the country personnel in municipal recreation departments, YMCA's, YWCA's, scouting organizations, and other social service agencies are reacting to the growth of community education with widely divergent views. While most system members consider its coming as an opportunity, many perceive community education as a threat. A recent national survey which attempted to assess the attitudes of community recreation administrators toward community education found that 32% of the community recreators felt that the establishment of community education threatened the existence of established community agencies.[14] The strength of the resentment held by some community recreators toward community education is illustrated by a statement which appeared in the news letter of a state recreation and park association recently warning its members (primarily community recreators) "to look out for the take over of community recreation by the opening of the schools for community education."[15] Analysis of survey results indicate that the basis for such concern stems primarily from a fear that community school-education programs openly compete with community recreation agencies for the same scarce tax dollars, and at the same time duplicate many of the services already being provided. Evidence that such concerns are not unwarranted is provided by the remarks of one YMCA Director:

> "For years our local YMCA has asked for the use of the schools for club meetings and organized sports, and for years we were told the schools could not be used for this. When the school board adopted the community-school concept, we were told the schools would be open to our use. Instead, the community-schools opened their own programs which were identical to and in direct competition to ours. I supported community-education, even went before the school board to get it installed. Now I can tell you I am unalterably opposed to it."[16]

While problems of competition and duplication do exist, the extent of such abuse is fortunately very small. Overall, it is apparent that most community educators rather than attempting to "build empires," genuinely practice the central tenets of community education concept—cooperation and coordination. As a result, most community recreation personnel (68%) agree that community education is working and working well.[17] A great number of recreation administrators perceive the establishment of community school-education in their communities as an opportunity to expand leisure services to community residents. Community recreators, who have for years advocated the productive use of school facilities for recreation both during and after school hours see the coming of community education as the vehicle for achieving this end.

The potential that community education brings to the community recreation system both in the form of conflict and promise has prompted a move towards cooperation between both parties at the highest levels. Recently, the National Recreation and Park Association (NRPA) joined representatives from the National Center for Community Education, the National Community Education Association (CEA) and the American Alliance for Health, Physical Education and Recreation (AAHPER) to collectively discuss and identify issues, problems and possible solutions regarding the relationship between community recreation agencies and school sponsored community education programs.[18] A major recommendation to come from that meeting was a call for all communities engaged (or preparing to engage) in community education to establish a strong formal system of communication between the school system and existing recreation service agencies to facilitate the joint development of programs and facilities.

Whether this spirit of cooperation and consultation can be transmitted to all local communities remains to be seen. Encouragement has been provided, however, by the growing number of cities where very productive alliances have been forged between community educators and recreators. In these communities professional staff members on both sides have adopted the positive attitude of putting the community first. All parties have realized that competition, duplication of services, and the undercutting and infighting related to jurisdictional disputes can serve to no one agency's advantage, least of all the tax paying public's. Perhaps, Mr. Ken Smithee, former President of the American Parks and Recreation Society, makes this point most effectively when he states that:

> "The job of providing for the public's leisure needs is so vast that no one agency can expect to do it alone. Accordingly, there is a place for municipal park and recreation departments, county departments, schools, private, and non-profit recreation agencies, and many others in meeting the recreational needs of any given locality. Cooperation and consultation—not competition—among agencies are the answer.

The professionals, who spend time in a community competing with and downgrading each other, are being counter-productive—and they, their organizations will ultimately be the losers in such an undesirable and needless situation."[19]

Undeniably, community education is here to stay. If present trends persist, the impact and influence of community education will grow considerably more significant in the years to come. It is crucial that all members of the community recreation system accept the inevitability, as well as potentiality, of its growth. Perhaps, initial efforts of system members could be directed toward clarifying agency roles and relationships. Determination of what services could be most appropriately and efficiently provided by each agency could provide the foundation for continued efforts at collaboration and coordination.

Special District Recreation. Several states, most notably Illinois and California, have passed legislation allowing for the establishment of special government districts for parks and/or recreation. In some states these special districts are referred to as "recreation and park districts" (California) and in other as "recreation districts" (Louisiana) or "park or parkway districts" (Illinois). Regardless of designation, these units of local government are created in most cases for the exclusive purpose of providing recreation and/or park services. Like school districts, they exist as autonomous government bodies, independent from county or city governments. State enabling laws generally provide special districts for parks and/or recreation with the following legal provisions:

1. A separate legal identity with a defined geographical service area and resident population.
2. A governing body, composed generally of three to seven elected or appointed board or commission members. (The terms commission or board will be used interchangeably here to designate the governing authority.) The governing body is commonly vested with ultimate control or policy-making authority over the conduct of the district's park and recreation functions.
3. Revenue producing powers. Commonly, special districts responsible for parks and recreation and empowered to levy their own general and special taxes and to issue general indebtedness and revenue bonds within prescribed statutory limits.

As with the previous organizational patterns discussed, the establishment of special district authorities for recreation has generated a number of proponents as well as opponents. Rodney[20] furnishes an excellent summary of the major arguments expressed for and against the special district plan. Those authorities who defend special districts commonly provide the following arguments:

1. A recreation district provides for fiscal independence and, thus, better continuity of services.
2. District boards and their professional staffs are free from political influences.
3. District boards can devote all their time and energy to recreation and park problems.
4. Greater flexibility in establishing and changing programs is possible under an organizational pattern that is focused upon one basic function.
5. District operation makes it easier to interpret needs directly to the people.
6. Unified long-range planning for programs and facilities can be given to a geographical area encompassing all the people, rather than being restricted to artificial political boundaries of a city.
7. Large districts that encompass a number of urban areas make for economy of operation and less duplication of service.

On the other hand, opponents to district organization argue that:

1. Establishment of a recreation district only aggravates government problems by adding another over-lapping taxing jurisdiction.
2. Independent-district organization fragments government services and creates problems for unified planning.
3. It is more economical to have one governing body provide for all services, rather than have independent boards plan separately for single functions.
4. A multiplicity of small recreation districts can neither plan effectively nor enlarge their services, owing to their limited tax base.

Despite the arguments pro and con, there is little question that in many states the district pattern of organization will continue to grow. The special district managing authority for recreation and parks has worked effectively in those states which have provided a strong foundation in the form of liberal enabling legislation. For example, the park district concept in Illinois has evidenced tremendous growth, expanding from 48 districts in 1934 to close to 300 in 1975.

Recreation as a Community/Human Service Agency. A recent development in California, which could signal a new trend in both the organizational structure and function of recreation services, is the creation of comprehensive social service departments. Among the growing number of California cities which have established such units are: Cerritos (Department of Human Affairs), Saratoga, Cardiff, Irving, Westminister, Brea (Department of Human Services) and Davis (Department of Life Enrichment). The organization of these departments has taken place in one of two ways: First, and most commonly, the city has transformed the traditional recreation and park agency in both organizational configuration and service role into the new social service department. Garden Grove is an example of a city which has made such a transformation (Fig. 9). The Garden Grove City Council in unanimously approving the

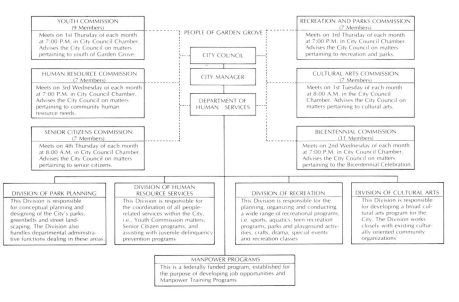

Fig. 9. Functional table of organization.

organizational change stated "it was the consensus that the traditional functions of recreation should be expanded more in the area of people-related services to greater serve the needs of the entire community." This broadened mandate translated into services ranging from youth counseling and referral to delinquency prevention and family service programs—services far beyond the role of the traditional recreation and park department.

The second method through which cities have formed community/human service departments has been through the reorganization and consolidation of existing social service agencies. Typically, this type of arrangement has led to the recreation services agency being assimilated into a larger comprehensive social service department along with health, family, rehabilitation and in some cases protective services. The intent of such consolidation is to enhance the coordination and effectiveness of the cities' traditionally independent and fragmented social service programs. A major attribute of such an organizational arrangement is its recognition of recreation as integral and important member of the social planning and human resources team. This advantage, however, may be negated by the realization that absorption of the once independent recreation agency into super department may result in recreation forfeiting much of its public identity and visibility. No longer would an independent board or commission or department head level executive be charged with exclusive authority for advocating and promoting recreation.

The recentness of the formation of comprehensive social service agencies makes it difficult to truly assess the ramifications for recreation agencies. It is apparent, however, that the "holistic" service philosophy is growing in recognition and popularity. While currently confined to California, it is quite possible that this form of organization may spread to other cities across the nation.

2. Private Non-Profit Subsystem

The private non-profit recreation subsystem is comprised of a loosely woven network of non-governmental, voluntary organizations. Serving a variety of specialized interests, these organizations play an important role in expanding and supplementing recreation opportunities provided by the public and commercial sectors. There are a variety of private organizations including youth-serving agencies, patriotic and fraternal orders, social clubs, and religious groups. The term private is used to describe these organizations because of their non-governmental status and almost universal membership requirements. All are basically non-profit in nature and heavily dependent upon voluntary financial contributions.

Most private groups were created primarily for the purpose of achieving a variety of socially desirable ends—character development, community service, vocational training and social fellowship. Recreation programs are provided as an important medium through which these social goals are to be achieved. Recreation, while not *the* essential purpose, is extensively employed as an important function of these organizations.

Youth Serving Organizations. A tremendous number of private agencies have been founded on a genuine concern for youth. There are currently over 300 youth serving agencies in the country with a combined membership in excess of 20 million.[21] In many communities, youth serving organizations are a prominent part of the private recreation subsystem. A number of community organizations devoted entirely to youth are the Boy Scouts of America, Camp Fire Girls, Girl Scouts of the United States of America, Boys' Clubs of America, Y.M.C.A., Y.W.C.A., and 4-H Clubs.

In summarizing the common characteristics of youth-serving organizations Hanson and Carlson[22] state:

> *In the first place, membership is usually voluntary on the part of the child. The program and leadership are designed to attract him on his*

own free will. The membership is open to all children regardless of race or religion, within the prescribed age and sex limitations.
The major organizations also tend to use similar methods of operation. They all function, in part at least, through small and continuous groups which have adult sponsorship but which retain a high degree of self-direction. The agencies attempt to base their programs on the interests and needs of youth, providing different groups for different age levels. Emphasis is placed on learning by doing.
Membership fees are kept low, with finances coming chiefly from public contributions. Leadership is largely voluntary and involves millions of adults as advisors, leaders, board members, and committeemen. The organizations are directed by lay boards at both national and local levels.

While a number of similarities exist among the youth agencies, it is important also to understand the differences that exist between them. Table 8 is an attempt to differentiate and classify several of the major youth-serving organizations along four basic dimensions.

As a major partner in the community recreation system, youth-serving agencies play a significant role in reducing the potential for undesirable social behavior on the part of many youths through the provision of healthy and positive recreation opportunities. With the tremendous amount of concern directed toward effectively serving this age group, youth-serving agencies will continue to be prominent members of the community recreation system.

Church Recreation. Most churches across the U.S. have grown to recognize the need for the provision of wholesome recreation to their members. Many churches at the community level, therefore, are actively engaged in the sponsorship of recreation activities. Historically, the churches' initial efforts were confined to bazaars, church socials and in some cases to organized sports leagues and concerts. More recently, however, as church leaders have come to realize the reality of increased leisure and its potential use for physical, social and spiritual development, many churches have initiated ambitious recreation programs complete with gymnasiums, resident camps, auditoriums and community centers. Some churches have become active in largely secular matters, assisting social agencies through the provision of day-care centers, programs for the aged, Head Start classes and a variety of other social, educational, and recreational services.

The Mormon Church was one of the first religions to recognize the positive attributes of recreation. One of Brigham Young's first actions upon arriving in Salt Lake in 1852 was to erect a social hall for recreation activities. Today with the establishment of Mutual Improvement Association, (MIA), the Mormon Church has one of the most highly organized church sponsored recreation systems.

Table 8. Comparison of Major Youth Organizations*

	Boy Scouts Camp Fire Girls Girl Scouts	Boys' Club Y.M.C.A. Y.W.C.A.
Program	Program structure developed on national level. The "stair-step" program method is employed—progression of members takes place through the passing of tests or the completion of projects. Outdoor-related activities such as camping receive major emphasis.	Program develops out of community needs and interests. National and regional program materials are made available to local agencies. Activities tend to be building-centered with indoor recreation and education programs emphasized.
Leadership	Dependent upon volunteers. Maintain a relatively small paid staff to recruit and train volunteers and promote the organization. Professional staff performs little face-to-face leadership with boys and girls.	Operate with paid professional staffs who perform administrative responsibilities as well as provide direct program leadership for the members. Volunteers used but not as extensively as first group of organizations.
Finance	Depend on funds from voluntary sources such as private donors, Community Chest or United Fund Contributions, and fund-raising events.	Rely on membership fees to augment voluntary donations.
Properties	Seldom own or rent community facilities. Use existing community resources such as schools, churches, and homes. Own camp properties.	Maintain own facilities, generally comprised of club rooms, gymnasium, swimming pool and activity rooms.

*Adapted from Hanson and Carlson, *Organizations for Children and Youth*, Englewood Cliffs, New Jersey, Prentice-Hall, Inc., 1972, pp. 9–12.

Under the direction of MIA, programs in dance, drama, sports and music are carefully prepared and disseminated to member churches across the nation.

The Jewish Welfare Board, under the direction of the Young Men's and Young Women's Hebrew Association oversees the conduct of hundreds of well-equipped Jewish Community Centers (JCC) across the nation. JCC's have expanded their programs to incorporate all age groups (especially seniors of late).

Catholic youth for decades have been served by Catholic Youth Organization (CYO), which in many communities has been an active sponsor of sports leagues, festivals and general recreation programs. Almost all of the Protestant religions have established their own youth organizations.

The Episcopalian Youth People's Service League, the Lutheran League, the Methodist Youth Fellowship, the Westminister Fellowship of Presbyterians, and the Baptist Training Union all serve as good examples of Protestant denomination youth organizations which emphasize recreation as a special part of their spiritual aims.

Authorities[23] suggest that the church has two major responsibilities with respect to recreation: (1) to provide recreation opportunities for its members; and (2) to assist other members of the community recreation system in the development of community recreation.

Membership Program. While the content and number of recreation activities and events will vary according to the denominational philosophy, financial capability and available leadership, Carlson, et al.[24] have summarized those recreation programs most commonly sponsored by church groups:

1. Camping and other outdoor activities, including church camping, family camping, camp conferences, and retreats in which Christian education is the main goal. Campers are introduced to recreation activities and are encouraged to pick up recreation skills wherever they are available.
2. Social recreation, including family nights, picnics, banquets, potluck suppers, game nights, bazaars and dances.
3. Vacation Bible schools, which run the gamut of recreation activities with the educational program.
4. Arts, crafts and hobby workshops.
5. Fellowship groups, youth clubs, Scout programs and adult interest clubs.
6. Sports activities, including bowling, basketball and baseball.
7. Volunteer services.
8. Study and discussion groups.

Community Recreation Responsibility. Beyond providing recreation for its own members the church can play an important role in enhancing recreation opportunities for the entire community. Listed below are a number of ways the church can contribute to the community recreation program.

1. Allowing the use of church facilities such as gyms, meeting rooms and dining halls for the conduct of community or neighborhood recreation programs.
2. The local ministerial association can play an important role in advising community recreation authorities on the adequacy and content of their programs. Members of the clergy would be welcome members on public recreation agency boards, community center advisory boards and so on.
3. Promoting the growth and development of community recreation. Encouraging its members to support recreation referenda, to serve in voluntary leadership roles for community recreation agencies and to participate in local programs are all ways in which churches can significantly help the development of community recreation.
4. Sponsoring youth-serving clubs and organizations such as Boy Scout or Girl Scout troops. Often churches can supplement school or municipal recreation after school programs through the sponsorship of their own club programs.

Social, Fraternal and Community Service Organizations. In most communities there are a variety of social, fraternal and Civic organizations for adults including country clubs, Jaycees, Benevolent Order of the Elks, American Legion and Kiwanis Club.

While the expressed purposes of these organizations generally range from providing fellowship to community service, recreation activities exist as an integral part of the organizations over-all operations.

Social-recreation pastimes which have been traditional favorites are dinner-dances, entertainment, discussion groups, banquets and an assortment of table games. Recreation acts as an important integrative device, serving to enhance and maintain the membership of the organization as a cohesive unit. In many cases, these private groups have constructed elaborate recreation facilities such as golf courses, tennis courts, auditoriums and swimming pools.

In addition to providing a host of recreation opportunities for their members, private associations can play a crucial role in the development of community recreation system. It is important that recreation professionals realize the significant contributions these private organizations can make.

Civic and fraternal groups can utilize the strength of their influence to cultivate favorable and wholesome attitudes toward community recreation. For example, they can spearhead fund-raising drives or recreation bond referendum campaigns, provide a source of volunteer leadership for program activities, donate time and energy toward the construction and development of recreation areas and facilities, and provide a supplemental reservoir of facilities for community use.

3. The Commercial Subsystem

The third and often the largest and most diverse component of a community's recreation system is the commercial recreation subsystem. The commercial sector is a fragmented assortment of many enterprises large and small. The "product" of the subsystem is a vast array of services including indoor tennis, bowling, roller skating, billiards, miniature golf, boating facilities and a host of other recreation opportunities. Commercial recreation enterprises operate in the economic marketplace, and as such are owned and operated primarily for profit.* This profit-orientation is the paramount difference between commercial operators and other members of the community recreation system. Unlike the agencies comprising the public and private sector, the continued existence of most commercial recreation firms is dependent upon their ability to generate a satisfactory profit-margin. Irwin Sanders[25] describes the commercial recreation subsystem as follows:

> The commercial subsystem is profit-making; it caters to "what the public wants," as interpreted by the individual businessman risking his capital in the economic venture; since it is competitive, in that a customer has many alternative ways of using his time, each establishment seeks to develop a clientele of regular patrons who return over and over again to enjoy the activity it provides. Often it is seasonal in character, which means that enough profits have to be gained over a few months to assure success for the year; this is particularly true of enterprises having to do with tourist cabins, ski resorts, professional football, outdoor swimming pools, and hunting to mention but a few cases in point.

The economic impact of commercial recreation enterprises on a national scale is astronomical, with estimates of recreation expenditures placed as high as $100 billion annually. While this figure is impressive, current evidence suggests that the requirements for success in commercial recreation are becoming increasingly difficult to attain. In fact, one report[26] reveals that while the overall arena of commercial recreation continues to "bustle" many firms, especially small recreation businesses, are running into increasing financial difficulties. Several basic problems such as rising costs, economic downturns, inadequate management and increased competition have often combined to seriously erode the

*The major exception is the provision of leisure facilities as "loss leaders." These are recreation facilities which do not directly pay for themselves, but represent investments which enhance the attraction of primary revenue generating assets such as apartments, condominiums and new housing developments.

profitability of a substantial number of recreation businesses. For example, it has been estimated that roughly 20 to 30% of the firms in the outdoor recreation and tourism industry are operating at a loss.[27] These problems have brought with them a change in the character of commercial recreation firms in cities across the U.S. Family operated "Mom and Pop" recreation businesses, which characterized the ownership pattern of the commercial recreation industry since its inception, are currently disappearing at a rapid rate. The increased capital requirements and management complexities necessary for sustaining a successful operation in a highly competitive arena have made it increasingly difficult for numerous small recreation businesses to survive. Corporations and franchise operations with their substantially greater capital resources and managerial expertise have emerged in the place of many independent commercial operators. Evidence of this trend toward franchise operations in communities is readily apparent in the theater, bowling, roller skating, camping and accommodations industries.

An important function performed by the commercial subsystem is that of service or product innovation. Over the years almost every new and innovative recreation service has been introduced to the public by the commercial recreation sector. This innovative role has emerged primarily as a result of trying to survive in a highly complex and competitive environment. Imperative to the survival of recreation businesses is the need to remain acutely sensitive to change in people's needs and desires. Failure to cope with change in the market environment can be fatal as demonstrated by the number of casualties among the circus and amusement park industries. Recent innovations such as indoor tennis centers and executive golf courses are more positive examples of the commercial recreation sector's response to a rapidly changing social environment. The popularity of these recent forms of recreation opportunity appears to reflect contemporary America's reverence for such values as speed, comfort and convenience. Invariably the public and private non-profit sectors of the community recreation system lag behind commercial operators in service innovation. Often it is not until after a new opportunity has been introduced by commercial firms and popularly accepted by the public that government agencies will then perhaps adopt the service as a part of their program offerings.

Relationship of Commercial Sector To Other System Members. Even though the mission of all three sectors is fundamentally the same—the provision of "need-satisfying" leisure services—commercial recreation operators have traditionally had little interaction with those involved in the public and private recreation subsystem. In large part, the communication gap that exists between these sectors is the product of the divergent value systems and service philosophies that underlie each of the areas. The public and private subsystem developed from a tradition of serving the underprivileged which public agencies later expanded into a concern for providing recreation activities with "equal opportunity to all." In achieving this end, the accent was placed on providing services primarily on a free or inexpensive basis such as parks, playgrounds and recreation centers. The personnel occupying leadership positions came essentially from human service fields (social work, physical education and recreation).

On the other hand, the commercial sector has been motivated in large part by a completely different set of values. The provision of services directed toward making a profit has been the primary goal of commercial operators. Economic considerations invariably outweigh social service considerations in the commercial recreation marketplace. Naturally, this orientation has attracted owners and managers with backgrounds generally in business and management areas.

Due to the historical differences in service and philosophical orientations, the degree of cooperative interplay between the sectors has been significantly limited. Occasionally, municipal governments have made public lands available for recreation development by private interests. Rarely, at the community level, however, have public agencies formed strong working partnerships with commercial interests in the form of joint financing, planning and/or managing agreements. While instances of commercial and public sector cooperation in the development of recreation opportunities of recreation are few, notable examples do exist such as Marina del Ray (Los Angeles County), Seven Seas theme park (Arlington, Texas), and Mission Bay Park (San Diego, California). In San Diego, for example, the combined efforts of the city Recreation and Parks Department, the U.S. Army Corps of Engineers, the State Harbor Commission and a host of representatives from private industry successfully converted what were in 1945 undeveloped wetlands into a beautiful, popular, well-designed recreation area. Mission Bay Park provides a wide range of recreation activities from waterskiing to swimming, from fishing to golf, from rides on excursion boats to helicopter rides from picnicking to sailing. Well integrated into the 4,460 acres of land and water are an attractive mix of motor inns, restaurants, entertainment lounges and commercial marinas. As partners in development, private commercial enterprise has spent about $19 million and governmental agencies approximately $30 million.

Currently, Mission Bay Park serves 3 million visitors annually.

While the potential for cooperative arrangements of a similar nature exist in many cities, the general (day-to-day) trend in most areas appears to be directed toward increased competition rather than cooperation between public and commercial recreation suppliers.

Over the past 30 years, the majority of public recreation agencies have gradually abandoned their total adherence to the concept of a free park. Recent economic conditions have accentuated this trend, rising inflation and the declining tax revenue base in many cities having made the provision of "pay as you go" public recreation opportunities increasingly prevalent.

While the bulk of public recreation services (most children's programs, park and playground use, etc.) are provided free, city recreation departments in growing numbers are operating revenue-producing facilities which heretofore were considered to be firmly a part of the commercial realm. Public management of ice rinks, bowling centers, indoor tennis centers, marinas and in a few cases amusement parks are good examples of this trend.

An increasing number of these facilities have been financed from private dollars through the issuance of revenue bonds. The source of the money used to buy back these bonds must come from the monies generated from the operation of the recreation facility itself. Therefore, the agency can only consider using revenue bonds for those recreation facilities which can generate a net income above operation and maintenance expenses. Adoption of this method of finance then, immediately suggests the introduction of a much greater concern for profit-generation to the operation of public sponsored recreation opportunities.

As the public recreation subsystem increasingly involves itself in the provision of revenue-producing facilities, the issue of government competition with private enterprise becomes a significant one.

While competition may produce some short run benefits for the recreation consumer, the dangers of unnecessary duplication and over-lap in the provision of services may have a much more deleterious effect in the long run.* The scarcity of "risk" capital in

* It is important to realize that competition can provide some valuable benefits. An inherent virtue of competitive systems is that they invariably encourage efficiency and an improved quality of service. When the continued financial viability of public (this is especially true in the case of government facilities financed by revenue bonds) as well as private commercial recreation services is dependent upon attracting patrons from the same target population, representatives from either sector cannot afford to operate facilities which are poorly supervised or maintained. The threatened loss of public support to competitors can act as an important incentive to the maintenance of high standards of operation.

the private sector due to high real estate costs and interest rates combined with the declining financial health of many cities has already made meeting the public's current demand for recreation a virtually impossible task. The increased possibility of both sectors investing a large portion of their limited development capital into competitive projects can only serve to accentuate the supply problem in the future. If the tradition of limited cooperation, accentuated by the trend toward increased competition persists, the recreation consumer will be the big loser. The inefficient allocation of scarce resources can only result in restricting the number of leisure opportunities eventually made available to the public.

To forestall such an eventuality, the members of local recreation systems will have to reassess their relationship to one another. Reaching some kind of understanding, however, as to the most appropriate service roles for each of the sectors will be an extremely difficult task. No clear lines of demarcation defining the service jurisdictions of the public, private non-profit and commercial sectors have ever been drawn. The diffused nature of the commercial sector in most communities compounds the problem—just trying to identify what might constitute representative input from a fragmented assortment of commercial businesses would in itself be an elusive task.

The most logical approach to establish a definable cooperative relationship between the various recreation sectors would be for the more consolidated and organized public sector to seize the initiative. Recognizing that it cannot possibly meet all of the public demand for recreation facilities because of its own financial constraints, a logical alternative course of action would be for public agencies to encourage the commercial sector to provide them. Offering incentives to private enterprise in the form of nominally priced public lands for commercial development, significantly reduced rates for city services (e.g., power, water, sewer), attractive lease agreements, and/or direct financial assistance could effectively stimulate more active commercial sector involvement in the provision of important local recreation services.

Those services that appeal to a special interest group such as indoor tennis, racquet ball, skating, boating, and that generate substantial revenue would logically be operated by commercial interests. The public recreation agency (in addition to assuming an active facilitative role with other system members) would more naturally (as a tax supported agency) concentrate its direct service function at serving the broad mass of potential clients through vehicles such as recreation centers, beaches, home-centers, parks and art centers. Mission Bay Park in San Diego, mentioned previously, is an excellent example on a grand scale of where the public sector "primed the pump" to successfully integrate a variety of government agencies and commercial interests. Perhaps this successful illustration of public and commercial sector cooperation should serve as the model for the development of community leisure opportunities in the future.

Power and the Community Recreation System

We would be remiss if before concluding this chapter we failed to mention an important dimension of the community environment—the community power structure and its relationship to recreation system agencies. In every community system there are influential individuals or groups of individuals who play a dominant role in the making of public decisions. It is imperative that recreation administrators recognize that the support of these "power elites" or "economic notables," as they are sometimes called, can significantly enhance the development of the community recreation system. Sociologists and political scientists have devoted much effort to answering the question of "who calls the shots" in American cities. While the methods of study employed and the results obtained vary, research has concluded that: (1) persons not elected to office, operating behind the scenes, play significant parts in the making of many important decisions, and (2) there are some persons, groups or combination of the former that wield a disproportionate share of influence in the community decision-making process.

The real question pursued by researchers today is not whether there is or is not a power structure, but whether the power structure is monolithic or pluralistic. Floyd Hunter,[28] who pioneered the study of community power in his study of "Regional City," advanced the concept of a centralized power elite. Employing the "reputational method," Hunter described a structure of power which closely resembled a sharply pointed pyramid in which very few had a great deal of influence over the outcome of community affairs. Having identified the influentials through the opinions of a panel of well-informed judges, Hunter concluded that "decisions were made by a handful of individuals who stand at the top of a stable hierarchy."

In contrast to Hunter's results, a study conducted by Robert Dahl[29] found a highly dispersed distribution of community power. Dahl used the "decisional" method of analysis, in which top leaders were identified because of the active role they played in the making of actual community decisions. Instead of finding a monolithic power structure or a single group determining policy in a broad area of issues, Dahl found a pluralistic power structure with influence distributed among several individuals and groups, each exercising some influence over a narrow range of issues and none dominating policy over a wide range of issues.

Subsequent studies support Dahl's findings that community power is less concentrated than Hunter's research and other earlier studies made it appear. Hawley and Svara[30] suggest that this difference "is often explained by observing that research methods are becoming more sophisticated and that we are more aware now of the complexity and subtleties of community power." While this explanation seems reasonable, it may also be that power in many American communities is, generally, becoming more diffused.

Despite the fact that the distribution of power is changing and appears to vary from one community to the next, it has been discovered by researchers that invariably, business or economic leaders exercise a great deal of authority. A number of studies[31] show the close relationship that exists between community leadership and affiliation with the business community. The predominant influence of certain members from commerce, finance and industry can be accounted for on several grounds. The control that business leaders can exercise over the wealth and resources of a community is a major factor in the structure of power and influence. Since money is such a vital ingredient to the conduct of campaigns and the operation of organizations, persons with access to money will undoubtedly play a prominent role in the determination of local issues. Another reason for the business leaders' influence on civic affairs is the respect and status they are generally accorded by the community. Bureaucrats and politicians are seldom held in as high esteem as professionals and businessmen. According to Peter Clark,[32] the business leader "represents" a complex of highly revered societal values such as wealth, achievement, efficiency, respectability and public spiritedness. It is this "success" image which distinguishes the man of great leadership capacity in the American society and assures his presence in the decision-making arena.

It is essential that administrators of recreation agencies strive to cultivate the support of top community leaders. The active support and/or endorsement of these influentials can be increasingly important factors in the growth and development of an agency's program. This is especially true in light of the current economic crisis. Presently, most park and recreation agencies, public as well as private, are facing a severe budget crisis as revenue and budget dollars decline. Support provided, in any number of ways, by civic and business leaders may make the difference in ensuring the continued viability of members of the recreation system. Listed below are a number of ways in which community influentials, working either behind the scenes or in the forefront of an issue, can provide invaluable aid to recreation and park agencies:

1. Spear heading (or at least donating time and dollars to) worthy fund-raising projects such as sending underprivileged to camp, the annual Special Olympics for mentally retarded youngsters, or the construction of a performing arts center.
2. Buying revenue bonds to underwrite the cost of the development of special recreation facilities such as tennis centers, golf courses, marinas, etc.
3. Serving on recreation agency boards, councils or committees.
4. Providing leadership for the establishment of a recreation foundation or endowment designed to attract bequests, donations, grants and gifts for the development of community recreation programs and facilities.
5. Sponsoring (e.g., providing manpower and underwriting the cost of) special program activities such as community-wide special events. On a national level, Ford Motor Company with the Punt, Pass and Kick Contest is an example of successful business sponsored recreation program.
6. Endorsing recreation and park projects such as the passage of a bond referendum or a fund-raising campaign. Endorsements can range from formal speaking engagements to civic organizations to just consenting to have a name placed on promotional materials.
7. Providing leadership for the establishment of non-profit corporation for the acquisition and improvement of recreation areas and facilities. For example, such a nonprofit organization could establish a tax-exempt lease-back financing program with the city recreation department for the development of golf courses, marinas and beach areas.

Influential people can mean the difference in attracting favorable community sentiment for recreation and park services. Community leaders perform an important symbolic function by just appearing on a recreation board or by positively endorsing a community project. The association of recreation with these persons who "represent" success and integrity to many can inspire the allegiance of many in the community. Perhaps more important, this ability to generate community support, whether real or imagined, seldom goes unnoticed by the community's political leadership who must often make the final decisions regarding budget requests, revenue sharing grants, etc. for recreation purposes. Not only can they lend the weight of their prestige and status to recreation, but as important, often the business acumen that a corporate president or bank officer can bring to a fund-raising campaign or building project is instrumental to its eventual success.

While the value of harnessing the support of business and community leaders is easily recognized, the little evidence available indicates that recreation agencies have been ineffective in attracting the backing of these important public opinion shapers.

Lawson[33] reports on two research investigations which assessed the relationship of community influentials to public park and recreation agencies in two major U.S. cities. Price in his study of Memphis, Tennessee, sought to compare how members of the black and white power structures perceived park and recreation services. Reputational and decisional methods were employed to identify the top 20 black and white influentials. A significant finding was the low status that both groups attached to park and recreation services. With regard to overall community priorities, black influentials ranked the provision of the park and recreation services 5th out of 12 issues studied, while white influentials ranked it 12th or last.

Vinton identified 34 persons holding positions of power in Indianapolis (all were male with a mean age of 62.5 years; three-fourths of which were members of the economic sector). Of this group, only 12% knew the name of the director of parks and recreation and 25% knew the name of one of the park commissioners. It was found that the influential people consistently regarded the status of the parks and recreation department as unacceptable.

In interpreting these findings, Lawson stated . . . "The inferences are quite clear. We had best get acquainted with those 60- to 65-year-old males who serve as officers or on boards of banking institutions, loan agencies and industry and who are members of prestigious social clubs and involve them in our programs."

With valuable rewards at stake, the recreation administrator must work hard to win the support of the influential members of the community power structure. Norton Long,[34] in his study of community power and influence, underscores the importance of this role, stressing the value of "civic staff men as integrators who mobilize or put together the influence of others to secure action on community projects." The task of attracting the support of community leaders may not be easy. With large numbers of issues, and people placing demands on influentials, it will require a concerted effort on the part of the recreation administrator to compete effectively for their limited favors, time and energies. The first important step is to identify those persons who play a dominant role in the making of community decisions. This can be accomplished in a number of ways. First, a list of those holding formal positions of authority in economic, religious, educational and governmental institutions can be drawn up. In addition, scanning the newspapers while conducting informal conversations with knowledgeable community residents can provide a list of names of those who have played a prominent role in community issues.

Convincing community leaders (through office calls, informal talks and actual participation in programs) of the over-riding importance of recreation to the sustained livability and vitality of the community generally will require much time and effort on the part of the administrator. Even if initial efforts to cultivate their support do not meet with success, the fact that an attempt has been made is in itself beneficial, especially in light of the future promise these contracts may hold.

Fortunately, recreation and park agencies have a number of legitimate grounds upon which to base their appeals for support to community business and civic leaders. First, it is important to recognize that those who exercise power unofficially do so for reasons that range from self-serving or business-serving to group-serving or community-serving.[35] This suggests, then, that the recreation administrator when attempting to enlist their support has a number of options or strategies available. For example, the administrator who uses the argument that "building new park recreation facilities will help to attract new business" in an effort to recruit the active support of a local bank president, may motivate the president for primary business-serving reasons. In this case the president may realize that more recreation amenities now may add up to increased bank deposits and capital later as new industries and people are attracted to an improved living environment.

On the other hand, an appeal to the "civic pride" of the industrialist or financier may be more fruitful. Civic leaders with a long-standing commitment and stake to the community may be motivated to support increased recreation opportunities purely out of their "public-serving" concern for the welfare of the city as a whole. This same concern for civic pride may motivate community influentials to back recreation and park projects on the basis that they will help to ameliorate serious community problems such as drug abuse, vandalism and juvenile delinquency. For example, in 1936 Frank Manley, then a public school physical education instructor, converted industrialist C. S. Mott's concern for the youth of Flint, Michigan, into what is today the multi-million dollar, internationally celebrated community-school concept.

The ability of business elites to win the adoption of proposals for civic improvements has been frequently documented. An important challenge facing community recreation directors today is to effectively cultivate the support of these influentials in the interest of expanding leisure opportunities for all community residents. The enlistment of the tremendous resources commanded by these people (heretofore barely tapped) exists as one of our profession's unfulfilled priorities.

Summary

In this chapter, the organization of community recreation services is viewed as a system comprised of three interdependent subsystems (public, private non-profit, and commercial) which are at the same time part of a larger community social system. Each of these subsystems is sufficiently different with respect to such aspects as finance, management philosophy, and target clientele to allow for their separate classification.

The operation of recreation programs and facilities has long been recognized as a legitimate function of local government. However, there has been no consensus within the public sector as to what constitutes the most appropriate administering authority for recreation. Variations in state enabling laws, historical precedent, and community traditions have resulted in the creation of several different types of managing authorities for public recreation services. Currently, throughout the country there is a strong trend toward uniting separate recreation and park agencies into one consolidated recreation and parks department. Recent developments in several western states, particularly California, will perhaps have an even more significant impact on the future identity of recreation departments. A growing number of western cities have formed single comprehensive social service departments in which recreation services have been combined with family, health, welfare and rehabilitative services. It is too early to tell, however, whether this new concept of social service organization will be adopted nation-wide. In recent years, the school's role in providing recreation services has changed significantly. The emergence of the community school-education concept has allowed schools to play an increasingly significant role in the provision of leisure opportunities. The rapid growth of community education has been viewed with mixed feelings by established members of the community recreation system. While most see community education as an opportunity to extend and expand their services, many perceive it as a threat to existing recreation agency programs.

The private non-profit subsystem is comprised of a loosely woven network of non-governmental, voluntary membership organizations. Prominent members of the private sector are youth-serving organizations such as YMCA's, YWCA's, scouting organizations, and the Boys' and Girls' Clubs. Social and civic clubs and religious groups make up the rest of the private sector.

The commercial sector refers to the fragmented assortment of business enterprises providing recreation services. Commercial enterprises operate in the economic market place, and as such are owned and operated primarily for profit. The character of commercial recreation enterprises is changing across the United States. The increased capital requirements and management expertise necessary for successful operation in a highly competitive arena have led to the gradual demise of the once characteristic small "Mom and Pop" recreation business. In its place has emerged a variety of corporate or franchise operations. The degree of cooperative interplay among the three subsystems has been significantly limited. An absence of cooperation has been particularly evident between the public and commercial sectors. While the few examples of commercial and public sector cooperation illustrate the tremendous potential of joint financing, planning and/or managing arrangements, the trend appears directed toward increased competition. Initial responsibility for reversing this trend lies with the public sector. By "priming the pump" through the provision of incentives to private enterprise public agencies could stimulate increased commercial sector involvement in the development of important local recreation services.

Finally, the importance of attracting the support of members of the community power structure—those individuals who play a dominant role in the making of public decisions—is discussed at length.

Recreation agencies have been ineffective in cultivating the support of community influentials. The tremendous potential that can be realized through their active endorsement suggests harnessing their support as an essential priority of recreation administrators.

References

1. Sanders, Irwin T.: *The Community; An Introduction To A Social System.* 2nd Ed., New York, Ronald Press, 1966.
2. Loomis, Charles P.: *Social Systems: Essays on Their Persistence and Change.* Princeton, New Jersey, D. Van Nostrand Co., Inc., 1960.
3. Sessoms, Douglas H.: Community Development and Social Planning, In S. G. Lutzin and T. S. Storey (eds.), *Managing Municipal Leisure Services.* Washington, D.C., International City Management Association, 1973.

4. Ibid: p. 110.
5. Meyer, Harold D. and Brightbill, Charles K.: *Community Recreation: A Guide To Its Organization.* 3rd Ed., Englewood Cliffs, New Jersey, Prentice-Hall, Inc., 1964, pp. 269–271.
6. Illinois Legislative Council, *Local Park Administration In Other States.* Publication 143, Springfield, Illinois, August 1970, pp. 1–2.
7. Sessoms, Douglas H., Meyer, Harold D., and Brightbill, Charles K.: *Leisure Services: The Organized Recreation and Park System.* 5th Ed., Englewood Cliffs, New Jersey, Prentice-Hall, Inc., 1975, p. 123.
8. Kraus, Richard, and Curtis, Joseph: *Creative Administration in Recreation and Parks,* St. Louis, C. V. Mosby Co., 1973.
9. Rodney, Lynn S.: *Administration of Public Recreation.* New York, Ronald Press, 1964, p. 75.
10. Arnold, Serena: *Trends in Consolidation of Parks and Recreation.* Management Aids Bulletin No. 41, Oglebay Park, Wheeling, West Virginia, National Recreation and Park Association, 1966, pp. 15–16.
11. Rodney: Op. Cit., p. 77.
12. Riegle, Donald: Congressional Statements on Community Education Development Act, *Community Education Journal,* Sept.–Oct., 1974, pp. 7–8.
13. Decker, Larry E.: Community Education—Purpose, Function, Growth, Potential, *Leisure Today,* April, 1974, p. 9.
14. Ellis, Taylor: *An Attitude Study of Community Recreation and Community Education: Cooperation and Conflict,* Unpublished study, Texas A&M University, 1975.
15. Ohio Parks and Recreation Newsletter, Newsletter, 1975, p. 1.
16. Greiner, James C.: Cooperation—Or—Conflict, *Community Education Journal,* Sept.–Oct., 1974, p. 15.
17. Ellis: Op. Cit., p. 5.
18. Artz, Robert: Cooperation: What the Community School Movement Can't Do Without, *Parks and Recreation,* October 1974, p. 36.
19. Greiner: Op. Cit., p. 62.
20. Rodney: Op. Cit., p. 82.
21. Hanson, Robert F., and Carlson, Reynold E.: *Organizations For Children and Youth,* Englewood Cliffs, New Jersey, Prentice-Hall, Inc., 1972, p. 5.
22. Ibid: p. 7–8.
23. Meyer and Brightbill: Op. Cit., p. 218.
24. Carlson, Reynold E., Deppe, Theodore R., and MacLean, Janet R.: *Recreation In American Life,* Belmont, California, Wadsworth Publishing Company, 1963, p. 204.
25. Sander: Op. Cit., p. 326.
26. House Subcommittee on Environmental Problems Affecting Small Businesses, *Small Business Enterprises in Outdoor Recreation and Tourism,* Washington, D.C., U.S. Government Printing Office, 1974.
27. Ibid: p. 11.
28. Hunter, Floyd: *Community Power Structure.* Chapel Hill, University of North Carolina Press, 1953.
29. Dahl, Robert A.: *Who Governs? Democracy and Power In An American City,* New Haven, Yale University Press, 1961.
30. Hawley, Willis D. and Svara, James H.: *Community Power: A Bibliographic Review,* Santa Barbara, ABC-Clio Press, 1972, p. 5.
31. D'Antonio, William V., et al.: Institutional and Occupational Representations in Eleven Community Influence Systems, *American Sociological Review* 26 June 1961, 440–446: Rossi, Peter H.: The Organizational Structure Of An American Community, in Amatai Etzioni, ed., *Complex Organizations: A Sociological Reader,* New York, Holt, Rinehart and Winston, 1963, pp. 301–12; Thometz, Carol E.: *The Decision Makers: The Power Structure of Dallas,* Dallas, Southern Methodist University Press, 1963.

32. Clark, Peter: Civic Leadership: The Symbols of Legitimacy, paper delivered before the annual meeting of the American Political Science Association, New York City, September 1960.
33. Lawson, Richard W.: Developing Effective Pressure Groups, in Anita Leifer (ed.) *Congress Highlights, Congress for Recreation and Parks,* Arlington, Virginia, National Recreation and Park Association, 1972.
34. Long, Norton: The Local Community As An Ecology Of Games, *American Journal of Sociology 64* (November 1958) 251–61.
35. Banfield, Edward C. and Wilson, James Q.: *City Politics,* New York, Random House, 1963, p. 245.

CHAPTER 6

The Delivery of Community Recreation Services

"Recognition of the pluralistic nature of the community lies at the heart of developing an optimum program delivery strategy for recreational services. The need to adopt differential approaches to programming to effectively accommodate the variety of needs and interests held by diverse client groups is a primary challenge facing recreation. Role flexibility is the key to effectively delivering program services in a highly pluralistic community setting."

Overview

This chapter will attempt to examine the characteristics of and functional differences between the major types of program delivery methods employed by community recreation agencies.

As one gets closer to the community he begins to appreciate that the community is far from homogeneous—that in fact it is comprised of a heterogeneous mix of sub populations which can be differentiated along age, income, ethnic and/or racial lines. Each of these segments, called client groups, (e.g., older people, blacks,

Chicanos, teens, American Indians, etc.) differs significantly with respect to its recreational preferences as well as its ability to take part in recreational opportunities. Though they may be interested in a particular activity, many potential clients do not have the time, money and/or means of transportation necessary to enable them to participate. Recognition of the pluralistic nature of the community (and the differences associated with heterogeneity) lies at the heart of developing an optimum program delivery strategy for recreational services. The need to adopt differential approaches to programming to effectively accommodate the variety of needs and interests held by diverse client groups is a primary challenge facing recreation administrators. Rather than treating the community as a uniform collection of clients, undifferentiated in their leisure wants and desires, this perspective views distinguishing the needs and interests of client groups as the essential purpose of the agency. The traditional focus of concentrating on what various groups have in common is supplanted by an emphasis on what is different and unique about population segments. Historically, the efforts of recreation agencies were directed toward providing "equal recreation opportunities for all." This ideal often

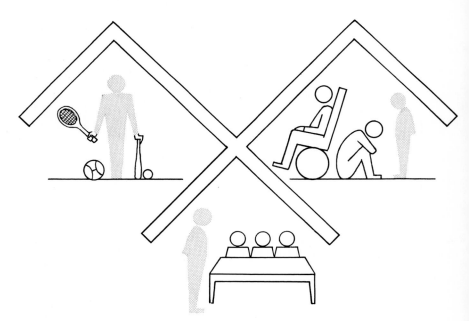

Fig. 10.

led to the development of standardized, uniform programs mass produced, mass distributed and mass promoted. Most often these programs were designed to meet the model expectations of the middle class. It was not until the emergence of the Civil Rights movement and widespread civil unrest that programs especially attuned to the needs and interests of different racial and ethnic client groups were provided in significant number.

The tumultuous 60's was a period of change and innovation for most recreation agencies. The recreation movement was not immune to the forces of social change. The revolutionary movements which altered the condition and consciousness of women, the poor, the aged and the young have had a profound impact on recreation departments. Many agencies realized that total reliance on their traditional approach to service was inadequate in the face of the changing and expanding demands placed upon them by newly "energized" client groups (e.g., blacks, women, handicapped, elderly, etc.). At the same time it became evident to many administrators that recreation departments could and should play a larger role in the amelioration of many social problems plaguing their cities. It was apparent that the provision of "fun" programs without meaningful social goals was a luxury that most cities were reluctant to support.*

The combined effect of these conditions led many recreation agencies to shift their program priorities as well as their methods of service delivery. A return by the park and recreation movement to issues of social concern was a prominent manifestation of this change. Outreach to youth and the economically disadvantaged, concern for the minorities, and increased services to the aged all received new emphasis. The emergence of the racial and ethnic identity movements stimulated many recreation departments to dispense with the white, middle-class model as the exclusive standard for providing program services. Many programs especially designed to meet the needs and interest of various racial and ethnic groups were initiated.

The reorientation in program focus was accompanied by an expansion of the methods used to make program services available to client groups. Many agencies recognized the need to adopt differential program delivery strategies to adequately cope with the increased range of client demands they encountered. Outreach,

---

*Kraus[1] in the conclusion of his national survey of municipal recreation departments commented that "the majority of urban park and recreation administrators accept the view that they must undertake a new and more socially significant role if their departments are to survive as a form of social service."

referral services, increased "synergetic" programming and other vehicles for decentralizing services were gradually integrated into the program operations of a growing number of agencies.

The remainder of this chapter will attempt to broadly describe and contrast the major service roles that are currently available to most recreation departments. The intent is not to single out the one best approach to the provision of recreation services. Instead, the intention is to convey the idea that *role* flexibility is the key to effectively delivering program services in a highly pluralistic community setting. The decision of what one approach or "mix" of approaches an agency should employ is influenced by a number of local conditions, such as client needs, financial condition of the agency, available resources, programs provided by other types of agencies and clientele to be served. The three primary delivery roles arranged on a service continuum have been identified as (1) the direct provider role, (2) the facilitator role and (3) the outreach role.

SERVICE DELIVERY ROLES

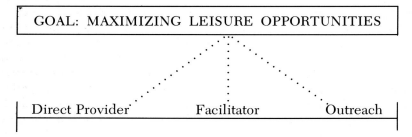

The Direct Provider Role

The traditional service approach role assumed by recreation professionals has been the Direct Provider role. This service model is characterized by a centralized agency-determined approach to the delivery of program services. Typically, the agency takes exclusive responsibility for planning and organizing programs, scheduling areas and facilities and developing organizational priorities. In effect, the recreation agency pre-assembles the essential program ingredients (e.g., leadership, materials, facilities, etc.) to create a number of immediate, ready-made participation opportunities. The participants' basic task is to pick and choose, "cafeteria style," from the array of opportunities made available to them. For the most part, then, participation opportunities are prescribed by the recreation agency's professional staff. Characteristically, in employing this approach, the professional staff relies on its knowledge of the recreational needs of community residents and provides leisure opportunities on the basis of what it feels is the "best" and "right" way to meet them. Generally, a minimum amount of input into the formulation and conduct of programs is required from service recipients. The relationship is analogous to the manufacturer-consumer roles found in the general market place. The recreation agency "produces" program activities, primarily based on the staff's "expert" opinion and the public's role is essentially one of "consuming" these ready-made products.

While the Direct Provider role may provide professional agency staffs with perhaps the easiest and most efficient method for delivering program services, the manner in which the approach is employed is open to criticism from several directions. First, and perhaps the major indictment against the approach, is that it presumes a knowledge of citizens' leisure needs and interests. Invariably, because programs are organized essentially on the basis of professional judgment, little or no attempt is made to systematically assess the leisure behavior patterns and preferences of community residents. Unfortunately, as many urban recreation departments discovered in the '60's, the practice of providing services without regard to clientele input can be hazardous. During the previous decade, the relevance of programs and the service priorities of many recreation agencies were severely challenged by displeased service recipients. It was discovered that the predominant number of agency-determined programs were available and attractive to only a narrow range of interest groups, while the needs of many client groups were going unserved.*

A second significant shortcoming of the Direct Provider service model relates to its facility-centered orientation. Generally this approach relies on the "center concept" as a means of delivering leisure opportunities. Participants are required to travel to recreation centers, community centers or schools to take part in ready-made recreation programs. An implicit assumption of this approach is that citizens will somehow have the means and ability to attend those activities offered on their own accord. The legitimacy of this assumption, however, has been challenged by experience which has shown that the center concept actually

---

*To minimize the occurrence of this situation, the major premise of the program planning model discussed in Chapter 7 (pp. 185) is that the program planning process must emanate from the needs and interest of community residents.

inhibits the ability of many individuals and groups to participate in recreation pursuits. Those most affected include the aged, the physically disabled, the housewife without a car and many others who are unable to travel the distance to the nearest recreation facility.

Despite apparent shortcomings the Direct Provider role remains the dominant method for deliverying community recreation services. The problems associated with its exclusive application, however, have led many recreation agencies to adopt additional modes of service delivery.

Facilitator Role

This broadened service approach emphasizes the agency's role as a facilitator or enabler of leisure opportunities, rather than just as an exclusive provider of ready-made, "packaged" activities. Adoption of the facilitator role is in effect an extension of the direct provider function. In addition to program initiation responsibilities, the recreation department as an enabling agent takes on the tasks of coordination, referral and technical assistance. This expanded orientation may entail the co-sponsorship of programs with other agencies such as the YMCA or the school district, the initiation of a leisure opportunity referral system, the offering of technical and consultative services to community groups (e.g., special interest clubs, nursing homes, etc.) and perhaps the provision of "seed" money to worthy community projects or agencies (Scouts, Y's, churches). Specific applications of this approach are endless, ranging from the provision of a comprehensive, interagency in-service training program for summer recreation personnel (e.g., life guards, day camp staff, playground leaders) employed by the private, quasipublic and commercial leisure service agencies in the community to the writing of a Title VII grant proposal under the Older Americans Act to provide a comprehensive, social, recreational and nutritional program for area senior citizens.

In most instances, members of the public recreation subsystem, (e.g. city recreation and parks department, school district) would logically be in the best position to assume the extra service dimension required of the facilitative approach. Government tax-supported agencies, such as municipal recreation departments, generally command larger budgetary and physical resources than other leisure service agencies. In addition, public agencies comprise the one sector of the community recreation system which is legally mandated to serve the recreation interests of the *total* community.

Implicit in an agency's adoption of the facilitator role is recognition of the fact that no one agency relying exclusively on its own resources can meet all the leisure needs of a community. Even the largest service agency, generally the public recreation department, cannot provide enough activities and facilities to accommodate the entire citizenry's demand for recreation. One natural dimension of the facilitator role, then, is the application of "synergetic" programming. This term, coined by Dunn and Phillips[2] refers to "the process of combining the unique resources of more than one agency to produce leisure services which could not be carried out successfully by one agency acting alone." Coordination and cooperation are the bywords of this approach to programming. Emphasis is placed on the development of joint-agency programs through such vehicles as interagency cooperative agreements, and on a broader scale, the formation of community wide recreation councils.

The facilitation of such integrative arrangements are increasingly justifiable in light of diminishing municipal budgets, rising maintenance and operation costs and greater service demands. The bringing together, for example, of all the various suppliers of recreational opportunities into a recreation council could result in a tremendous expansion of service economies and programs. Initial information exchange between council participants could lead to the development of joint purchasing agreements, pooled staff training programs and the resolution of community problems (e.g., inadequate transportation to recreation facilities, vandalism, etc.). Later, other tasks may be identified as important by council members, such as the collective sponsorship of a community wide recreation needs survey (this process is discussed at length in Chapter 7).

Potentially, then, a variety of purposes could be achieved through a coordination mechanism such as a recreation council. The council's most significant contribution, however, may lie in its helping participants to understand the interdependencies that exist between all members of the community recreation system—to make them cognizant of the fact that the presence of any one member of the system can and most often will have tremendous bearing and impact on the other members of the system. Rather than leaving the effects of these associations to chance (with resultant conflict problems and diseconomics), the recreation council provides a vehicle for eliminating uncertainty from system relationships so that all members working in closer harmony can benefit from the more productive and efficient delivery of their services.

Tangible evidence for the benefits of synergetic programming has been provided in Dunn and Phillips' national survey of cooperative interagency programs. The majority of respondents reported synergetic programs to be "a great help," resulting in (1) stretching public dollars, (2) enhancing public relations, and (3) helping to keep their recreation agencies dynamic. Commenting on the role that municipal recreation departments can play in fostering such benefits, one respondent, the administrator of a municipal park and recreation board stated:

> *"I submit to you that it is the responsibility of the municipal recreation departments to extend the arm of their total community program through cooperative planning and working with other agencies within the community. If you do not want to cooperate with other agencies, hundreds of excuses can be found to enhance this attitude and the total program in your community will thus be limited to the financial and physical resources of the municipal department. However, if an attitude of community cooperation is adopted, tremendous good can be accomplished . . . No longer are you limited to the assets of the municipal department, but the sky is the limit and the total resources of the community can go to work for a total community recreation program."*[3]

In adopting the facilitative role, the recreation agency is in effect expanding its definition of what it believes to be its service constituency. This perspective perceives *other* leisure service agencies (e.g., YMCA's, churches, etc.) as primary service targets as well as the traditional recipients—individuals and special interest groups. The provision of financial and technical assistance to other agencies can become *as* integral a part of a recreation department's mission as is the provision of direct service programs to community residents. As a result, the agency is in a position to serve the leisure needs (albeit in a more indirect fashion) of far more people than it would through exclusive use of the Direct Provider role.

The facilitative function can further be expanded to include the recreation agency assuming the role of a referral agent. In this instance, the agency would act as a broker, providing a connection between the recreational needs of community residents and the supply of recreational opportunities available to satisfy them. The key task of recreation staff would be to match expressed recreation interests with the most appropriate available leisure opportunities. An important first step in implementing such a service would be to inventory all existing leisure opportunities available within the community or perhaps in the surrounding geographical region. This survey could include information on participation opportunities provided by youth-serving agencies, private parties, state parks, hunting preserves, commercial water-based recreation enterprises, and so forth. The existence of a community recreation council would expedite the collection of necessary data. Once the information was collected (this would be an on-going task, continually in need of up-dating and revision) the recreation agency would be in a position to provide a vast amount of information regarding recreation opportunities to interested individuals or groups in the community.

Commenting on the feasibility of a recreation agency establishing a leisure opportunity referral service Myron Weiner states:

> *"It is not inconceivable that with the proper technologically based system the municipality will have a leisure hot-line to assist families in selecting from a variety of weekend recreational/leisure options recorded on their telephone/computer connection; then, once the family's choice is made, reservations will be completed and even an itinerary will be plotted."*[4]

By adopting the facilitative approach (characterized by such activities as synergetic programming, referral and technical assistance), the recreation agency transcends a preoccupation with the development of its own programs to emphasize providing services which enable individuals and other organizations to expand and improve their own leisure opportunities. In doing so, the recreation agency makes great progress toward increasing the leisure self-sufficiency of its clientele as well as maximizing the limited resources it has at its disposal.

The Outreach Role

The third major role that a recreation agency can assume in delivering program services is the Outreach role. Bannon defines outreach as "the effort that takes place when a social service agency, such as recreation, reaches out and assists through personal contacts those citizens systematically excluded from, unaware of, or unreceptive to an agency's service or those of related agencies."[5] The concept is not new; social welfare agencies have been successfully employing outreach methods since the 1930's. It has only been within the last decade, however, that recreation departments have in increasing numbers adopted outreach programming methods. A primary reason for the slow incorporation of this concept into recreation agencies is that Outreach represents in effect a contradiction of traditional operating methods. As David Gray suggests, recreation departments' historical reliance on the Direct Provider approach has resulted in the growth of a "chain-link fence" mentality.[6] This perspective views the primary concern of the recreation agency staff to be with the operation of recreation centers and facilities. "It identifies the primary tasks as surveillance of grounds to assure compliance with rules, safety, proper use of equipment; development of a schedule for use of the facility; planning and execution of a program of activities with the staff in face-to-face leadership roles . . ."[8] Gray concludes that such a facility-oriented perspective often charges recreation personnel not with the development of people, but with the management of a center, not with service to the community, but with the supervision of grounds.

Conversely, the emphasis of outreach programming is on reaching out beyond the confines of a recreation facility to assist needy clientele groups. It perceives the recreation worker as a "community figure," one who can operate effectively in the community without *any* facilities. There is no precise model to guide this kind of professional. The social climate conditions the nature of the tasks to be performed. Depending on factors such as need and available resources, outreach programming can range from extending program services into community settings such as nursing homes and hospitals to the implementation of recreation advisory councils; from the promotion of community organization activities to the adoption of roving program leaders.

Roving Leader Program. A significant commitment to outreach programming has been made by several recreation agencies (particularly YMCA's) across the country in the form of the Roving Leader Program. The Roving Leader concept represents a creative approach for providing recreation and social services to hard-to-reach, delinquency prone youth in inner cities.[8] The Roving Leader is generally assigned to a specific geographical area within the community. His "turf" becomes street corners, alleys, pool halls; any place where young people hang out. The major function of the Roving Leader is to stimulate youth to participate in agency programs, to encourage them to use community facilities, and at the same time to introduce them to essential community resources in education, health, employment, and related social services. Achievement of these ends is not a short-term undertaking. Building the rapport and confidence necessary to effect change may take months, sometimes years. Over time the Roving Leader program has broadened its initial focus on youth to now include work with any citizens in need of special attention, from preschoolers through senior adults.

The elderly in particular can benefit from the extended service efforts of a recreation agency. Ironically, unlike many delinquent youths, seniors may have the will but not the means to participate in recreation opportunities. Plagued by low, fixed incomes, physical disabilities, lack of transportation and an assortment of other problems many older adults are not in a position to participate in the regular, "drop-in" programs customarily offered by recreation agencies. They simply can't or won't come to a recreation facility. Outreach efforts, then, directed toward bringing program services to the elderly—to the homebound, to rest homes, to nursing homes, to Title VII nutritional centers, would greatly expand the numbers of seniors being served. Even if an agency did not have adequate resources to directly provide for such an effort, it could still, in a more indirect fashion, make a significant contribution to senior outreach. For example, the recreation department, possibly in concert with other social service agencies, could provide an ongoing training program to assist nursing home staff, volunteers, county extension home-aid specialists, and others to become more knowledgeable in recreation leadership methods, techniques and materials.

Underlying a recreation agency's committment to outreach programming is a strong holistic service philosophy. The decision to augment extended service programs is based on the conviction that recreation service to many clientele groups has little meaning or impact if the agency fails to recognize, or attempt to deal with those constraints (racism, illiteracy, malnutrition, lack of transportation, lack of awareness, etc.) that impede the ability of the disadvantaged to participate in recreation activities. Likewise, recreation agencies must share in the amelioration of broader social problems plaguing cities (rising juvenile crime rates, unemployment, impoverished social as well as spiritual conditions) if they are to remain viable, adequately funded, members of local government.

Summary

This chapter provided a description of the expanded service opportunities available to community recreation agencies, and at the same time suggested the need for integrating these roles into a comprehensive, adaptive service delivery strategy. In a social climate characterized by complexity, diversity and rapid change, role flexibility is essential if the agency is to satisfy the divergent needs and demands of its many client groups. The three roles discussed, Direct Provider, Facilitator, and Outreach, represent three options available to agencies in carrying out their service responsibilities. Elements of all three service methods can be employed interchangeably as changing circumstances and conditions demand. The application of these expanded role models is predicated on the beliefs that (1) no one agency relying exclusively on its own resources can possibly meet all the leisure needs of a community, and (2) recreation services to remain truly viable must work toward alleviating those social problems and constraints that impede the ability of many individuals to participate in leisure opportunities.

No reliable "cookbook" for designing the most appropriate mix of delivery approaches exists. Developing the optimum marketing strategy for recreation services requires the careful gathering and analysis of information regarding the kinds of client groups seeking satisfaction and the resources available for satisfying them. Methods for achieving these ends will be discussed in the next chapter.

References

1. Kraus, Richard: *Urban Parks and Recreation: Challenge of the 1970's.* New York, Community Council of Greater New York, 1972, p. 68.
2. Dunn, Diana, and Phillips, Lamarr A.: Synergetic Programming or 2 +2 =5, *Parks and Recreation*, March 1975, p. 24.
3. Ibid: p. 26.
4. Weiner, Myron: A Systems Approach to Leisure Services, In S. G. Lutzin and T. S. Storey (eds.), *Managing Municipal Leisure Services*, Washington, D.C., International City Managment Association, 1973, p. 5.
5. Bannon, Joseph: Outreach—*Extending Community Service in Urban Areas.* Springfield, Charles C Thomas, 1973, p. XIII.
6. Gray, David, and Pelegrino, David: *Reflections on the Recreation and Park Movement*, Dubuque, Iowa, Wm. C. Brown Company, Publishers, 1973, pp. 288–289.
7. Ibid: p. 288.
8. The *Roving Recreation Leader Guide*, Office of Recreation and Park Resources, University of Illinois, Urbana — Champaign, 1969.

CHAPTER 7

The Program Function

"The effective development of a recreation program, one which truly satisfies participant needs, is built upon the systematic integration of such elements as collecting and analyzing 'need' data, organizing and coordinating staff efforts through the use of systematic forecasting methods, conducting the event and evaluating the outcome."

Recreation Program: The Opportunity Complex

This chapter will focus on the implementation of recreation programs. Emphasis will be placed on the essential tasks of planning, organizing and evaluating. The total array of opportunities provided by recreation agency is commonly referred to as its program. This complex of opportunities usually includes a broad range of organized activities (sports, arts and crafts, music, drama, etc.) as well as a variety of physical resources (swimming pools, recreation centers, playgrounds, etc.) all of which seek to enrich the quality of community life. The essential task facing municipal recreation agencies is to maximize or sufficiently expand this array of opportunities to effectively satisfy the diverse leisure needs and interests of community residents.

As we have seen in Chapter 6, the concept of program has been expanded tremendously in recent years. Service to other agencies in the form of technical and financial assistance is now increasingly viewed as a legitimate aspect of the program function. In addition,

179

outreach efforts, referral services and synergetic or cooperative programs are being employed by public recreation agencies in greater numbers than ever before. Also, more emphasis today is being placed on the development of recreation areas for unorganized, self-directed use. The constant pressures for more ball diamonds, golf courses, and picnic areas, coupled with the more recent boom in bicycling, tennis, jogging and racquet ball provide excellent examples of the increasing need for recreation areas and facilities which allow for self-directed use. Use of these areas requires little or no paid leadership or formal organization, attracting those who prefer more independent or spontaneous use of their leisure time. The popularity of these opportunities is growing in a society where people, especially the young, are demanding as Bull states "greater discretion over time and place at which recreation activities can be carried out."[1]

While the nature and scope of the program function in many agencies have expanded to accommodate a number of new roles, the prominent element of the programming task continues to be the provision of organized recreation activities. For most recreation agency personnel, the majority of hours of each working day are allocated to the organization of program activities such as instructional classes, leagues, workshops or special events. The implementation of such activities normally requires that members of the recreation staff take primary, if not exclusive responsibility for planning and promoting the activities, staffing them and for providing the necessary facilities and equipment. Examples of recreation activities which can be provided in this manner are numerous, encompassing such elements as the highly organized (community-wide and special events), the informal (table games, reading), the physical (sports and contests) and the aesthetic (cultural and performing arts).

Several methods for classifying this myriad number of activities into logical categories have been established. These classification schemes have varied tremendously according to the criterion used to segregate them, e.g., form, type, season, active or passive, indoor or outdoor and so on. To illustrate the scope and magnitude of recreation activities one of the most comprehensive classification schemes is presented here:

I *Arts and Crafts*[2]

Elementary
  Paper bag crafts
  Puppets
  Plaster carving
  Carving, soap, wood
  Drawing
  Finger painting
  Clay modeling
  Copper foil
  Vegetable printing
  Stenciling
  Basketry
  Gimp craft
  Finger weaving
  Card weaving
  Hooking
  Spatter printing
  Papier mache
  Candle making
  Mobiles
  Whittling
  Wood stamping
  Shell craft
  Tie dyeing

Intermediate
  Games, checkers, puzzles,
    bean bag, box hockey
  Leather, modeling and
    tooling
  Simple metal jewelry
  Wood carving
  Wood working (hand)
  Basic ceramics
  Painting and sketching
  Block printing
  Dry paint etching
  Hand and simple loom
    weaving
  Tin can craft
  Art metal craft
  Plastics

Advanced
  Leather carving
  Jewelry enameling
  Painting
  (Advanced levels of activities as listed)

II *Dance*

Folk Dance
  American Folk Dances
    Square dance
    Round or couple dance
    Longways dance
    Circle dance
    Solo dance
  Folk Dance of Other Lands
    Ethnic groups
Social Dance
Dance mixers
Ballet

Creative Rhythms for Children
  Free rhythms
  Identification rhythms
  Dramatic rhythms
  Rhythms games
    Singing games
    Simple folk dances
Modern Dance
  Conditioning and free
    exercise
  Art of movement
  Concert dance
  Tap, clog, character dance

III *Drama*

Blackouts

Ceremonials

Charades

Children's Theater

Choral Speech

Community Theater

Creative Drama

Demonstrations

Dramatization

Festivals

Formal drama

Grand Opera

Imagination Plays

Impersonations

Light Opera

Marionettes

Monodrama

Monologue

Musical Comedy

Observances

Operetta

Pageants

Pantomime

Peep box

Plays

Puppetry

Script-in-hand

Shadow Plays

Shows

Skits

Story reading

Story telling

Stunts

Symphonic Drama

Tableaux

Theater in the Round

IV *Games—Sports—Athletics*

Informal Games and Activities

Ball games—Dodge-ball, Circle Pall Ball, etc.

Circle games

Goal games

Hitting or Striking Games

Net Games

Running Games

Tag Games

Stunts

Relays

Apparatus Play

Individual and Dual Sports

Individual—archery, bicycling, boating, bowling, fishing, etc.

Dual—badminton, fencing, horseshoes, table tennis, etc.

Team Sports

Combative Sports

Women's and Girls' Sports

Co-recreation Sports

V *Hobbies*

Collecting
  Stamp(s)
  Antiques
  Firearms
  Models
  Books
  China
  Paintings
  Others
Creating
  Writing
  Wood-working
  Sculpture
  Painting
  Photography
  Cooking
  Gardening
  Others

Educational
  Reading
  Ornithology
  Astronomy
  Horticulture
  Entomology
  Zoology
  Sciences
  Others
Performing (use of body skills)
  Hiking
  Swimming
  Hunting
  Fishing
  Magic
  Camping
  Chess
  Bowling
  Canoeing
  Tennis
  Others

VI *Music*

Singing
  Informal singing
  Community sings
  Choruses
  Quartets
  Ensembles
  Glee clubs
  Solos
Listening
  Home music
  Records
  Radio
  Television
  Concerts
Creating
  Song making
  Other music making

Playing
  Rhythm instruments
  Melody instruments
  Harmony instruments
  Fretted instruments
  Bands
  Orchestras
  Chamber music groups
Rhythmic Movement
  Purely rhythmic
  Simple interpretation
  Singing games
  Folk dances
  Play party games
Combined Activities
  Folk dancing
  Musical charades
  Shadow plays
  Pageants
  Talent and variety shows
  Others

VII *Outdoor Recreation*

Nature Activities
  Scenery and observation
  Collecting
  Nature experiments
  Gathering wild food
  Nature trails
  Nature talks and exhibits
  Nature games
Outdoor Living
  Informal fun
  Basic campcraft skills
  Camping
Miscellaneous
  Museums
  Zoos
  Arboretums
  Parks and forest preserves
  Gardens

Outdoor Arts and Crafts
  Projects (Use of natural
    materials)
  Wood
  Bark
  Fiber
  Minerals
Trips and Outings
  Tours and travel
  Informal outings

VIII *Reading, Writing, and Speaking*

Reading
  Great Books program
  Book review clubs
  Reading classes
  New books club
  Reading the classics
  Mystery story club

Writing
  Business and social writing
    club
  Writing for fun
  Technical writing
  Creative writing
  Newspaper writing
  Contesting

IX *Social Recreation*

Activities
  Games
  Informal drama
  Music
  Dance
  Co-recreation sports
  Relays
  Arts and Crafts
  Novelty events

Events
  Parties
  Banquets
  Informal drama
  Outings
  Dances
  Snow and ice sports
  Progressive games program
  Family recreation
  Teas and coffee hours

X *Special Events*

Exhibits of Objects
  Hobby show
  Science fair
  Arts and crafts exhibit
  Flower show
  Doll show
Mass Activities
  Folk dance festival
  Winter carnival
  Celebrations

Performances
  Circus
  Talent show
  Concert
  Dance exhibit
Social Occasions
  Veterans' Day parade
  Cherry blossom festival
  Others

The preceding list illustrates the broad range of activities that would warrant consideration in the establishment of a comprehensive community recreation program. The remainder of this chapter will focus on the processes involved in planning and organizing activities such as these into a viable community recreation services program.

The Program Development Process

The following model (Fig. 11) is an attempt to identify and logically order the major components in the recreation program planning process. It is intended to be descriptive not prescriptive. Primarily, the paradigm is meant to *identify* the many variables which may be a part of the planning process and which may either impede or enhance the agency's ability to deliver program services.

PROGRAM DEVELOPMENT MODEL

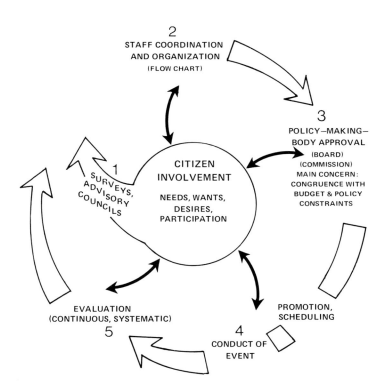

Fig. 11. Program development model.

It is hoped that it will provide a meaningful framework for practitioners to analyze the planning process in their agencies; and at the same time, give students and others with little experience in the field practical insight into the actual mechanics of recreation programming.

Identification of Needs and Interests. Fundamental to the notion of providing recreation opportunities is the existence of a condition of need for such services. It seems logical therefore, that the program planning process should emanate from the needs* and interests of community residents. The underlying assumption is that the analysis of leisure behavior patterns and recreational preferences should provide an informative and objective foundation upon which to make decisions regarding the allocation of program resources.

While the identification of the community's recreation needs seems a logical place to start the planning process, few recreation agencies systematically attempt to collect, for example, user preference and satisfaction data. Instead they rely on tradition and professional experience in the formulation of program services. While the collection of "need" data can be complex and time-consuming, providing recreation services solely on the basis of professional considerations without regard to clientele input can be a hazardous practice. First, an assumed knowledge of a community's recreation needs and interests is presumptuous, especially in light of the fact that recreation as a profession has done so little to systematically measure the impact of the services it provides. The administrator who believes he's getting the job done because certain "tried and true" programs continue to be popular year after year, may in fact be missing the boat. It is possible that the same group of people are being consistently attracted to the same programs, while the vast majority of potential clientele are going unserved. Second, it is becoming increasingly difficult in a period of economic scarcity to justify expenditures for more recreation on the basis of emotional appeals, based on what the recreation administrator "feels" the community needs in the way of leisure opportunities. The chances of procuring adequate financial support for recreation seems to be greatly enhanced when the professional is armed with hard data to support his claims. The recreation staff's request for funds would logically have much more credence in the

---

*Recreation need is defined as the degree to which recreational opportunities are perceived to be necessary or desired in a community. The concept of need can be manifest as an expressed preference for particular recreation activities, as a normative standard, and/or as the comparative adequacy of existing opportunities.[3]

eyes of the "city fathers" if, for example, they could demonstrate that 75% of the community wants the new service.

A number of methods are available for identifying the recreation needs of a community. The data collection technique that is used most frequently is the comprehensive recreation survey. Survey methods have improved to the point where remarkably valid results can be obtained from a relatively small sample of the total population. Through the use of *random* sampling techniques (e.g., each resident has an equal opportunity of being selected), a representative sample can be drawn which accurately describes the recreation interests of the total population. Using such a representative sample, recreation agency personnel can interpret and take action on the survey results with a high degree of confidence. Community recreation surveys can be employed for a variety of reasons. Data can be collected on:

1. *Expressed Needs and Interests: The recreation activity preferences of children, youth and adults. Current rates of participation as well as projected preferences (e.g., reflect what person would like to do rather than what he actually does).*
2. *Attitudes and Opinions: The way people feel about (e.g., level of satisfaction) the existing programs and facilities made available to them. Why people are* not *participating in available recreation programs. Whether community residents would be willing to increase their financial support for recreation services, as well as how much and in what form (increased property taxes, fees and charges, etc.).*
3. *Available Resources: The current and potential community resources (e.g., buildings, swimming areas, etc.) available for meeting the recreation needs of the people.*
4. *Demographic: Information describing the composition of the community's population: age, sex, income, etc.*

The information obtained from the analysis of survey data can prove to be extremely important to determining such things as: program priorities, the degree to which taxpayers are satisfied with current services, the chance of passing a bond referendum, the ability of people to pay for services, and the availability of skilled volunteers.

While survey information can be extremely valuable to the planning process, it is not a completely accurate method for identifying the recreational needs of a community. It is important to recognize that people's recreation preferences are limited by their previous experiences. A person may not express an interest, for example, in tennis or one of the performing arts simply because he or she has never participated in those forms of activity. It has been shown, however, that simply exposing a person to a new recreation opportunity can stimulate a great deal of interest in that particular activity. This suggests that rather than providing services which merely attempt to satisfy the expressed needs of a community, recreation leaders have the additional professional responsibility of introducing new programs and services which hopefully provide new and challenging need-satisfying outlets for people. To effectively meet the expressed desires of a community, as well as cultivate new life-enriching experiences, requires that the recreation agency attempt to accurately read the pulse of the community. Carefully collected and analyzed survey data integrated with information provided continuously from other "need" monitoring sources, such as neighborhood recreation advisory councils and program evaluation, can aid immeasurably in this task.

Another method for identifying needs as a basis for determining program planning priorities is through the application of a comparative need measurement device. The use of this approach in determining need is based on the belief that people are *not* equal in their need for local recreation services, and that various social, economic, and environmental characteristics in addition to population density are critical to a realistic assessment of recreation need.[4]

The process of assessing the need priorities among communities and neighborhoods has long been a part of the social welfare field. This precedent has been adapted to the field of recreation most prominently in the form of the "recreation needs instrument" developed and applied by the City of Los Angeles.[5] Application of this instrument provides the comparative priority of need for local recreation services in an urban setting.

The instrument was developed in the basis of three assumptions:

1. *There are measurable social characteristics and neighborhood recreation resources which indicate comparative need for recreation and youth services by areas, communities, or neighborhoods in an urban setting.*
2. *All citizens have important basic needs for recreation services, but due to different socioeconomic characteristics and interests, their needs can be met in different ways.*
3. *Priorities in community-subsidized recreation services should go to those experiencing maximum social pressures from density of population, number of youth, low income, and evidence of social disorganization.*

Variables used in the calculation of the "need index" are Youth Population (5 to 19 years of age), Population Density, Median Family Income and Juvenile Delinquency Rate. The three variables comprising the "resource index" are: (1) number of full and part-time professional staff hours per 1000 population per year

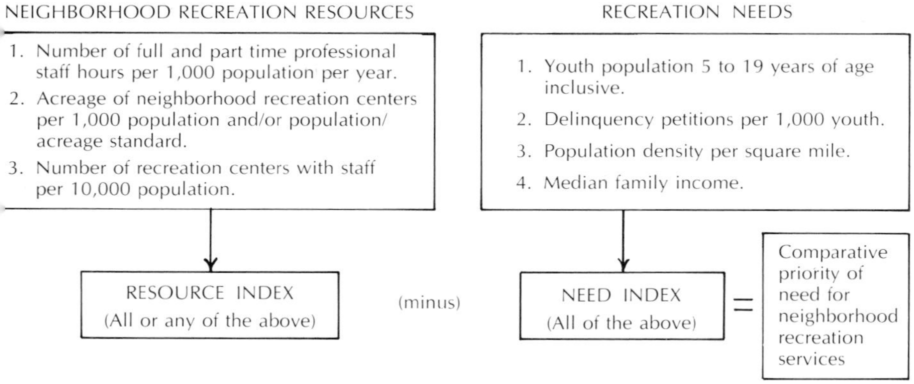

NEIGHBORHOOD RECREATION RESOURCES

1. Number of full and part time professional staff hours per 1,000 population per year.
2. Acreage of neighborhood recreation centers per 1,000 population and/or population/acreage standard.
3. Number of recreation centers with staff per 10,000 population.

RECREATION NEEDS

1. Youth population 5 to 19 years of age inclusive.
2. Delinquency petitions per 1,000 youth.
3. Population density per square mile.
4. Median family income.

RESOURCE INDEX (All or any of the above) (minus) NEED INDEX (All of the above) = Comparative priority of need for neighborhood recreation services

Fig. 12. Formula used to determine comparative priority of need for neighborhood recreation services.

in a neighborhood; (2) average of neighborhood recreation centers per 100 population; and (3) number of recreation centers per 10,000 population. By comparing the "need index" with the "resources index," a "comparative priority of need for neighborhood recreation services" can be established.

While the "recreation needs instrument" is not without certain conceptual limitations, the application of such a model for determining needs or comparative priorities is worthy of consideration by program planners.* Perhaps recreation staff members could increase the utility of using the priority method in their particular communities by substituting or including other more relevant variables into the model. For example, they could expand the service population to consider more than just the youth age-group on the "need" side of the equation, and include privately and commercially provided recreation opportunities as well as public recreation centers on the "resources" side. The results of such an analysis can provide a quantitative framework for determining the relative program needs between census tracts or neighborhoods within a city. Within each of these geographical sub-units, recreation planners can further refine the analysis by identifying the specific needs of a particular neighborhood through the use of more qualitative methods such as advisory councils and surveys.

*For a Critique of the Recreation Needs Instrument the reader is referred to comments by William Hendon in *The Journal of Leisure Research*, Spring 1969, p. 189.

Combining these methods not only establishes the relative priority of need for the overall community, but also identifies more specifically the degree to which the recreational needs of neighborhood "X" differ from those of neighborhood "Y".

The use of methods for identifying the recreational needs of a community, such as surveys, comparative need assessment devices, and advisory groups, is the cornerstone to effective program development. The information derived from these sources provides a solid and objective planning base for the intelligent allocation of program resources.

Staff Coordination and Preparation. Whereas the first step in the program development process focuses exclusively on the identification of recreation needs and interests, through the collection of data, the second phase emphasizes staff planning and organizing activities. During this phase the "need information" is translated into specific "action plans" in the form of programs and services. The formulation of new programs and the modification of existing offerings are staff tasks characteristic of the second stage in the planning process. The process involved in program preparation and modification can require a considerable amount of effort on the part of agency staff. Initially, the recreation staff, preferably working in close cooperation with citizens' groups (such as the P.T.A., Church Councils, neighborhood advisory councils, and interagency coordinating committees), should determine the scope and character of new program offerings. For each particular program, then questions should be raised, such as: what will the program attempt to accomplish?, and who's the program going to be geared for?, how much is it going to cost?, when will it be held?, and how will it be delivered? Answers to questions such as these provide the nucleus around which the staff can begin its organizational efforts. Generally, the preparation and organization of programs entail attending to a number of manpower, money, materials, time, facilities and publicity requirements. A specific technique for coordinating all these tasks is discussed in detail later in this chapter (refer to Flow Chart Method).

Policy-Making Body Approval. After the recreation staff has agreed upon a new program idea and developed plans for its implementation, the third, and possibly the most critical phase of the planning process begins: the securing of approval from the policy-making body. Once the staff has formulated a new program it generally must present the proposed service idea to its board or commission for approval. Approval from the policy-making body is essential, particularly if the new program request requires the expenditure of additional monies or represents a new direction in service orientation (e.g., Roving Leader Program, Title VII funded Senior Citizen Nutrition Program, etc.).

Approval authority in the case of a municipal recreation department would normally rest with the recreation commission (in many cities, ultimate budgetary consent resides with the City Council). Often the policy-making body (e.g., board or commission) perceives its central role as making sure that any new recreation programs or services provided by the agency remain congruent with certain budgetary and policy constraints. Unfortunately, all too frequently, policies regarding the provision of program services are not clearly defined. Too often tradition and/or the attitudes and values of individual commission members will act as the unwritten guides to the types of program services offered by an agency.

Table 9. Goals of Phoenix, Arizona, Department of Parks and Recreation

Primary Goals:

1. To provide adequate physical facilities and . . . program opportunities to make it possible for the people of the community to become self-sustaining in their leisure.
2. Promote and further the organization, administration, financing and operation of community recreation.
3. To meet recreational needs with maximum effectiveness and with minimum expense.
4. To hold and preserve for the future, land, water and air spaces to assure essential freedom of choice in recreational experience.

Secondary Goals

1. Identify community recreational needs.
2. Identify goals and objectives and develop a master plan . . . to achieve them.
3. Develop and maintain high standards of professional leadership.
4. Instill confidence and a feeling of respect among employees at all levels.
5. Maintain effective communication within the department and between the department and the community.
6. Encourage interagency cooperation.
7. Provide activities which are recreational, educational, cultural, character-building, and which have carry-over value for all people . . .
8. Provide specialized leadership, information and advisory services on all phases of recreation and leisure activity.
9. Control, safeguard and maintain public recreation areas and facilities.

Goals for Recreation as a Profession

1. Unite forces of all agencies dealing with recreation.
2. Promote conservation of natural resources and personal resources.
3. Promote favorable recreational legislation.
4. Promote and maintain a high degree of professional ethics.
5. Create a favorable public image of the profession.

Many recreation agencies, however, have developed written policy statements reflecting their goals and objectives. Preferably, the professional staff and board or commission members will include representative input from the larger community into the development of a policy statement.

The policies established by recreation agencies will vary from one community to the next depending on the mix of such local factors as the type of legally established managing authority, the nature and scope of the community recreation system, the wishes of community residents, the political environment, the philosophical background of the administrator, and the values held by board members. Within the context of established policy (whether it be clearly written or implied by previous action), it is the responsibility of the executive, the Director of a YMCA or the Superintendent of a city recreation department, to justify new program ideas to his or her policy-making board.*

The ability of the executive to successfully "sell" the proposed program or service change to his board is directly related to how well the groundwork was laid by the staff in the preceding, coordinating and organizing base of the planning process. A poorly conceived request, without adequate and objective justification, will invariably be rejected.

The administrator can enhance the probability of receiving a favorable response from his board or commission by preparing adequate justification data in the form of: (1) a clearly established and identified need for the service, (2) a realistic appraisal of projected cost and operational requirement (e.g., manpower, equipment, etc.) and (3) anticipated outcomes of program (e.g., increased numbers of people served, new skills learned, additional revenues realized, etc.). The more effectively this justification documentation is interpreted by the executive to his board, the greater the likelihood that the program will be granted.

The importance of infusing data concerning community need and involvement of citizens into the process of program adoption cannot be overemphasized. Program proposals grounded on a comprehensive appraisal of community needs, and combined with the

---

*It should be understood that policies are not static by dynamic guidelines for action. Both the board and professional staff should be recognize that policies "may be changed at anytime, as either circumstances or departmental philosophy change, or when the need arises for a new or more flexible course of action. However, when such changes are carried out, it should not be done at whim, but only after careful deliberation." Effective monitoring of the leisure needs and interests of community residents through surveys and evaluative feed-back devices will help keep policies congruent with changing community service demands.

support of involved and concerned citizens have a far greater chance of being adopted than those defended by timeworn emotional philosophies.

Citizen Involvement. Citizen involvement is portrayed as a central element in the program planning process, one which *can have* significant impact on each component of the model. Citizen participation in the planning of recreation activities can occur in a number of ways. Legislative boards and commissions, advisory councils, special interest groups are several common vehicles for facilitating citizen involvement. Of course, an important but less direct form of input can be secured through the collection of survey information. Almost all recreation agencies guarantee citizen involvement in some form through their legally constituted lay commissions or boards. While some administrators feel this provides enough (sometimes more than enough!) citizen participation, the trend is definitely toward involving community people more fully in the process of program policy and development through vehicles such as recreation advisory councils. Advisory councils are usually comprised of interested citizens representing a certain neighborhood or geographical area within the city. They function in purely an advisory capacity and as such, unlike the board or commission, have no legal authority. Acting as the "go between" between community residents and professional staff members, advisory councils can provide valuable assistance to recreation agencies. For example, their responsibilities can comprise such activities as (1) assisting in the planning and conducting of programs, (2) raising funds to support community recreation services, (3) providing volunteer assistance, (4) promoting program services provided by the recreation agency and, (5) lobbying as an advocate group for the continued support of community recreation services.

While the use of citizen involvement in program planning can be extremely valuable, one aspect of its application deserves a word of caution. The administrator who views advisory councils and other citizen participation devices primarily as "ammunition" to create a citizen lobby to support and safeguard departmental interests runs the risk of alienating his board. The appearance at the city council meeting of 75 senior citizens to vociferously argue in support of new programs for the aged could positively influence the decision made by council members. If, however, members of this policy-making body (or a board-of-directors, or commission) were to get the feeling that the recreation administrator was trying to intimidate or pressure them through a "show of force" by department sponsored citizen groups, the long-run consequences could be devastating to both the agency and the administrator. The reaction of the policy-makers, who feel that an attempt is being made to circumvent their authority and/or put them on an uncomfortable "hot seat," could be to slash future program requests or ultimately force the administrator to resign. For those recreation agency administrators considering a program of citizen involvement it would be wise to follow the advice of Dr. Joe Bannon who suggests that a primary "responsibility of the administrator is to make sure that citizens groups understand that their relationship to the recreation and park board is as an ally not as a threat. Overall goals and objectives of the two groups are in fact, identical, as all seek to improve parks and recreation."[7]

Conduct of the Program. Clearance for the implementation of the new program idea is in effect provided when the proposal is approved by the policy-making body. During this phase, the recreation staff puts into action the plans formulated in the second or organizational step of the planning model. Necessary equipment is purchased and dispensed, program leaders are trained and assigned, publicity is released, participants are registered, facilities are made ready — all culminating with the implementation of a recreation program (e.g., instructional class, workshop league or special event).

Evaluation. The last step in the planning model is evaluation. During this phase the recreation agency attempts to assess the effectiveness of its program services. Evaluation is viewed in the model as a continuous, on-going process. Participant and staff feedback is continuously fed into the planning process in an effort to determine whether programs are producing a desired level of participant satisfaction. In other words, are the programs satisfying the needs of community residents?; more specifically, are they meeting the objectives for which they were established (e.g., developing new skills, improving physical fitness, involving the entire family, bringing about desired behavioral changes, paying their own way, etc.)?

Analysis of feedback data can lead to the identification of discrepancies which may exist between the actual and desired outcomes of current programs, and as a result provide a sound basis for making the necessary changes.

Despite the importance of the evaluation process, a recent national survey conducted by the Urban Institute concluded that evaluation efforts of park and recreation agencies "seem to be quite limited in scope and sporadic."[8] The Urban Institute survey found that current evaluation practices, when applied, emphasized the use of quantitative, input-oriented measures. Indices such as attendance, space standards (e.g., number of tennis courts per 10,000 residents) and unit or per capita cost of programs have been the most commonly used measuring tools for assessing agency performance. These measures are not without utility. Systematic and accurate attendance counts, for example, can provide valuable information (e.g., identify peak-use periods, seasonal use trends, percent of available activity space and time utilized) which can result in a more efficient allocation of staff and physical resources. Analysis of program offerings on a cost basis can also provide valuable information to the recreation planner. By integrating, for example, the estimated cost of program offerings (including costs for personnel, maintenance, facilities, etc.) with attendance data, the recreation agency can generate cost per capita figures. Each unit of service or program (e.g., recreation centers, playgrounds, swimming pools, special events or sports, aquatics, cultural arts, etc.) can be compared on this "cost of operation per unit of attendance" measure and related to overall agency priorities.

However, while quantitative measures such as attendance and unit cost figures do provide valuable data, they do not provide an answer to the most important question, what effect or value is the program experience having on the participants? Traditional measures exclude factors such as degree of satisfaction derived from participation, amount of personal growth and skill development, and perhaps more importantly, why people chose *not* to participate in existing opportunities. Commenting on this point, the Urban Institute report concluded that "statistics collected . . . generally reflected this concern with recreation resources and dollars expended rather than with the clientele for these services. Measurement of inputs is important, but it is hardly sufficient if a government cares about the effect or impact of its services upon the public."[9]

Recognizing the deficiency in current evaluation practices, the Urban Institute, under contract to the Bureau of Outdoor Recreation, developed a set of measuring devices designed to collect recreation effectiveness data. The principal device used to collect most of the information on program effectiveness is a scientifically designed citizen survey. The survey focuses on the participant's recent perceptions of existing community recreational opportunities. In a sample of neighborhood households, respondents are asked to rate the cleanliness, safety, crowdedness, hours of

operation, condition of equipment and facilities, and helpfulness of
program staff. Other data collection techniques are incorporated
into the method which allows the agency to systematically
accumulate information on physical attendance.

An important dimension of the Urban Institute's survey
instrument is its effort to collect information on *non-users*. Non-use
is a significant problem besetting urban park and recreation
departments. It is estimated that use levels seldom exceed 10% of

Table 10. Illustrative Recreation Objectives and Measures of
Effectiveness[10]

Objectives
Recreation services should provide for all citizens, to the extent practicable, a
variety of leisure opportunities which are accessible, safe, physically attractive and
enjoyable. They should to the maximum extent, contribute to the mental and
physical health of the community and to its economic and social well-being.
Measures of Effectiveness
1. Overall Citizen Rating: (Overall Enjoyableness)
    a. Percent of households which feel that recreation opportunities are good.
    b. Percent of households which feel that recreation opportunities are poor.
2. Overall User Rating: (Enjoyableness)
    a. Percent of user households which feel that recreation opportunities are good.
    b. Percent of user households which feel that recreation opportunities are poor.
3. Crowdedness: (Enjoyableness)
    a. Percent of user households which feel that the amount of facility space is
        poor.
4. Facility Upkeep: (Physical Attractiveness)
    a. Percent of user households which feel that the facility cleanliness is poor.
    b. Percent of user households which feel that the maintenance of the
        equipment is poor.
5. Helpfulness—Attitude of Staff: (Enjoyableness)
    a. Percent of user housheoulds which feel that helpfulness—attitude of staff is
        poor.
6. Hours of Operation: (Accessibility)
    a. Percent of user households which feel that the hours of operation are poor.
7. Safety: (Safety)
    a. Percent of user households which feel that safety is poor.
    b. Number of serious accidents per 1 million citizen attendance hours of use.
    c. Number of deaths per 10 million citizen attendance hours of use.
8. Participation: (Enjoyableness)
    a. Percent of citizens who have used a city facility or program one or more
        times during a given time period.
    b. Percent of citizens who have not used a city facility or program one or more
        times during a given time period, categorized by reason for non-use.
9. Attendance: (Enjoyableness)
    a. Total attendance at city facilities or programs.
10. Hours of Attendance: (Enjoyableness)
    a. Total citizen attendance hours at city facilities or programs.
11. Physical Accessibility: (Accessibility)
    a. Percent of citizens who live within ½ mile of a city recreation facility.
12. Variety: (Variety)
    a. Average number of different programs per facility.

the total possible park users.[11] This fact underscores the critical importance of including non-user data in any effort to determine departmental effectiveness. Other valuable information that an applied (the Urban Institute recommends linking effectiveness measurement to the annual budgeting and program planning process) system of effectiveness measurement can provide are:

1. *Help identify priorities and support budget preparation.*
2. *Identify trouble spots and objectively address ad hoc issues.*
3. *Compare the level and need for services in various parts of the community and for various population segments.*
4. *Prepare annual status reports on the effectiveness of community services.*
5. *Evaluate programs and activities.*
6. *Establish a baseline from which future changes can be measured.*
7. *Project the future impact of recreation facilities and programs.*
8. *Answer public questions.*
9. *Provide information for the preparation of an annual report.*
10. *Help identify targets for future activities.*
11. *Identify areas where coordinated action among both public and non-public recreation suppliers is needed.*
12. *Help assess overall staff performance.*[12]

While the Urban Institute method represents a new direction and improvement over traditional efforts at evaluating recreation services, its application potential is perhaps constrained somewhat by time and cost considerations. The initial cost of its implementation alone, estimated between $20,000 to $40,000 for a jurisdiction of 500,000 and between $15,000 to $30,000 for a city of about 250,000 people, may be a deterrent to its use in some communities. It is quite possible that a city may choose, however, to modify the method (e.g., draw smaller sample, alter or limit the measurement indices, etc.) developed by the Urban Institute to better reflect its own objectives and financial capabilities.

A second evaluation method which focuses on the impact or effectiveness of the recreation experience is the participant interview. The intent of the participant interview approach is to establish a direct line of communication between representatives of the recreation agency and program participants. Application of the participant interview method is a relatively simple and straight forward process. Active participants are selected at random (from program registration lists) and asked to share their feelings, observations, and recommendations regarding the activity in which they are engaged with a recreation agency representative. The dialogue established between participant informants and agency staff (not necessarily the leader of the program being evaluated) allows for in-depth feedback or such aspects as quality of leadership, adequacy of physical setting, degree of participant satisfaction, and appropriateness of program content. Interviews could be established during the middle or at the end of various programs, or at both times. Staff availability, time and the nature of the activity would determine the time and frequency of the interviews. While time-consuming, the immediate feedback provided by the interview method could prove extremely valuable to the program staff. Information gathered on participant satisfaction could be integrated with data of broader based effectiveness to provide a more comprehensive basis for making planning and budgeting decisions.

Whether one or a combination of the preceding evaluation devices is used, measurement of program effectiveness should be an integral and routine function of recreation agencies. The continuous infusion of staff and participant feedback into the planning process is essential to producing desired levels of participant satisfaction. The planning model does not end with evaluation. In effect, the program evaluation information, which reflects the outcome of the planning process, then becomes a valuable input into the continuous cycle of program planning. Program evaluation data in combination with survey information, citizen input and professional judgment become the building blocks for the continuously evolving program planning process.

The model visualizes program development as an involved, challenging and time-consuming process, in which the recreation professional has a variety of tasks to perform. The effective development of a recreation program, one which truly satisfies participant needs, is built upon the systematic integration of such elements as collecting and analyzing "need" data, organizing and coordinating staff efforts, developing activity flow charts, proposing and justifying new requests, conducting the program and evaluating the outcome.

Program Organization and Implementation

While the preceding section provided a comprehensive over-view of the recreation program development process, this section will concentrate on one key element of the programming process—the staff's role in organizing and implementing a particular recreation event or activity. A useful organizational tool—the flow chart method—is introduced.

The effective development of recreation programs such as playgrounds, day camps and community-wide special events requires a considerable amount of careful planning and preparation. Normally programs of such magnitude involve significant manpower, material, time and space requirements. For example, an annual Fourth of July celebration sponsored by a Recreation Department, including such traditional activities as a parade, an "old fashioned" picnic, entertainment, and a fireworks display could entail the training and coordination of as many as a hundred people and the ordering and dispersing of literally tons of equipment. Haphazard or last-minute planning of the day-long event could easily result in a ragged parade, missing entertainers, a delayed or cancelled fireworks display—all adding up to a tremendous disappointment to thousands of community residents.

The Flow Chart Method (hereafter abbreviated as FCM) of planning is a technique which attempts to eliminate oversight, the uncertainty of chance and last-minute "scrambling" from the planning process. Basically, FCM is a systematic forecasting process which attempts to account for and sequentially set a precedent for each work requirement in the organization of a program. It represents the application of many elements of the Operations Research technique, P.E.R.T. (Program Evaluation Review Technique), to the planning of recreation activities. The Flow Chart Method separates the entire program into its component parts and evaluates each of these areas as *what* is to be done, *when* it is to be done, *who* is to do it, and *how* long it will take. The various parts are then combined and fitted to a "time line" on a precedence basis to provide the planner with an overall view of what needs to be accomplished. The application of FCM to the development of a Playground program is included to illustrate the steps involved in the actual use of this planning process (Fig. 13).

Certain requirements seem universal to the successful organization of most program activities. Invariably, recreation program planners have to be cognizant of money, manpower, materials, time, facilities and publicity requirements. Very few programs can succeed without trained leadership or supervision, adequate space, appropriate equipment and supplies and/or ample promotion. Therefore, FCM begins by dividing the entire program into its essential components. In this process, the planner identifies the major requirements or functions necessary for the completion of the program. In the Summer Playground Program example, five major functions are identified: manpower, materials, facilities, program and publicity. Each of the major functions is then analyzed independently. To start, the planner lists, in no particular order, the activities or tasks he considers essential to the completion of each major function. For example, a random list of all activities involved in meeting the manpower requirement could include hiring personnel, conducting employment interviews, completing a leader's manual, preparing an in-service training session, and so on. After the random lists are completed, the planner then sets a priority for the various activities within each of the major functions. The next step in the FCM is to project a time line. This line represents the estimated length of time necessary to complete all the planning requirements. In the Summer Playground example, approximately six months are allocated to sufficiently prepare for the eight-week program session. The flow of activities begins in January with a review of the previous years' evaluations of the playground program and concludes with two days of in-service training on June 26th. Between the first and last activities, a variety of related tasks are arranged in logical order on the flow chart diagram.

The placement of all these activities on the time line is the most difficult and time-consuming, but also the most important step in the application of FCM. The planner must select activities from each of the already major function areas given priority (e.g., manpower, materials, etc.) and place them on the FC diagram with respect to priority or urgency for completion and estimated length of time necessary for completion. Obviously, some activities or

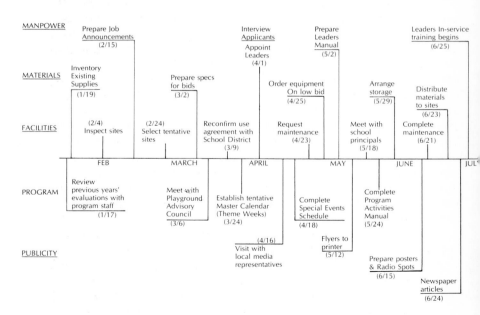

Fig. 13. Flow chart summer playground program.

tasks have to be completed before others can be initiated, and these will therefore receive precedence on the diagram. The decision of where to place the other activities will most often be a function of such factors as local conditions or circumstances, the experience of the programmer, time and/or personal preference. Regardless of what order is finally established, the crucial factor is to account for, in some logical manner, all necessary work requirements. The diagram illustrates the sequence which should be followed, as well as the degree of inter- and intra-dependence which exists between the tasks. Once a natural flow of activities is established, the flow chart diagram acts as a roadmap, helping to keep the planner on course resulting in the elimination of costly and sometimes embarrassing errors. The dates enclosed in the parentheses beneath the various tasks on the diagram are suspense dates indicating when the work must be completed. The suspense dates correspond to the location of activities on the time line.

In addition to the obvious attribute of increased service coordination and efficiency, FCM provides a number of other important benefits. Using the flow chart technique the planner is in a better position to anticipate and prevent potential problems. Having all the project requirements identified immediately before him, enhances the planner's ability to make adjustments within the established time/activities network should it become necessary. When the flow chart diagram is completed, the planner should have a clear picture of what is to be done, when it is to be done, and how long it will take.

While initially time-consuming and subject to imperfections, the FCM is eminently superior to many other program planning, or non-planning, approaches. Too often programmers rely solely on their memory of past experiences to guide their planning efforts. While some experienced program planners may be able to operate effectively in this manner, attempts by most to store and organize in their minds the myriad number of tasks involved in organizing a major program (there are over 30 individual elements in the Playground example alone) invariably lead to the poor allocation of time and resources.

The FCM also facilitates the delegation of responsibility to subordinates. When all requirements for a program have been accounted for, the supervisor can share the diagram with his or her subordinates and together they can easily identify those activities or tasks for which the employees will be responsible. With suspense dates already established the administrator can readily assess the compatibility of project deadlines with the schedules of his staff. During this process, the employee receives exposure to the full scope of the overall program event and gains an appreciation of how his efforts will contribute to the final product. For the inexperienced program planner exposure to the FCM can prove to be a valuable in-service training device. The opportunity to prepare a time/activities network for a special program under the supervision of an experienced programmer is an excellent learning experience for the new employee. The FCM can also be a valuable reference tool. Most programs are provided on a seasonal basis from year to year. Good examples of seasonal programs and special events should be maintained. Each year rather than starting from scratch, references to the flow chart diagrams will help provide the members of the program staff with a comprehensive and accurate picture of their time and work requirements for the upcoming season. Access to a complete record of FCM diagrams will be especially beneficial to program specialists new to the agency.

For all its many advantages, the use of the Flow Chart Method does not guarantee a successful program. FCM is only as good as the time and effort invested in its development. However, while not a panacea, it can act as a highly effective coordinating device, resulting in a more efficient use of scarce human and physical resources.

Summary

The principal objective of this chapter was to provide a comprehensive overview of the recreation program planning process. A descriptive model was used to graphically illustrate the many variables which can affect the agency's ability to deliver program services. A major contention of the planning model is that suppliers of recreation services should make themselves more aware of their clients' needs and desires. Program opportunities should be developed in view of what people want rather than what the suppliers think they should have. The traditional reliance of recreation agencies on professional intuition and attendance data for planning purposes is not sufficient in light of the changing patterns of leisure behavior and the emerging new and often more diverse forms of recreation activity. Several improved methods for assessing community recreation needs and interests were suggested including: community recreation surveys drawn from representative sample populations, neighborhood recreation advisory councils, and a variety of program evaluation feedback systems. The integration of elements from all of these "need" monitoring sources can aid immeasurably in ascertaining existing participation patterns, current levels of client satisfaction, projected recreation preferences, reasons for non-participation and the answers to many other vital questions. This information then becomes the corner-stone for the organization and implementation phases of the program development model. The need for more rigorous evaluation to measure the effectiveness of program services was stressed. The non-user/non-participant (as well as the user/participant) was identified as a crucial denominator in the effectiveness measurement process.

Finally, the Flow Chart Method—a systematic forecasting device—is introduced as a tool which recreation staff can employ in the actual organization and implementation of program events.

References

1. Bull, Neil C.: One Measure for Defining a Leisure Activity, *Journal of Leisure Research*, Spring, 1971, p. 120.
2. Athletic Institute, *The Recreation Program*. Chicago, The Institute, 1954.
3. Mercer, David: The Concept of Recreational Need, *Journal of Leisure Research*, Winter 1973, pp. 37–50.
4. Dunn, Diana: Recreation, Open Space and Social Organization, in Betty Van der Smissen (ed.) *Indicators of Change in the Recreation Environment—A National Research Symposium*, Pennsylvania State University, 1974, p. 264.
5. Staley, Edwin J.: Determining Neighborhood Recreation Priorities: An Instrument, *Journal of Leisure Research*, Winter 1969, pp. 69–74.
6. *Focus on the Recreation Division:* Phoenix, Arizona, Parks and Recreation Department, 1972.
7. Bannon, Joseph: Do and Don'ts of Citizen Involvement in a Good Park and Recreation Program, *The American City*, April, 1971.
8. The Urban Institute: *How Effective are Your Community Recreation Services?* Report to the Bureau of Outdoor Recreation, Washington, D.C., Urban Institute, April 1973, p. 3.
9. Ibid: p. 3.
10. Ibid: p. viii.
11. Carberry, Michael E.: *Activity Analysis: A Research Tool For Planning Leisure and Recreation Services* Nashville, Tennessee Department of Conservation, Planning and Development Division, 1975, p. 5.
12. Urban Institute: Op Cit., p. 5.

SECTION III

The Summary

CHAPTER **8**

Ecology of Recreation and Leisure Service: New Management Considerations

"Problems from one segment of the community are often symptoms of larger, more complex community problems. Unless each component of the leisure service delivery system is dealt with as a whole, no viable solution will be achieved in understanding the dynamics of what contribute to and affect leisure behavior."

The Human Service Professional

The recreation movement has not been immune to the forces of social change. The social revolution which altered the condition and consciousness of women, the poor, the aged and the young has led to significant changes in the recreation and leisure services field as well. Change has been most readily evidenced by shifts in program orientation and the adoption of a broadened service perspective. Recreation and leisure service is increasingly becoming incorporated into the wider, more encompassing human service profession. The new human service professional (which incorporates allied health fields; social work; community diversion programs, including community treatment, delinquency and adult prevention and half-way house programs; recreation and leisure

207

service field, etc.) transcends simply the dispensing of service or provision of areas, facilities, equipment and/or leadership for individuals. It is recognized that the professional has a responsibility to counsel, to teach, to work with people, to establish professional relationships, to function as a community liaison, to supervise and act as an agent of change.

The emerging human service profession would aid greatly in the improvement and simplification of the delivery of services in all the above mentioned areas. It would accomplish this by enabling one person to meet a client's diverse needs while making effective performance the criterion for licensing and promotion.

Humanism and Recreation and Leisure Service

Much of the contention of the development of the new human service profession, an eclectic fusion of the helping fields, reflects a growing adoption of humanism as a philosophical foundation. Humanism is seen as a way of life, a belief and conviction that emphasizes mutual respect and recognizes human interdependence. The humanistic approach aims at the development of the highest potential of the individual. The recreation and leisure service field is seen increasingly moving toward expanding its delivery service continuum to incorporate an enabling approach which transfers the responsibility for leisure choices, decisions and behavior to the individual. Such a self-directed approach is also recognized by health care fields. Bower comments.

> *"An interaction between the client and the clinician [following diagnosis and analysis] that involves the client in the exploring, analyzing, and understanding of the difficulties promotes a concomitant sense of responsibility by the client to the outcome. It acknowledges the rights and freedom as an individual. To create this kind of climate a humanistic approach is needed."*[1]

The human service professional seeks ways to maximize one's growth and discover the intrinsic and environmental conditions that make self-actualization possible. As the nurse plans care and consideration of the client as a *participating member* of the health team, so too in recreation and leisure service the individual must be encouraged and viewed as part of the decision making process, if not *the* major decision maker. Respect must be given the participant or potential user regardless of the difference in goals. Goals developed by recreation and leisure service agencies must be meshed with participant or potential user goals.

Value of a Humanistic Approach to the Participant

In a society where trust of government leaders and representatives of the helping professions has diminished and whose institutions in general are under questioning and being challenged as being unresponsive to the social changes which are occurring at an ever increasing rate, a different approach to meeting human needs seems evident. A humanistic approach makes the individual more comfortable. The individual knows what is being designed and programmed for him because he is involved generally in the program planning and decision-making; the individual feels the leisure service catalyst knows that he is a unique person because the professional staff member took time to learn about him. If the participant needs to ask questions, discuss a problem, obtain information or assistance, he knows that he will be helped and will be encouraged to do so.

Factors that Affect the Humanistic Relationship

There are several important interdependent factors which affect the ability of leisure service personnel to create a humanistic relationship. They include *(a)* the social environment, *(b)* the physical environment (setting), *(c)* the organization and its delivery approaches, and *(d)* individual participants. All of these are put into motion by the ability of the leisure service professional to provide guidance while creating a humanistic relationship.

Creating a Helping/Growth Environment. The leisure service professional has a major responsibility for creating an environment that is conducive to problem solving, the resolution of conflicts and the fostering of a growth situation which will move the individual participant to the realization of his optimum potential.

The physical environment of the playground, community center or park needs to provide the individual with a non-threatening milieu and one which will result in a motivating climate. For example, Gold suggests that the human response to plants has such potential for making cities more interesting, exciting, and beautiful places to live. They can provide a new and needed dimension of visual order, respect, aesthetics, diversity, love and joy. He suggests we have only begun to explore the unique potentials of plants to:

> *"(1) provide sensory diversity, (2) screen visual blight, (3) provide learning experiences, (4) encourage social interaction, (5) encourage people to walk to save gasoline and improve health, (6) reduce urban crime and violence, (7) encourage a possible return to the central city by suburbanites, (8) increase the use of urban parks to reduce the overuse of wilderness areas, and (9) convey a new sense of stewardship for the urban environment."[2]*

The environment created by plants, shrubs, trees and grass may actually help reduce levels of environmental stress as there is evidence which indicates that sight, smell, sound and touch of plants can lower the rate and frequency of crime and vandalism through well designed and maintained recreation areas with reference to the use of plants.

The policies, procedures, rules and regulations of the supervised and unsupervised recreation areas reflect the agency's interpretation of acceptable community norms. Unless they are truly reflective of the diverse and changing needs of a pluralistic society, the goals and objectives of the agency will not represent and even frustrate and possibly lead to the exclusion of certain community members from enjoying the recreation and leisure service offerings.

Interpersonal Environment. It is essential that the interpersonal climate of the leisure setting provide an opportunity for humanistic relationships to be developed and encouraged. Free and open communication is essential. A safe environment will make people feel at ease and not threatened but unless leisure service personnel have an awareness for individual participant attitudes, values and needs, the setting will be sterile and not conducive to spontaneous, self-expressive behavior. Accordingly, personnel should have an awareness of their own attitudes, prejudices and values. While it would be unrealistic to expect leisure service workers to be nonjudgmental, all human beings make judgments, since each individual has his own unique value system. In a humanistic relationship if the worker finds that he is in opposition or in conflict with the client's value system, he would then acknowledge the difference and deal with it. It is important, then, that leisure service worker accept his prejudices and biases. To accept the participant means he acknowledges his difference and accepts him for what he is and what he believes. Ultimately, the ability to accept the individual participant not only allows for open and free communication, but creates a trusting relationship, a vital component for the development of the individual.

Humanism and professionalism are seen as fundamental to the facilitation of growth potentials. A humanistic approach seeks to develop an individual's optimal potential. It is concerned not only with the factors that affect the individual's experience and action, but also with liberating the individual from the impact of these factors so that he can pursue his freedom and growth. The professional character of the relationship lies in the leisure service worker's ability to give of self while providing direction for the individual participant.

Holistic Theory and Recreation and Leisure Service

Human beings respond not only in a unique manner, but also as a total organism. What happens in one area of the community system affects the other components. So too what happens in one part of the human organism affects the whole. Wholeness implies that the individual is seeking his optimum potential as a complete well-integrated whole. Each person strives to be alert, to grow, to develop, and to perform the acts of daily living with interest, enjoyment and satisfaction.

Problems from one segment of the community are often symptoms of larger, more complex community problems. Unless each component of the leisure service delivery system is dealt with as a whole, no viable solution will be achieved to understanding the dynamics of what contributes and affects leisure behavior. Unless the factors that create the symptoms are discovered (under an activity philosophy the likelihood is slim) and corrected, individuals will not be adequately served. The whole community must be considered when attempting to provide a leisure framework conducive to human growth and development, as no part of the whole functions without its impact on the other parts or components and on the whole.

The philosophy of recreation and leisure service delivery will increasingly be predicated on a premise that it must assume equal responsibility with other city services in responding to the total needs of citizens either as a direct service agent, broker or catalyst. At least five factors in recent years have served to spark this recognition and growing commitment.

1. *Social Responsibility of Cities.* The League of California Cities[3] issued a position statement which called upon each local government unit to assume responsibility for identifying all community social needs, and for planning, coordinating, and evaluating programs to alleviate social problems within its boundaries. It further indicated that cities should insure the delivery of all essential social services either by serving as an advocate or catalyst to insure the most effective delivery of service by the appropriate public and/or private agencies or by delivering such services themselves.

While the League position statement has application to California and serves only as a suggested guide, it is expected that municipal and county governmental agencies throughout the country will also see that they have similar mandates.

2. *Social Service Element in the General Plan.* Cities and counties are gearing themselves to plan and adopt a social services element in their overall general plan, and as part of the overall

planning process. The social services element is seen as a method for determining city and/or county goals and objectives and for establishing standards and priorities to meet community social needs. The social services element should address the needs of *all* city and/or county residents. Some of the possible components might include the following:

> a. *Dependency Avoidance Services.* For example, employment de-velopment services, income maintenance, counseling.
> b. *Health Services.* For example, alcohol treatment, drug abuse, mental health, physical health, emergency care, disease prevention.
> c. *Individual and Family Services.* For example, education, housing, crisis intervention.
> d. *Justice, Rehabilitation and Protective Services.* For example, affirmative action, minority and community relations, crime preven-tion, legal assistance, consumer protection, rehabilitation, civil rights.
> e. *Transportation Services.* For example, transportation for the poor and elderly, rapid transit.
> f. *Leisure Services.* For example, educational programs, recreation, cultural activities, self-help services.

Such a social services plan should include an operational and implementation plan which delineates the allocation of resources, and it should be revised yearly to reflect changing needs, priorities and funding.

3. *New Federalism.* Federal and many state resources have fostered and nurtured a multiplicity of human services, many of which relate to park and recreation goals and objectives. Some federal and state programs have required cooperative arrangements with other human service agencies as a condition of funding.

4. *Humanistic Perspective.* It has been indicated previously that there is a growing awareness of the fact that a person's enjoyment of a leisure experience and degree of participation are influenced by forces and problems that relate to *other* aspects of daily life.

5. *Academic Approach to Viewing the Whole Person.* Colleges and universities have changed and expanded their park, recreation, and leisure studies curricula to emphasize an interdisciplinary approach to meeting human needs.

All of these factors stress the importance of governmental agencies and have implications for all leisure service departments, whether they be private, voluntary or quasi-public, to provide service to meet the total needs of the individual and/or family in a unified rather than a fragmented manner. Leisure service agencies in cooperation with other human service agencies should seek to eliminate the overlapping and duplication of services, and to identify service gaps. Social services planning should be related to and coordinated with physical, economic and environmental planning.

Events in recent years (including the energy crisis, resource shortages, continued crime problem, unemployment and financial insolvency of a growing number of American cities) indicate that every major crisis highlights the crucial need to better identify and improve our interrelationships. This requires greater cooperation among all human service agencies so that management techniques are employed to insure maximum participation of the various departments in the development of social goals.

Ideological Transition of America's Social Structure.

The change by leisure service agencies to incorporate a humanistic, developmental philosophical approach to social services delivery is a recognition that there is a broader continuum of providing leisure opportunities and ideological shift. The "activity" centered delivery approach for many years served as the philosophical perspective which saw the purpose of recreation and leisure service agencies to provide a full array of activities to members of the community.

An ideology is the framework of ideas that integrates and synthesizes all aspects of a community's being — political, social, economic, cultural, ecological and others. Ideology legitimizes a community's institutions — business, government, universities — and thus it underlies the authority and the rights of those who manage the institutions.[4]

In recent years there has been growing recognition that the traditional ideology of recreation and leisure service agencies, which has become incoherent and lost acceptance, has reduced community direction. It is seen by government that a "communitarian" approach as opposed to an "individualistic" ideology is more effective in solving community problems. The individualistic ideology revolved around the nucleus of the traditional "American way" which has extolled the values of individualism, private property, free competition in an open market place and limited government involvement. The communitarian ideology views the individual as an inseparable part of a community in which his rights and duties are determined by the needs of the common good. Government should play an important role as the planner and implementer of community need. Individual fulfillment and self-respect are the results of one's place in an organic social process. The perception of reality requires an awareness of whole

systems and of the interrelationships between and among the
wholes. This holistic process is the primary task of science.

There are increasing demands placed upon all American
institutions to participate more actively in social, cultural, and
political programs designed to improve the quality of American
life. There is a need for change toward a sensitive and flexible
planning capability on the part of management of major institutions. The necessity of all human service agencies to bring homo
sapiens in better harmony with the physical and social environments requires an ecological/humanistic foundation. The growing
self- and social consciousness with respect to the governance of
public and voluntary bureaucracies has led to the need on the part
of human service agencies to facilitate more participation in this
governance by the clients who are served, as well as those doing
the service, including lower levels of the hierarchy. In the
twentieth century conditions of continual change have led to an
emergence of the human/behavioral sciences and a deeper
understanding of the complexity of human behavior.

Future Considerations

It is expected that in the near future the philosophical
justification for leisure services will be expanded to include a social
services component, which sees recreation activity serving as a
threshold for the individual to realize certain human benefits. The
goal of leisure services will be human development. D'Amours
comments: "The state of responses to environmental stimuli in
search of positive feedback and achievement will take the place of
the traditional understanding as a state of being, a series of
activities performed during leisure time. The approach will be
integrative, holistic, as the segmentation of human behaviours into
work and leisure behaviours becomes less and less significant."[5]

Such a philosophical approach will require colleges and
universities to continue to include a multi-disciplinary approach in
the preparation of prospective professionals capable of solving
complex interrelated social problems. Such a social empathy will
necessarily permeate the delivery of leisure services and require
personnel to have a community organizer/developer competency.
Such a competency will require leisure service personnel to have
the ability to counsel, guide and advise people on activities and
resource use and also to relate human beings to the natural world.
With the growing number of avocational subgroups emerging (a
reflection of a new sense of community evolving which centers on
shared interests and mutual compatibility), leisure service person-

nel will need to be able to relate to a wide range of clienteles with possible conflicting goals and life styles. Therefore, it is expected that there will be a contraction of current types of program structures, including playground and recreation center model forms, and an increase in approaches of a personalized, self-paced nature with minimum supervision and direction from agency personnel. In his study on the future of the leisure service field through the collation of views of recreation educators and practitioners, D'Amours reached the following general conclusion:

> "... the study demonstrates that there will be a shift from a segmentalist activity-oriented approach to an integrative, multidisci- plinary and human-oriented approach in the domain of recreation professional preparation. The new professional will have to perform in different manners. It seems that the fundamental role of a recreation professional will be that of helping relation vis-a-vis the client, as counselor, guide, advisor. Leisure behavior will be considered less and less as a special kind of human behavior performed during free time. A more holistic approach will take place and those particular behaviors, which provide man with a sentiment of self-realization and achieve- ment, will be privileged among others. The justification of professional intervention will refer to social welfare benefits and to the accelera- tion of human development rather than to the ever-increasing amount of free-time and its activity use."[6]

The humanistic philosophy is an attempt to view the whole person and the interrelationships of the human experience. By adopting a humanistic perspective leisure service agencies recog- nize that there is a wide diversity of human values and efforts should be made to allow for divergent life style modes of expression. By recognizing the plurality of human needs and the diverse means required to facilitate their fulfillment, leisure service agencies will better be able to provide opportunities for leisure expression.

References

1. Bower, Fay Louise: *The Process of Planning Nursing Care: A Theoretical Model.* St. Louis, The C. V. Mosby Co., 1972, p. 26.
2. Gold, Seymour, M.: The Green Revolution in Urban America, *Parks and Recreation 10*:26, February, 1975.
3. Action Plan for Social Responsibilities of Cities, League of California Cities Annual Conference, October, 1973, San Francisco, California.
4. Martin, William F. and Lodge, George Cabot: Our Society in 1985—Business May Not Like It, *Harvard Business Review,* 149, November-December, 1975.
5. D'Amours, Max: The Views of Recreation Educators and Practitioners on the Future of the Leisure Service Professions as a New Source of Guidelines for Recreation Higher Education, A Delphi Study on the Future of the Recreation Profession, University of Quebec, Trois-Rivieres, August, 1975, p. 22.
6. D'Amours: *Ibid.,* p. 23.